The Edward[...]

The Edwardians is an 8-part BBC t[...] in the lives of a number of people who lived in the early years this century. By choosing a diversity of characters, the programmes are able to show a number of aspects of English life before the First World War.

Some of the characters are well known, others are less so. They are Baden-Powell, Horatio Bottomley, Arthur Conan Doyle, Marie Lloyd, David Lloyd George, E. Nesbit, Charles Rolls and Henry Royce, and Daisy Warwick. In this background book, Peter Brent studies their lives – what they did and how they lived – and relates them to the period as a whole.

The photographs on the back of the cover are as follows:

Conan
Doyle

Horatio
Bottomley

E. Nesbit

Lloyd
George

Daisy Warwick

Charles
Rolls

Henry
Royce

Baden-
Powell

Marie
Lloyd

who is flanked by two of her music-hall colleagues

Gus Elen

George Formby Snr

The Edwardians

by Peter Brent

British Broadcasting Corporation

The Edwardians was first broadcast on BBC 2 starting in November 1972. 'Baden-Powell' (played by Ron Moody) was written by John Prebble and directed by Robert Knight; 'Horatio Bottomley' (Timothy West) was written by Julian Bond and directed by Alan Clarke; 'Conan Doyle' (Nigel Davenport) was written by Jeremy Paul and directed by Brian Farnham; 'The Reluctant Juggler', a play in which several well-known music-hall artists are featured (Georgia Brown plays Marie Lloyd), was written by Alan Plater and directed by Brian Farnham; 'Lloyd George' (Anthony Hopkins) was written by Keith Dewhurst and directed by John Davies; 'E. Nesbit' (Judy Parfitt) was written by Ken Taylor and directed by James Cellan-Jones; 'Mr Rolls & Mr Royce' (with Michael Jayston as Royce and Robert Powell as Rolls) was written by Ian Curteis and directed by Gerald Blake; 'Daisy' (Virginia McKenna) was written by David Turner and directed by James Cellan-Jones. The series was produced by Mark Shivas.

The illustrations between pp. 112–13 are from the Radio Times Hulton Picture Library, except for the photographs of E. Nesbit and Conan Doyle in his living room, which are from the Mansell Collection.

Published by the British Broadcasting Corporation,
35 Marylebone High Street, London W1M 4AA

ISBN 0 563 12349 4

First published 1972

Printed in England by Cox & Wyman Ltd,
London, Reading and Fakenham

Contents

Introduction · 9

Baden-Powell · 17

Horatio Bottomley · 43

Conan Doyle · 71

Marie Lloyd · 97

Lloyd George · 121

E. Nesbit · 147

Mr Rolls and Mr Royce · 171

Daisy Warwick · 201

Further Reading

I have referred, to a greater or lesser extent, to a number of books which have been written about the personalities recorded in this book. Doris Langley Moore's work on E. Nesbit was indispensable. For the Edwardian era I would recommend *The Strange Death of Liberal England* by George Dangerfield (MacGibbon & Kee 1966).

Baden-Powell
Baden-Powell, by W. Hillcourt and Lady Baden-Powell (Heinemann 1964)
Baden-Powell: a biography, by E. E. Reynolds (Oxford University Press 1942)

Horatio Bottomley
The Rise and Fall of Horatio Bottomley, by A. Hyman (Cassell 1972)
Horatio Bottomley: a biography, by Julian Symons (Cresset Press 1955)

Conan Doyle
Life of Sir Arthur Conan Doyle, by John Dickson Carr (John Murray 1949)
Conan Doyle, by Pierre Nordon (John Murray 1966)
Conan Doyle, his life and art, by Hesketh Pearson (Methuen 1943)

Marie Lloyd
Our Marie, by Naomi Jacob (Hutchinson 1936)

Lloyd George
Tempestuous Journey: Lloyd George, his life and times, by Frank Owen (Hutchinson 1954)
The Real Lloyd George, by A. J. Sylvester (Cassell 1947)

E. Nesbit
E. Nesbit: a biography, by Doris Langley Moore (Benn 1967)
Magic and the Magician: E. Nesbit and her Children's Books, by Noel Streatfeild (Benn 1958)

Rolls and Royce
Rolls of Rolls Royce, by Lord Montagu of Beaulieu (Cassell 1966)
The Magic of a Name: Sir Henry Royce, by Harold Nockolds (Foulis, 3rd ed. 1972)
History of Rolls Royce Motor Cars, by C. W. Morton (Foulis 1964)

Daisy Warwick
The Countess of Warwick, by Margaret Blunden (Cassell 1967)
My Darling Daisy, by Theo Lang (Michael Joseph 1966)

Introduction

THE NINE people the stories of whose lives are briefly related in this book were Edwardians in the sense that what they did, and how they lived, reached crisis or apogee during a particular period, and in their way they help to illuminate the period as a whole and parts of the social structure that existed – and changed – during it. Yet there never really was, in the strict sense, an Edwardian 'era'. There was the decade between 1901 and 1910 during which Edward VII reigned, to which one may tack on the four years which led up to the beginning of the First World War. These fourteen years make, in retrospect, a curious episode, lit as they are both by the afterglow of that bright, imperial sunlight which blazed throughout most of the Victorian period, and by the false dawn of a century which would never see the light of day, that other, optimistically awaited twentieth century which might have been, but which was so soon to be overtaken and irrevocably altered by the cataclysm of the 1914–18 war.

Yet the roots of that war lay partly in the high chauvinism, the unquestionable pride and patriotism, which the successes of the nineteenth century had produced in the breasts of the British. (It would be pointless here to consider the jealousies and rivalries these successes had produced elsewhere.) Even at the turn of the century the supremacy of Britain in the world was a matter which did not need to be discussed by most Englishmen: it was one of the given facts of their situation.

For that reason it is significant that the period begins with the Boer War, a slightly contrived adventure in which the high idealism and the murky commercialism which had in paradoxical alliance built and sustained the Empire were very clearly to be seen in operation. It was idealism which criticised the Boers' treatment of the Africans, patriotism which wanted to support the English-speaking *Uitlanders* of the Transvaal, imperialism which led to the troop movements that provoked Kruger's ultimatum. But it was the hunger for land and gold and personal glory, particularly that of Cecil Rhodes, which provided the real energy; without it the British Government might have deplored, but it is doubtful if they would have acted. The Boer War itself was, in a sense, a warning of the greater disaster to come as it dragged drearily on to its undramatic and strangely magnanimous conclusion. For a minority of people the exposure it gave to some of Britain's real motives overseas undermined their patriotic certainties, but they were comparatively only a handful. Of the men and women dealt with here, it is noticeable that only David Lloyd George came out in wholehearted opposition to the war – and he, of course, was rather self-consciously a maverick and ostentatiously Welsh rather than English.

How widespread this unquestioned and unquestionable patriotism was and how deeply it was felt can be gauged by the careers of two very different men: Baden-Powell, who was lifted to hero status on the wave of emotion which followed Mafeking, and Horatio Bottomley, that eccentric financier who throughout the first two decades of the century manipulated the self-congratulatory pride of his fellow-countrymen in the most sinister, if profitable, manner. For Baden-Powell chauvinism was natural, a part of his being and something which he expected to be part of the being of others. Probably Horatio Bottomley too believed what he so vigorously expounded in his newspaper, *John Bull*, but the cynicism in his raffish armoury allowed him to expose and exploit the essential mindlessness behind the mood of patriotic sacrifice which animated so many millions of people, especially during the First World War. He could do so, just as Baden-Powell could put love of country so high on his Boy Scouts' list of virtues, precisely because such feelings were so strong and widely held. Indeed they had to be – what else would have supplied the energy to run an Empire or the rationale persuading the down-trodden to accept poverty and injustice? It is no coincidence that the kind of blind patriotism so familiar to the Edwardians has declined as social equality has become both more widely desired and nearer realisation.

But for the pre-1914 British chauvinism was the cement which held the social fabric together, the ultimate expression of six centuries of nationalism. It was expressed in the various 'racial' theories current at that time in Britain, postulating the supremacy of the 'Anglo-Saxon race', a non-existent ethnic entity believed in even by such men of high intelligence and wide tolerance as Conan Doyle. It led eventually to the hysteria of the war years, when young men crowded to serve in the trenches, and those who did not received white feathers for their 'cowardice' from well-spoken but vituperative ladies. That it was echoed in parallel patriotisms as blind and overwhelming in most of the other great countries of Europe was what led in the end to the inevitable tragedy. And when one considers how that enthusiasm was used and manipulated by the kings and the statesmen, by the jealous, the paranoid and the power-hungry, one might come to the conclusion that only by the relatively small scale of his operations did Bottomley avoid a much more respectable niche in the history of those times.

Patriotism was, however, only one of the forces working upon Edwardian society. Most easily to be seen were the technical innovations, particularly perhaps in transport. The motor-car and the aeroplane during this period changed from being objects of highly technical and widely suspect experiments and became instead items in the clutter of the everyday world. They were still rare and still exciting, but they had become part of the expected scenery in which an Englishman might spend his days. In this way there was opened up a route to success for a new race of entrepreneurs with engineering skill, a route which the Sopwiths, the Morrises, the Royces and their rivals were quick to take.

Social mobility may have been generally on the increase, but the appalling and continuing gap between the rich and the poor divided the country like an abyss. Children still ran barefoot through the slums, while at the other end of the scale the Duke of Sutherland could pin £1000 notes to his wife's pillow while she slept. When, in 1899, Daisy Warwick and her husband, the Earl, turned their estates into a limited liability company, it was registered with a capital of £120,000 – and that was at a period when they were beginning to be worried about their declining fortunes. At the time of the Boer War Lord Lonsdale from his own estates offered to supply the War Office with 208 officers and men, three machine guns, four ambulances, a detachment of trained nurses and nearly 300 carts. Yet when, in 1901, Benjamin Seebohm Rowntree carried out a social survey in York, he found nearly five thousand people living two or more to a room, in houses some seven hundred of which had to share a water supply – in 170 of these, there was only one tap to five houses. Partly as a result of these conditions and partly because of increased industrialisation, rivers which were only seasonally polluted at the turn of the century had by 1908 reached a state in which no fish could live in them: the countryside, like the towns, was being poisoned. Drunkenness was rife, with many of those appearing before the magistrates only in their teens. The drinking of methylated spirits was widespread – not to be wondered at when many families had an income of less than £1 a week and methylated spirits sold for fourpence a pint.

A result of these conditions was the increasing pressure for change and reform, led by the concerned middle-class intellectuals of the Fabian Society and more directly by the newly formed Labour Party: Keir Hardie entered Parliament in 1896, wearing his cap and rough tweed suit with a dour bravado which put in their place the jeers of the silk-hatted. By 1906 there were twenty-nine

Labour Members in the House. It was this pressure for reform which led to the Liberal victories from which Lloyd George profited, and which provided the support for his more radical proposals. (Paradoxically, by its insistence on more direct confrontation and opposition to established authority, it was also one of the prime factors in the Liberals' decline.) Behind this pressure there lay, at least in part, the consequences of an earlier reform measure, the Education Act of thirty years before. There was growing up in Britain during the Edwardian years a whole population which was beginning to take literacy for granted.

This new reading public took on a role that had never been played before by any but a few sections of the middle class. They became the spectators at the game, the crowd who from the stands and terraces sent out their applause, their 'oohs' of horror, their 'aahs' of pleasure or adulation, their chorused insults, sarcasm and abuse. The aristocracy, which had been able during the previous century to hide its frequently dubious escapades from the scrutiny of the lower orders, now found themselves overlooked. Their names appeared in the new popular Press, their affairs and adventures, frequently exaggerated, enlivened the dreary mornings of a million junior clerks and chambermaids.

In the forefront of this interest stood the King, just as he had in the decades preceding when he was still Prince of Wales. His mode of life, moulded by the years in which, shielded from responsibility by his autocratic mother, he had rebelled against the repressive tenets of his education, provided in its pursuit of pleasure a model for the *haute monde*. Near him stood the libertine gentlemen and ladies, the strange foreign aristocrats and the thrusting self-made millionaires who were the members of his extraordinary set. His mistresses became matter not merely for Court gossip, but had names which every housewife in the country knew. A metropolitan knowingness spread throughout the land and across the class barriers.

In terms of sexual morality, it was only the middle classes which needed to be enlightened. The working classes were only slowly succumbing to the more rigorous notions of respectability which bound their immediate 'betters'; in their realism about the relations between men and women, they much more resembled the majority of the aristocracy. Their attitudes were reflected in the music hall, from the stages of which, by rhyme and wink and innuendo, entertainers like Marie Lloyd conspiratorially reassured their audiences that they at least knew what was what. It is no wonder that the death of Edward in 1910 seemed a heavy blow for the people to bear, and that they looked forward with very little enjoyment to the prospect of seeing on the throne the colourless George V.

Of the people in this book, two at least, Lloyd George and Daisy Warwick, lived lives of an extraordinary promiscuity, matched by that of E. Nesbit's husband, Hubert Bland. Marie Lloyd married, disastrously, three times; E. Nesbit herself entertained several lovers, even if only in self-defence; Horatio Bottomley paraded his string of chorus girls as openly as he did his racehorses. So five of them led complex and adventurous sex lives, a fact which, when one puts it together with the self-advertisements of Frank Harris or the nineteenth-century peregrinations of the vigorous but still un-identified 'Walter', makes one feel a renewed respect for the ac-complished manner in which the late Victorians and the Edwardians hoodwinked themselves and, to some extent, us about the real nature of their sexual behaviour.

The adventures, both intellectual and sexual, of Daisy Warwick and E. Nesbit do however throw some light on the changing con-dition of women – a change which was accelerated and finally acknowledged as a result of the 1914–18 war. After a century during which they had become more and more chattels, the passive admirers of male industry and invention, the child-bearers, without rights or needs, women were beginning to move out into the world once more. Throughout this period they agitated for the vote, for divorce reform, for changes in the disciminatory property laws, and more intimately, to free themselves from the imprisonment of the corset. They began to take part – in the arts, in politics and in business. They began to take their places in the universities and thence in the professions. The days when the impoverished and half-educated female could find no occupation but that of governess were largely over.

New ideas, new opportunities, new machines and techniques. Wider education, for both the working-class child of ability and the middle-class girl. New politics, offering the poor a chance of rep-resentation. New social legislation, some of it devised by new-style politicians like Lloyd George. The twentieth century in that first decade must have seemed to many full of promise. A new King was on the throne, a new life-style was softening the public austerities of the old; the Widow of Windsor had vanished, and with her going would vanish the old repression, the old dreariness. A new era was dawning. Many must have seen the world in these terms.

Yet, half instinctively, there were many others who realised that an era was actually drawing to a close – the era of British supremacy. Built on an industrial lead which had already disappeared, involving enormous responsibilities and expenditure, the Empire must have seemed to these not a source of pride but of suspicion, a vast, intractable area the very existence of which posed a continuing threat to the peace and serenity of Britain. For them the Boer War was the evidence. When they glanced about them, they saw the rest of Western Europe drawing near like wolves – with Germany, many-fanged, in the lead and with a very dangerous gleam in its eye. It was therefore to the United States they looked; it is extraordinary how much traffic there was at this time across the three thousand miles of the Atlantic. Heiresses moved west to east, men of reputation confirmed their status by moving east to west. Daisy Warwick, Conan Doyle, Baden-Powell – all, like so many of their countrymen, were intrigued by the possibility of basing, on the shaky foundation of the 'Anglo-Saxon race', some permanent connection between these English-speaking nations. Such a plan, attractive to so many, suggests that the serenities of Edwardian England hid deep anxieties about the future.

That future, in the terms in which they must have set it out for themselves, was as we know never to be reached. Their time, their logic, came to an end in August, 1914, and the four grim years that followed; the Europe they tried so hard to revive in the Twenties was different, harder, wilder, more hysterical – post-operative, shell-shocked. Many of them survived into it, but for most of them it was unfamiliar territory and they wandered through it in some bewilderment, trying with less and less success the gambits and ventures which had once ensured them so much success. Even when they appeared to be successful – Baden-Powell is a notable example – their activities were predicated on beliefs which time has made to seem more and more irrelevant.

To say there is no continuity between that period and our own would be absurd, but it is not the continuity they must have hoped for, looking forward. For us, looking back, they seem, in their avowed certainties, their assurance, the division they made between their public and their private faces, their poverty and their wealth, both very familiar and incredibly strange. They stand there, in that sunlight in which nostalgia always bathes them, they peer arrogantly out at us, we smile, we nod encouragingly – but in the end, we can never quite understand them.

Baden-Powell

BADEN-POWELL was to the Edwardian era rather what Lindbergh was to the American Twenties. Each was not only a hero acclaimed by millions of his fellow-citizens, but represented in himself those aspects of heroism thought at the time to be most admirable. Lindbergh was the apotheosis of Man commanding nature with the aid of the machine – in one sense, the archetype of the United States citizen in the twentieth century. Baden-Powell was equally the archetype of the Englishman of the imperial era, a storybook soldier sallying forth against the enemies of the Crown wherever they dared to raise their heads, even if that should be on their own soil. His adventures while helping to 'pacify' people of diverse hue, continent, religion and political persuasion seemed to the British of that time an indication that theirs was indeed the highest known peak of human development. When he crowned all these with his dogged and cheerful heroism at Mafeking, itself culminating in a success, which, while of course only natural in retrospect, had appeared for a while dangerously in the balance, he became their champion, peerless and beyond reproach: the incarnation of Kipling man.

Baden-Powell's father had been a clergyman and scientist, an authority on optics, a Fellow of the Royal Society, a man who had worked with the great Herschel and in 1827 became Savilian Professor of Geometry at Oxford. He was also prolific in other ways – he married three times, by his second wife becoming the father of three children (one of them later to be a judge of the Chief Court, Lahore), and by his third wife of ten, seven of whom survived infancy. The second son, George, became an MP and was knighted. It was the fifth son, Robert Stephenson Smyth, taking his name from his godfather, the engineer who had devised the 'Rocket', who became Lord Baden-Powell, hero of the Boer War, founder of the Scouting movement. He was born in 1857; three years later the last child was born, and a month after that Professor Baden Bowell was dead.

The children, however, did not thereby lose all contact with intellectual society. Their mother was friendly with luminaries from the worlds of art and science whom she entertained at small dinner parties: Robert Browning, T. H. Huxley, the botanist Hooker, Jowett, the physicist Tyndall; Ruskin regarded with approval young 'Stephe' Powell's paintings, Thackeray on one occasion bribed him with a shilling to return to bed (writers on the whole prefer to hold the social spotlight untramelled by the competition of small boys). That a high moral tone prevailed may be deduced from the 'Law's For Me When I Am Old' which Baden-Powell wrote out for himself just after his eighth birthday. It begins, 'I will have the poor people be as rich as we are, and they ought by rights to be as happy as we are. . . .', and ends '. . . you cannot be good with only praying but you must also try very hard to be good'.

The name 'Baden' was only added to the family name by his mother in 1869, and shortly afterwards that slightly snobbish hyphen dropped into place. This was just after 'Stephe', as the family still called him, had been sent to Rose Hill School, a prep school where his father had been a pupil sixty years earlier. After two years it was decided that he should go on to public school – although the headmistress said she would be happy to keep him without payment, 'so great is his moral influence on the rest of the school'. Young Stephe won a scholarship to Fettes, the Scottish school – but, recommended by the Duke of Marlborough, a Governor of the school, found himself going as a Gownboy Foundationer to Charterhouse.

He seems to have been an ideal public-school boy. He was possessed of various talents, all of which he placed at the disposal of the relevant organisations. He could sing – he joined the choir. He played musical instruments – he became the cadet corps' bugler, a violinist in the orchestra. He took part in amateur theatricals. He became a useful goalkeeper, although employing tactics we should now think rather dubious: as opposing forwards prepared to shoot, he would give vent to ear-splitting yells and whoops, putting them off their stroke, whereupon he would clear the ball upfield. He helped in the formation of the Rifle Corps. In the Upper School he became one of the select twelve who made up a secret social club known as 'The Druids'. At the same time he managed to keep about him an air of aloofness, to keep people guessing as to whether he might be joking or serious, thus preventing anyone from taking him too lightly. This picture of a boy totally acceptable to his peers is completed by the fact that in the classroom his performance tended to be indifferent.

In 1876, Charterhouse drawing to a close, Baden-Powell travelled to Oxford to see about the next stage of his progress through life. Here, however, he met with a setback, being turned down by both Balliol (despite Jowett's friendship with his father) and Christ Church. Only then did Stephe, now 19, consider the Army as an alternative. Open Competitive Examinations for ninety commissions were being held; he was of the right age (and, after all, background) with an uncle a colonel, so he crammed during the short time that remained to him, then struggled through a dozen arduous days of examinations, to emerge fifth in the Infantry list, second in the Cavalry, having put his name down for both branches of the service. By coming in the first six, he avoided what would otherwise have been an obligatory two years at Sandhurst. Instead he was gazetted to the 13th Hussars, a crack cavalry regiment, and within three months was on his way to India, a sub-lieutenant off to play his part in Britain's imperial destiny. In his kit, with a foresight which was rarely to desert him, he carried the texts of all the plays in which he had appeared at Charterhouse.

As a young officer in a fashionable regiment, Baden-Powell had his money problems. His mess bills tended to be among the lowest; when he wanted to play polo, he had to train his own ponies (deprivation has many relative meanings). Yet his talents allowed him to become popular – he could act and sing and paint scenery, after all, abilities perhaps more acceptable than horsemanship or an aristocratic lineage in a place as steeped in tedium as the military cantonments of Lucknow. He passed further exams, caught the inevitable fever, went to Simla for a month's leave. Again his acting talents proved invaluable – he performed before the Viceroy, Lord Lytton, and the C-in-C, India, with the result that high-level intercession got his leave extended, enabling him to continue regaling those happy audiences in their little England high among the alien mountains. But back in Lucknow his fevers returned, there was a suspicion of hepatitis, there were headaches and dizziness; a year after landing in India Baden-Powell was on his way back to England again, on sick leave.

By the autumn of 1880 he had returned to Bombay, this time equipped with a certificate in musketry. One can sense him sniffing the heavy air of Maharashtra for excitement – there had been battles, defeats, marches and victories in Afghanistan; Roberts, until then not widely known, had become Roberts of Kandahar after his march of 313 miles in twenty days and his subsequent beating of Ayub Khan, the anti-British 'dissident' leader. With his regiment posted to Afghanistan, Baden-Powell hastened to follow, and after some difficulty among the passes and peaks of the Hindu Kush arrived in Kandahar in December. He was soon busy, patrolling, reconnoitring, on one occasion using his skill as a draughtsman to prepare the maps which were later to explain the defeat of an earlier British army at the court martial of those who had commanded it. As usual he organised the 'theatricals' which kept the regiment happy, performing notably in *The Pirates of Penzance*.

When the political decisions had been taken and it was time for the British column to return to India, it was Baden-Powell who commanded the escort which fired the salute when the Union Jack came down. His adventures, however, were not entirely over – on the return journey, preparing himself to repel horse-thieves, he examined a pistol which he had lent to his batman, experimentally pulled the trigger and shot himself in the calf.

While convalescing he developed his less martial skills, working at his French and his Hindustani, brushing up his musical and dramatic repertoire, and preparing the articles and sketches he was now beginning to send back to the *Graphic*, an illustrated periodical in London which paid him a guinea for each of them. He spent the next three years in the ways then common among the officers quartered in India; the difference was that he did a little more than was expected from most of them, becoming director of the regimental theatre, manager of the brass band, musketry instructor, riding master, instructor in reconnaissance and scouting (his Afghan experience coming in useful here), and a member of a highly successful regimental polo team, as well as working hard at the office duties with which he had been burdened when appointed adjutant. He also, around this time, discovered the sport of pig-sticking. He seems to have had little difficulty in picking up the tricks of this mounted confrontation with an enraged boar, for in 1883 he won the Kadir Cup, proof of the highest level of accomplishment.

Not content with this, he began work on a book, based on the instruction he was giving in scouting. There is no question that he was ambitious, always keeping a cool eye on how his own situation might be advanced by his activities. The Army in India, after all, was swarming with eager and hopeful young officers, most of them with much more behind them in the way of money, breeding and connections than he had. He can hardly be blamed for trying every means he knew and using every talent he had to further his career. When he undertook his book, which appeared in 1884 under the title *Reconnaissance and Scouting*, he wrote, 'Even if it did not sell more than twenty copies it would be a grand advertisement for me – because I could send copies to all the boss quartermaster-generals, Wolseleys, etc . . .' Sir Garnett Wolseley was Quartermaster-General of the British Army; he was to cross Baden-Powell's path several times later, always with happy results for the young officer.

He sent sketches for exhibition in Simla, where the 'best people' spent their pleasant, promiscuous summers. He bought and broke horses of a quality which would get him talked about. He went to endless trouble to find new material for the entertainments he put on and starred in. When Queen Victoria's third son, the Duke of Connaught, visited India, he found himself caught up in a constant whirl of self-display – one day as the young officer who had drawn those splendid maps of the Afghan battlefield, another as the expert on pig-sticking, a third as the star of *Box and Cox*.

He shared a bungalow with an officer named McLaren, but nicknamed 'The Boy' because of his youthful appearance; when Baden-Powell had met him first, he had assumed him the son of the regimental doctor. One wonders why it was the most immature-looking of all the officers in the regiment that Baden-Powell chose as his closest friend. Between the lines of his official biographies, one can sense a boyish, play-acting delight in at least the appearance of a Henty-like derring-do. He did not shirk from danger, certainly, and he was not in an odious sense a 'show-off', but he seems to have revelled in the game-like elements which accompanied war in those far-off days and places. He enjoyed prominence and he enjoyed exploits, special events which one can imagine him romanticising even as he described them to himself as 'real-life' adventures. And it is this kind of immaturity which one senses in his sexual personality, too, a kind of immaturity, indeed, which the sequestered life of a British cavalry officer in India can have done little to dispel.

He was twenty-seven by this time, and a captain; his name was one sometimes mentioned in high places and often seen in the newspapers. He was daily in company of the Duke of Connaught. Yet when he received a note from an unnamed young lady, he forwarded it at once to his sister, with a letter which, while joking, might have been written by someone ten years younger: 'What do you think of this from a young lady? I had told her I would take her for a ride on an elephant to see a big native fair – only she must be prepared for jeers from the Artillery mess as we went by and also she must get Mrs A. to chaperon me. I warned her that if she attempted to make love to me I should immediately get off the elephant and walk home with Mrs A.' But he pacifies any nervousness his mother might feel at these goings-on – '... behind my sleeve I grin the grin which only I can grin' – and then, perhaps facetiously, adds, 'I'm going to wait until I'm a major and then it will be a £50,000 girl at home.'

In 1884 the 13th Hussars were sent to South Africa, there to be held in reserve in case trouble, which had swirled around the borders of the Transvaal, should break out again. Here Baden-Powell wrote another of his useful little books, *Cavalry Instruction*. He also did a ride of 600 miles in three weeks, in order to bring some reality to the maps the Army was using, mapping, sketching and describing the terrain he passed through. But he did not, as he seems to have hoped, see any action – by the end of 1885 he was in England again. Reconnaissance, however, seems now to have become a way of life with him. In 1886 he appeared at the German army's summer manoeuvres in an effort to assess the potentiality of a new machine gun. Seen at an inopportune moment by a sentry, he pretended to be drunk, thus being led to safety instead of dragged into danger. Attempting to observe the Russian manoeuvres later that year, he made a slip – he did not salute the passing entourage of Tsar Alexander III. Arrested, he found himself under surveillance in his hotel (those were gentlemanly days and to be English was to be half-excused for any crime). He and his brother Baden, who was with him, decided on a plan – they talked in a loud voice about their intention to leave by train, then nipped aboard the ferry for Copenhagen, thus outwitting the sinister machinations of the Tsarist police.

In 1887 Baden-Powell was once more promenading the defences and potential battlefields of Europe. He examined the fortifications of Antwerp, he hobnobbed with Uhlans, he observed the inspection of the French forces by General Boulanger. In his heart was the hope that France was on the verge of seeking revenge for 1871 and that he would be able to watch the subsequent events, publicly and lucratively, as a war correspondent. But in the end there was no war. Baden-Powell returned to England and his own manoeuvres. Here again his efforts brought him to the attention of his superiors. He had met Torsten Nordenfelt, inventor of the machine gun named after him, and had got the use of one, mounted on a carriage. This he used during the Grand Military Tournament, one event among the thousands which marked Victoria's Jubilee. Shortly afterwards, Wolseley, still Quartermaster-General, came to see him: what did he think of the gun? Baden-Powell waxed enthusiastic, harnessed up the carriage, and galloped off with the gun and the General over the dunes of Seaforth. By September the Nordenfelt gun was going into use with the cavalry.

Soon Baden-Powell was on his way to South Africa again. His uncle, now General Smyth, had been put in command there and, not for the first time, asked him to become his ADC. Although suspicious of office soldiering, Baden-Powell now took the opportunity to go abroad, arriving in Cape Town early in 1888. Desk-work bound him for a while, as he had feared. Northward, however, in Zululand, Dinizulu and his impis were besieging Umsinduze. Threatened by the Boers, once his allies, this son of Cetywayo had called on the British, who had replied by annexation as the simplest way of ensuring that the march of the Afrikaners remained within bounds. Dissatisfied with this, Dinizulu had turned on his hoped-for protectors. Now the local magistrate, Pretorius, with a few hundred men, was trapped in this small town. Four hundred mounted men, with two hundred police, were formed into a relief column. Baden-Powell was taken from behind his desk and made staff officer to the column's commander.

Once in Umsinduze, the column settled to the protection of the town, while Baden-Powell was sent off on his favourite game, reconnaissance. He found an interpreter and Zulus who would work for him. He traversed the local countryside, and sent them even further afield. Finally he located Dinizulu and his army, hidden on the scarred and rocky slopes of a mountain called Ceza, near the borders of the Transvaal. Smyth moved his HQ close and prepared to attack, but had to wait four days until confirmation of this order came from Cape Town. By then Dinizulu was gone. The Zulu resistance collapsed, the desk once more claimed Baden-Powell; not exclusively for administrative work though. In 1889 he brought out a book that earned him surprisingly wide and generally favourable reviews: *Pig-sticking or Hoghunting*.

Baden-Powell fell ill again and, as before, returned to England. He did not remain inactive long, but talked his way into the post of secretary to Sir Francis de Winton, a member of the Royal Commission appointed to consider the political problems of Swaziland. While on the way there, he was among those presented to the President of the Transvaal, Paul Kruger – 'Oom Paul', the grim old 'uncle' who would be causing him and the rest of Britain so much trouble within a very few years.

When Swazi independence was guaranteed, Baden-Powell returned to find his uncle General Smyth now Governor of Malta. He invited Baden-Powell there as his military secretary, and thus the next three years were for this ambitious officer, now in his early thirties, rather routine and even boring. But in the process he became Intelligence Officer for the area, and was thus able to indulge his passion both for reconnaissance and amateur dramatics by travelling about the countries of the Mediterranean basin in various disguises. The most imaginative was that of lepidopterist.

Covered in the nets and bottles of the dedicated butterfly-collector, he made his way to Cattaro (now Kotor) in Yugoslavia, there to draw endless fanciful insects, the delicate patterns of whose wings actually concealed outline plans of the local fortifications. He managed to watch the manoeuvres of the Austrian army from a spot only two or three hundred yards from the vantage point where Franz-Josef, the Emperor, had himself been placed with his two colleagues, Kaiser Wilhelm and the King of Saxony. He watched the Italian manoeuvres while ostensibly engaged on various studies of dawn on the Alpine slopes, sketches to which the artistic Italian officers responded with some enthusiasm. And in Turkey he discovered that some new guns which had intrigued him and others for some time were just the old guns after all, covered with a tarpaulin by the wily Turk in order to give potential enemies the idea that they were something especially dangerous and secret.

Sir Henry Smyth's governorship came to an end and in 1893 Baden-Powell was back in England. His eldest brother, George, had just got married: 'I think it's a rare good thing for him,' he had written home, 'and I hope the example will not be set in vain for the rest of the family (always excepting me – I'm too young yet!)', He was now thirty-six. He rejoined the 13th Hussars, now in Ireland, as a Major and once more began to build up his journalistic output; he was, after all, by no means a rich man.

In 1895, however, he was away again – this time to the Gold Coast, assigned to the staff of Sir Francis Scott. The British were setting off on one of their periodic forays against the Ashanti, a warlike people who had for three centuries made a fat profit out of the supply of slaves, until the fading away of that trade early in the nineteenth century had left them without a market. Their raids on their neighbours still had their logic, since they believed in a religion which prominently featured the blood sacrifice. The British had tried to put down this practice and, as a result, had found themselves involved at intervals in four Ashanti Expeditions. The score now stood at two-all; Sir Francis Scott planned to win the final rubber.

Baden-Powell organised a levy of local men, marched them through jungle to the town of Prahsu, there recruiting more men and training those he had. Then he moved on, both scouting the area ahead and preparing a route for the army, following closely behind. In Kumasi, the Ashanti capital, King Prempeh held a council of war. His scouts appeared, watched the column for a while, then stepped away into the jungle again. But no one opposed the advance, and within a short time the troops of the British column were marching among the huts and wooden walls of Kumasi, observed by the King wearing a black and gold tiara. Finally, to everyone's surprise, the King got down from the throne on which he had been carried, walked to where Sir Francis was seated among his officers, and quietly surrendered.

The Governor arrived in Kumasi – formality was all and total surrender could only be made to him. Late one night, in Prempeh's daub-and-wattle palace, the chiefs quietly gathered. But Baden-Powell was suspicious and posted himself beside a secret path he had found, which led away from the palace and out into the jungle, where who knew how many warriors waited for the signal to leap into battle. He had his men wait deeper in the shadows, so that if the chiefs tried to slip away in order to call up their followers, he would be there to prevent them.

It was three in the morning before the first of the chiefs came hurrying past, to find himself ambushed and quietly tied up. At intervals the others came, each trying to sustain a secrecy he imagined unbroken. Each was captured – the last, so the story runs, by Baden-Powell himself. Thus, in the morning, Prempeh had to make his submission, only to fall into one of those imperialist traps which always waylaid the African when trying to deal with the civilised white man. The Governor had demanded indemnity for the wrongs done – 50,000 ounces of gold. Prempeh said he could only produce 680 ounces immediately. The Governor thereupon arrested him, the queen mother and all the leading chiefs and ordered Baden-Powell to search for the gold he was convinced was there. Thus the Major found himself ransacking the royal palace, despoiling the royal burial places and trampling through the sacred fetish houses of the Ashanti people – all this, as was the custom of the day, without a thought as to what it might mean to those who saw it, or to those who would remember it through the seven colonial decades that were to follow. He did not discover the gold, carried, as he supposed, into the jungle by the priests; he seems to have been disappointed that he did not turn up the Golden Stool which was supposed to contain the soul of the Ashanti people.

Back in England, it was only a few months before Baden-Powell, now a Brevet Lieutenant-Colonel, found himself appointed Chief of Staff to Sir Frederick Carrington and once more travelling to Africa. The Army was on its way to put down a rising by the Matabele, a branch of the Zulus. Rhodes, then energetically carving out large pieces of southern Africa for an empire he must have thought of as almost his own property, had done a deal with Lobengula some years earlier. When this king of the Matabele realised how one-sided the arrangement actually was, he struck violently back. The forces of the British South Africa company under Dr Jameson – Rhodes's private army led by Rhodes's private general – smashed this attack on them; Lobengula fled, then died. In 1896 Jameson went on his famous raid against the Boers (see p. 213) and was defeated ignominiously. Heartened by this, and by the prophecies of their god, M'Limo, the Matabele under their new leader, Mlugulu, rose again with all the force of their old desperation. They planned to descend on Bulawayo, 'the place of killings', and destroy all the white people there. Some, however, attacked too soon and thus gave warning of the doom that had been planned. The settlers built barricades around the town, determined to remain; soon they were reinforced by the Matabele Relief Force under Major Plumer, and, in June 1896, by Carrington's column from England.

Conditions in Bulawayo were difficult. Baden-Powell wrote in his diary, 'I live on bread, jam and coffee, and that costs five shillings and prices are rising.' He worked, by all accounts very efficiently, as Chief of Staff; in addition, he took on the necessary scouting duties, as usual. At the beginning he worked with an American, F. R. Burnham, who had learned his bush-craft in the Indian wars. Later, and for his longer trips in the field, he travelled with Jan Grootboom, a Zulu who also knew a number of tricks Baden-Powell was happy to learn. He was himself by now an efficient scout – Vere Stent, a war correspondent, described him on one of his missions: 'Wearing soft rubber shoes, he used to spend his nights prowling about the Matoppos [the hills where the Matabele hid], spying on the rebels, calculating their numbers and locating their camping grounds. ... One night, after much persuading, he took me with him. ... Soon we were amidst the great giant boulders of the Matoppos, where he seemed completely at home. He led me by a rough footpath on to a kop. Peering over this, we could see, not 500 yards distant, the fires of an impi. Signing to me to be silent, we watched for a few minutes and then, on a sign from Baden-Powell, we moved off by another path. "Never return by the same road you took." ... It was with a sigh of relief that I found myself once more safely in Plumer's camp. Once was enough. I never asked to be taken again.' A year later a trooper described him, heading a column which drove up from Bulawayo into Mashonaland: 'He wore the typical "Baden-Powell" hat, a blazing red shirt with a large neckerchief, the knot at the back, breeches and leather gaiters, in which was a sort of pocket containing a revolver, so that when mounted on his pony he only had to stoop down to draw a revolver from either leg.' It is clear that he had lost none of his sense of the dramatic, and this had its effect, certainly on the Matabele, who were said to call him *Impeesa*, 'the wolf that never sleeps'.

On one of these raids Baden-Powell found himself in somewhat bad odour with his superiors. He had captured Uwini, one of the priests of M'Limo, who had taken refuge with his men in a maze of caves and underground passages. To force his followers to surrender, Baden-Powell had him court-martialled and executed on the spot. His men surrendered, but there was a move from Cape Town to have the Colonel himself court-martialled; instead, Carrington ordered a commission of inquiry which exonerated him.

There is no doubt that his experiences on this campaign taught Baden-Powell much about scouting, both from his own experience and from working with the experienced men who were his colleagues. After the uprising had been put down and peace made at an Indaba arranged by Jan Grootboom and attended by the remaining Matabele chiefs on one side and Cecil Rhodes on the other, Baden-Powell wrote a book, *The Matabele Campaign*. In it he both emphasised and described the value of scouting: 'Suddenly my boy gave a "How!" of surprise, and ten yards off the track picked up a leaf – it was the leaf of a tree that did not grow about here, but some ten or fifteen miles away; it was damp, and smelled of Kaffir beer. From these signs it was evident that women had been carrying beer from the place where the trees grew towards the Matoppos (they stuff up the mouth of the beer-pots with leaves), and they had passed this way at four in the morning (a strong breeze had been blowing about that hour, and the leaf had evidently been blown ten yards away). ... The men would not delay to drink up the fresh beer, and would by this time be very comfortable, not to say half-stupid ... so that we were able to go and reconnoitre more nearly with impunity. ...' Later, he adds, 'We English have the talent of woodcraft and the spirit of independence already inborn in our blood to an extent to which no other nationality can claim, and therefore among our soldiers we ought to find the best material in the world for scouts.'

Promoted to Brevet-Colonel, Baden-Powell was now in the odd position of being of higher rank than his commanding officer in the

13th Hussars. After a short spell in England, therefore, he was once more sent away to India, this time to command his own regiment, the 5th Dragoon Guards. He seems to have been a popular CO, bringing into play all his experience of commanding men. As one subaltern later wrote, 'We all felt ready to do anything for, or go anywhere with, him.'

Although in command, with the health, training, morale and the quarters of his men his constant concern, Baden-Powell found time as always to make his journeys – the longest several weeks' trip to Kashmir. He made a voyage high into the narrow valleys and rocky defiles of the North-west Frontier, where he managed to involve himself in one of those isolated skirmishes which went to make up the continuing love-hate war the British carried on against the Pathan. He went hunting, but, as he wrote, 'I could never bring myself to shoot an elephant.... It strikes me as an impertinence to put an end to a wise old creature a hundred and fifty years old and of such massive proportions.' He played polo again, and recovered his skill at pig-sticking; he acted, as so long before, in Simla's operetta – and offered the gossips of that self-regarding place a chance to notice the attentions he paid to one of the play's leading ladies.

In December 1898 manoeuvres were held some ten miles from Delhi. Of the twelve regiments participating, Baden-Powell's 5th Dragoon Guards came first in scouting, manoeuvring, parade movements, assault at arms and the condition of the horses. It must have been with some satisfaction that he left in the following spring for a long leave in England. Probably he looked forward to it; he was now in his early forties and might have felt that he deserved a rest. Yet he liked to be seen and to make himself noticeable to those who might be useful. As he wrote to his mother about his acting at Simla, 'You may think it an awful waste of time on my part, but there was a lot of nasty cool calculation underlying my taking the part....'

Two weeks after his arrival in England, he was summoned to the Commander-in-Chief, Lord Wolseley, and ordered to go at once to South Africa. The *uitlanders* or foreigners in Paul Kruger's Transvaal, most of them British, had been growing restive because of their lack of political power. Kruger wanted any concessions on that score to be balanced by a withdrawal of British suzerainty over a country the Boers considered their own. The resultant disagreements and tensions had, by 1899, grown to look like the harbingers of violence. Now Wolseley wanted Baden-Powell to raise two regiments of mounted infantry and to see to the defences of Rhodesia and Bechuanaland, where their frontiers marched with those of the Transvaal. In Bulawayo, a town now blessed with electric light and transformed from the bare settlement he had known only a few years earlier, he was reunited with two old friends – 'The Boy' McLaren and Plumer, now a Colonel. He organised his two regiments, one based on Bulawayo and the banks of the Limpopo, the other on Ramathlabama, in Bechuanaland, a tiny place twenty miles north of Mafeking. By September he could write to his mother that his two regiments were 'raised, mounted, equipped and fed for three months to come'.

War preparations continued. Kruger bought arms from Europe, Britain sent her soldiers from the corners of the Empire, although most were due to arrive from India. Baden-Powell had remained clear of Mafeking, since to base his soldiers there would be to alarm the Boers. Now he received permission to mount a guard over the stores which were accumulating there and, since no one had specified the size of that guard, moved in his whole regiment. By October, as the situation worsened again, he was fortifying the town, building a double line of defences while demanding from Cape Town guns which were never to arrive. He had some 750 men under arms, some local, some volunteers, most untried. He introduced 300 Africans as an auxiliary force, to be used for guarding cattle, as watchmen, as civil police. He posted notices warning passers-by that he was laying a ring of mines to defend the town, then let off dynamite in an explosion which convinced Boer spies that he was indeed doing so – as he probably would have done, had he had any. He built shelters to protect women and children. And, in the middle of all these hectic preparations, he read and passed the proofs of his new book, *Aids to Scouting*. On the afternoon of 11 October 1899 Kruger's final ultimatum to the British came to an end. The Boer War was under way.

Baden-Powell's first act was to send some two hundred women and children to safety in Kimberley (the Government later refused to pay their fare – 'Nor will I!' wrote Baden-Powell in his diary). Then he sat down to wait for the arrival of the large force of Boers which he had himself seen a few days earlier on a scouting expedition preparing their *laager* only a few miles away, just inside the Transvaal. By 13 October that force had arrived, moving in from every side, well armed, mounted, provisioned and determined. Baden-Powell had done what he could; now he would see how well his foresight would stand the test of actual events. He was about to become the hero his story-book life seems always to have prepared him to be.

He felt he knew why it was necessary to hold Mafeking – not only because it governed some of the approaches to Kimberley and even Cape Town to the south, or stood as a crucial outpost for Bechuanaland and Rhodesia to the north, or even because by remaining in British hands it threatened the flanks of the Transvaal itself, but because fifteen years before it had been the scene of a British stand against the Boers and more recently it had been Jameson's base before his sortie to Johannesburg. It had so great a propaganda and emotional value for the Boers that if it fell, it was said that all the Dutch in the Cape would rise in unison with their Transvaal cousins. It was for this reason that nine thousand Boers, led by Cronje, 'the Lion of the Transvaal', now invested the town.

Baden-Powell began his Standing Orders with the words, 'Bluff the enemy with show of force as much as you like', and his own first manoeuvre showed that he intended to keep to that directive himself. He sent out his armoured train on a sortie and, when it came under heavy fire, reinforced it. After four hours the Boers retreated. Baden-Powell predicted in his diary, 'This smartly fought little engagement will have a great and lasting moral effect on the enemy.' Later, shelling began; after the first bout of this, Cronje asked the garrison to surrender. Baden-Powell contemptuously dismissed the demand. The shelling continued. Several days later Baden-Powell sent a message by runner to Colonel Plumer: 'All well. Four hours' bombardment. One dog killed.' Plumer passed the message on to London; when the newspapers printed it, the public seized on the words as typifying what they imagined the war was about, what England stood for.

Cronje, believing the town mined and nervous of the armoured train, ordered up cannon to belabour Mafeking into submission. He warned Baden-Powell of this, offering to allow civilians to leave. Baden-Powell refused, thus helping to initiate a correspondence which, often with surprising humour and always with politeness, both men continued until Cronje's departure. But Cronje's threat turned out to be a real one – from the end of October Mafeking was shelled almost every day by ponderous siege guns manufactured in the European works of Krupp and Creusot.

Major Lord Edward Cecil, Baden-Powell's Chief of Staff, formed the Mafeking Cadet Force. There had been something of a problem with the energy and unharnessed enthusiasm of the young boys who remained. Now, drilled and dressed in khaki, they became the garrison's messenger service. In their spare time, they drilled or played improving games.

Cronje now decided on a closer siege. He pushed his men forward, until they were digging in not more than a mile from the outer line of defences. Baden-Powell decided on counter-attack, and sent a force out at night which, creeping up the Boer flank, turned and cleared the length of the most advanced trench. The besiegers, retreating, were mistaken by their own men in the reserve trenches for the advancing ranks of the British; desperate shooting continued long after Baden-Powell's soldiers had returned safely to the besieged town.

Using carbide and old biscuit tins, a searchlight was devised and rushed from place to place, until the Boer besiegers imagined that Baden-Powell had a battery of them. Realising that because of the distance he could not actually see the wires which the Boers had strung up before their trenches, Baden-Powell ordered posts to be set up in front of his own defences and every man to behave as if wire had indeed been stretched in place. The Boers took note and, as with the mines, redoubled their caution. Ruses of this sort confounded the enemy and raised the morale of the defenders. To raise that even higher, Baden-Powell called up all his old talents, once deployed to gain the attention of a Viceroy. He put on plays, concerts, sports, even baby shows, enabled to do so by the strict Sabbatarianism of the Boers, who every Sunday called a punctilious halt to the war.

After a month Cronje, impatient, moved away. He left three thousand men and the artillery, under the command of General Snijman. Thus the siege wore on to Christmas, but on Boxing Day Baden-Powell suffered his first defeat. A force sallying to take a Boer stronghold found the enemy waiting and prepared, and lost more men and officers than they could afford. However, the improvising spirit continued: a gun, cast in 1770, was found and made serviceable; then another on the same model was manufactured in the railway foundry.

Naturally enough supplies were running low. It was in February 1900 that the defenders began to slaughter horses, thus releasing horse fodder, especially oats, for human consumption. An infestation of locusts was put to good use; fried, they were surprisingly palatable. Baden-Powell eased the clogging of the local economy by producing his own money; he printed his own Mafeking stamps (these used his own head – against his will, he always insisted). But, at the perimeter, ammunition was beginning to run low. Plumer tried to get a column through at the end of March, but failed. Baden-Powell suffered a few days of anguish when it was thought that his old friend, 'The Boy' McLaren, had been killed; but had his morale restored to some extent when he learned that he was only wounded, although a Boer prisoner.

Runners more or less regularly brought through letters, and Baden-Powell was able to receive personal news from England for the first time. 'You are the hero of the day,' his sister Agnes wrote. 'Your photo is in all the shops now, and on inquiring they say yours is first favourite. . . .' Queen Victoria sent her restrained but heartfelt commendations. And 'Creaky', the great siege gun which had plagued them, after a final bombardment, was silently withdrawn. In mid-May, however, what Victoria had called Baden-Powell's 'ever resourceful command' was put to the test: a force of Boers broke through a weak spot in the defences and began firing the African houses. Outside the town, Boer forces gathered. Baden-Powell realised they were waiting for a signal to attack. He sent a note to his wounded friend, McLaren, which said in part that 'the Boers made an attack on us and we have scuppered the lot'. As he had known they would, the Boers intercepted and read his note – the morning was subsequently made more cheerful by the sight of hundreds of sullenly disappointed Boers climbing out of their advanced hiding-places and glumly going back to their own investing lines. The garrison turned at its leisure on the remaining attackers within the perimeter and soon forced them to surrender.

At three in the morning of 17 May Baden-Powell was woken up by someone shaking him. It was his brother, Baden, Intelligence Officer of the Relief Force. After 217 days Mafeking had been relieved. In London there was frenzy. The theatres emptied, while the streets and squares filled with crowds of shouting, cheering people. News-boys raced along packed pavements, selling copies of their extra editions. 'Hurrah for Mafeking!' was the cry, 'God save the Queen!' – and 'Three cheers for B.-P.!' After a year of gloom, when Britons in some dismay had seen their army defied by heterogeneous if determined congregations of farmers, hemmed in at some points and beaten at others, the victories which they had assumed theirs by natural right were once more beginning to occur. Mafeking, which had seemed a symbol of their refusal to accept defeat, now became in its relief a herald of triumph to come – and Baden-Powell personified Mafeking.

There were always two opinions as to the actual value, in military terms, of Baden-Powell's holding operation. Charged with guarding a frontier, he had allowed himself to be cooped up in an unimpressive railhead. Although always under pressure, he had never had to suffer a sustained attack by the Boers, who were, in any case, unused to siege warfare. Surrounded though he was, he was always able to keep lines of communication open to the south. In some ways the siege of Mafeking was one of the best-reported actions of its kind in the history of warfare. Those who had always suspected him of a deliberately eye-catching flamboyance (with some justification, as his own letters bear witness) now thought of Mafeking as another of his exercises in self-advertisement. Yet in fairness, he never really had the forces to control that whole frontier area; by settling in Mafeking, he stopped Cronje's advance for over a month and in a war of small armies tied down several thousand Boers and a proportion of their artillery for the whole period of the siege. Not only that, the British hold on Mafeking had a high moral value; while Baden-Powell remained there, the Boers could not think themselves victorious – despite Magersfontein and Colenso – nor the British as entirely defeated. As for his reputation, it was several months before he could have had any idea of the impact his stand was making in Britain and none of his dispatches, although they appeared in the Press, was ever written for that purpose. More damaging were criticisms about his lack of concern for the Africans, whose rations were markedly lower than those of the Europeans. But Baden-Powell was a man of his time, essentially a Victorian buoyed up by ideas of racial and national superiority – few British officers of the day would have acted differently.

The moment the line to the south was open, some five hundred telegrams descended on Mafeking and Baden-Powell. From England he heard that his London home was being inundated by the flood of letters, cables, poems and tributes. But it was not until he rode into Pretoria to meet his C-in-C, Lord Roberts, that he realised that his status now was that of imperial hero. The crowds that welcomed him bayed as they must have during some Roman triumph. (While there, he was interviewed by a young journalist whose scoops and exploits were themselves interwoven with the history of the Boer War – Winston Churchill.)

For most of that summer Baden-Powell traversed South Africa, playing a sort of complex military chess with commando leaders like de Wet. But Milner, the High Commissioner, wanted the country put on a peace-time footing and, to do that, insisted that a mobile police force should be established. Baden-Powell, since Mafeking the youngest Major-General in the British Army, was the man chosen to found this corps, the South African Constabulary. Thus, as Roberts and then Kitchener painfully brought the war to an end, Baden-Powell formed and trained this para-military force, among other things designing its uniform. They took as their slogan the words 'Be Prepared'.

In Britain the Queen died; the turn of the century had brought a new king to head a new era. In South Africa the war dragged on, the Boer fighting his elusive guerrilla campaign. Baden-Powell's SAC, therefore, found itself used, not against criminals or for the peaceful purposes Milner had envisaged, but as an auxiliary to the Army. Under pressure of work Baden-Powell fell ill; he came back to an England primed to put him through the circus-tricks it demanded of its heroes. He did what he had to do – an audience with the King, the presentation of a Sword of Honour, a vast family luncheon – but most of the time he kept out of sight, travelling on occasion under an assumed name.

In South Africa again Baden-Powell saw the war end and his new force begin its intended peacetime work. But in 1903 the army asked to have him back, to serve as Inspector-General of Cavalry. From this position of influence he helped reorganise the cavalry, a task dear to his heart but, given the technical developments then overtaking the horse in other spheres, less far-sighted than he may have hoped. In 1907, at a dinner of some splendour, attended by army men already famous, or about to become so in the war which Baden-Powell was among those beginning to expect, he came to the end of his military career.

It is hard now, through the solidity of his reputation, to realise what this must have meant to him. Action had been his whole life, for preference action where an audience could appreciate it. He needed admiration, although the adulation he received after Mafeking was always too exaggerated and indiscriminate for him to enjoy. Now, at fifty, the adventures, the excitements in faraway places, the grudging respect of 'savages' whom he was able to beat at their own game, thus proving the natural superiority of Englishmen, the saddling-up, the parades, the mess-table jokes, the comic operas, the wild animals a ride away to be shot or sketched – all that was over. And the future offered nothing but old age and an ignominious death, leaving behind no more than a footnote in the history of a minor war: Mafeking.

In a way, however, this new inactivity allowed an old preoccupation of his to rise to the surface. All his life he had played games. His expeditions and battles, costumes and uniforms, had always been an extension of boyhood play, something which was only a more rigorous and public version of the hiding and tracking he had done in The Copse, a section of rough, wooded country near Charterhouse in which he had spent as much time as he could when a schoolboy. He had not, as yet, married. His closest relations were with his mother, his sister, his brothers, his friends. In essentials, therefore, this famous man had spent a lifetime as a child, accepting the responsibilities of the playing field or of a school prefect, while avoiding many of the personal responsibilities which mark the adult. He was, in short, a man who understood what boys enjoyed because their condition was so close to his own. At the same time his army career had given him an organisational ability which he still had the energy to put to use. It is no wonder that such a man, with all the charisma his reputation gave him, should have been the ideal person to found a youth movement which spread, first through Britain and then throughout the world.

The foundations of the Boy Scout Movement lay, of course, not only in Baden-Powell's character but in his experience. His thirty years face-to-face with the unruly minions of Empire and his adventures in both Africa and India were of the greatest importance; so, paradoxically, was the respect he had for certain of the African customs he had come across, most particularly the initiation ceremonies of the Zulus. But everything that he had learned about the way of the wild and of the 'savage' who inhabited it could now not only be put on display, but put to use and, he hoped, passed on.

The idea gathered speed almost without his conscious volition at first. The book, *Aids to Scouting*, the proofs of which he had corrected at Mafeking, proved to be a best-seller – partly because of the heroic name which adorned its cover. Then, in 1903, he had been greatly impressed by a rally of the Boy's Brigade which he attended. He had told the founder of the Brigade, Sir William Smith, 'that I would willingly change places to be in his shoes and look upon these splendid lads as my own'. When Baden-Powell had pointed out that if the Brigade could introduce more variety into its training methods it would attract even more boys, Sir William had suggested that Baden-Powell should rewrite his Army training book on scouting in a way which would appeal to boys.

From then on Baden-Powell was fired more and more by the idea of offering the growing lads of an imperial power the methods and training which would not only fit them, in a purely technical way, for the tasks that faced them, but which would also extend and strengthen their characters. By 1906 the first outline of a proposed training scheme was ready, and he sent it to Sir William Smith for his opinion. The objective of the scheme was, in his own words, 'to develop among Boys a power of sympathising with others, a spirit of self-sacrifice and patriotism. . . .' This was to be done by making 'Boys observant of details, and to develop their reasoning powers, and at the same time to inculcate in them the spirit of self-denial and of obedience to duty'.

What he needed was a medium through which to spread his ideas. His meeting with C. Arthur Pearson provided that. Pearson was a publisher, a man who from working as a clerk on the magazine *Tit-Bits* had moved on to found magazines and buy newspapers of his own. He was not an unadulterated idealist, but it may be that what the Scouting Movement needed at the time was precisely someone with the commercial awareness which could smell a profit in the association between the writings of Baden-Powell and the young people they were addressed to. In fairness one ought to add that Pearson was also known for his philanthropic work, despite Joseph Chamberlain's opinion of him as 'the greatest hustler I have ever known'. (Coming from a close associate of Cecil Rhodes, this may of course have been intended as a compliment.)

Another spur was the arrival through the post, in 1906, of a book entitled *The Birch-Bark Roll of the Woodcraft Indians*, by a man called Seton. This Englishman, living in the United States, had learned his skills during a childhood spent in the Canadian backwoods. His articles on 'American Woodcraft for Boys' had been the cause of 'tribes' of boys, called 'Seton's Indians' or 'Woodcraft Indians', coming into existence all over the United States. Baden-Powell, by agreement with Seton, obtained permission to incorporate some of the games and techniques Seton had worked out in his own forthcoming book.

In 1907, while on his last trip as Inspector-General to examine the condition of the cavalry in Egypt, he drafted out a new outline of his intentions, heading it 'Boy Patrols'. His object, he wrote, was to make 'the rising generation, of whatever class or creed, into good citizens or useful colonists'. The proposed organisation was to give, 'under the name of "Scouting", a novel and attractive form of training in manly qualities'. He then settled down and wrote the full text of the book which would launch the Scouting Movement. Almost at once its methods were tested. Baden-Powell had arranged that this should be so, taking a small island, Brownsea Island, among the indentations of the Dorset coast, for this purpose. His book finished on 23 July, he took a party of twenty boys of mixed social background to the island on 29 July. By the end of his month's stay, he was convinced that what he was doing was on the right lines, offering training and enjoyment to the age-group at which he was aiming.

Pearson provided an office, one room in Henrietta Street in London. He guaranteed the Movement financially for its first year and brought out a weekly, entitled *The Scout*. Most important of all, he brought out *Scouting for Boys* in six fortnightly parts. Selling at fourpence each, the first appeared in January 1908. From now on Baden-Powell was busy again, addressing meetings, writing articles, answering the rising spate of correspondence. Early in 1909 new offices were needed and taken in Victoria Street. By July there were over 400 Scoutmasters on the official list. By the end of that year, scouting was spreading to countries overseas, not all of them English-speaking, and its headquarters, a ten-room office, had a paid staff of fifteen, with eight unpaid volunteers. There were local committees throughout the country and the Empire, the patronage of the King had been obtained – and Baden-Powell's work had been recognised by an honour nothing he had done in the Army had earned him: he was now Sir Robert Baden-Powell.

In 1910 he resigned from the Army, giving up even the work he had been doing for the Territorials (in the course of which he had, incidentally, made a controversial speech predicting that Germany would become Britain's major enemy). The scouting movement grew, it seemed, without limit, fostered by his imaginative awareness that its units, and even its individuals, should be left to develop as far as possible without supervision. It was for this reason, for example, that he dismissed any idea of making army-style drilling a part of scouting; discipline of that sort was not his objective. What he wanted to encourage was self-reliance.

Perhaps the success of this movement he had started released something in him, permitted him some personal development which his earlier life had denied him, or for which it had not been necessary. In 1912, travelling to a lecture tour in the United States, he was introduced to a fellow passenger, Olave St Clair Soames. He remembered her – he had seen her once, two years earlier, walking her spaniel in Knightsbridge, and had been impressed by her gait. Maybe there was more about her that had impressed him then; now, together with her every day, he seems to have fallen almost instantly and unexpectedly in love. Although she was only twenty-two, with a father not much older than Baden-Powell himself, now fifty-four, she found herself in love with him. He was, after all, a hero, a famous man, upright and slim, with an endless variety of stories and a most practised manner of telling them. Thus, by the time their liner was steaming across the Caribbean on its way to its first stops in the West Indies, she was writing in her diary, 'Up before dawn to see him and kiss him. See Venezuela coast in the dim distance. . . .' And, a few days later, 'I'm so happy all day with him . . . Even when we try to be serious the imp of mirth steps in. We feel and think alike about everything. Perfect bliss.'

He travelled the United States, surrounded now by the business and the propaganda – and the success – of scouting. He moved on across the world – Japan, China, Australia, New Zealand, South Africa. Everywhere he was received at worst with respect, at best with tumultuous delight. And in many places he could see how the movement he had started just a few years earlier was spreading without apparent hindrance across these enormous distances.

In October 1912 Baden-Powell, now fifty-five, married Olave Soames, in a ceremony pared down to simplicity. They honeymooned – at the beginning in Lord St David's Roche Castle, in Pembrokeshire, later by camping out, in a style which must have revived in Baden-Powell memories of other skies and different canvas, in the mountains and deserts of Algeria. Two years later, Baden-Powell's mother, now aged ninety, died and personal grief merged into the emotions which Europe's greatest disaster now aroused in everyone. It was expected that the Scouting Movement might find the war a setback; on the contrary, boys saw the Scouts' uniform as a miniature version of that which their fathers wore and flocked to join, giving an emphasis to the movement's patriotic elements greater perhaps than even Baden-Powell had intended. Thus, when the war ended, the Boy Scouts – now including in the organisation both Cubs and Guides – were stronger than they had been before and poised to continue their world-wide expansion.

In 1920 the first World Jamboree of the Scouting Movement was held, long delayed by the four years of war, but now planned and organised with all the vigour which the movement itself was showing. The venue was the great exhibition hall at Olympia in London, and there on 30 July Scouts from every corner of the world marched past the Duke of Connaught, with Baden-Powell and his wife near him in the Royal Box. For eight days the boys performed the tableaux and sketches which had been devised to illustrate their methods, philosophy and way of life. On the last day Baden-Powell was there again, to see the closing ceremony.

At the end of the performance, made up of those items which had given most pleasure or caused most interest throughout the week, the arena filled with Scouts. A lane marked by the flags of all the nations represented was formed, and Baden-Powell walked solemnly through it to the dais from which he was to close the Jamboree. But before he could speak the clear voice of a boy intoned, 'We, Scouts of the world, salute you, Sir Robert Baden-Powell – Chief Scout of the World!' It was a title he had not devised or even heard of. As he stared down at them, the multi-coloured flags dipped in salute.

There were to be other Jamborees, he was to earn other titles. George V created him Lord Baden-Powell of Gilwell. He was to travel again, and to meet great men. Before he died in 1941, he was to see another war begin against the enemy he had predicted so many years before. But that moment at Olympia, in August 1920, must have been the greatest of his life.

Horatio Bottomley

SQUAT, florid, rhetorical, bloated, altogether unlikely, Horatio Bottomley remains one of the minor enigmas of history. Not that anything he did was mysterious – it is in its very obviousness that his own mystery lies. Why did it take so long to find him out? He was a magician the power of whose spells we can only recognise now by the number of princes he turned into toads, the number of men he turned into gulls. How he exerted that power, of what precise nature his spells were, we can never really know; we should have had to meet him to understand that and even then, as we ruefully counted our losses, we would probably have been no wiser. He fascinated: one can say little more than that. He was an ugly, pouch-eyed, dew-lapped little hypnotist and among those who played rabbit to his snake were some of the coolest and most cunning men in the country.

Horatio Bottomley was born in 1860. There is some possibility that he was the illegitimate son of one of the most famous Radicals and free-thinkers of the time, Charles Bradlaugh; there was a very strong resemblance between them, and Bottomley used to claim him as his father. But Bottomley's claims were usually more baroque embellishments of his personality than strict statements of historical fact. In any case, within five years he was an orphan, both his mother and his putative father having died and before he was ten he had been admitted to Sir Josiah Mason's Orphanage in Birmingham. He was taken in there partly because George Jacob Holyoake, another Radical leader and a founder of the Co-operative Movement, was his uncle. It was with his Holyoake relations that he stayed when, at the age of fourteen, he came back to his native London; for a while he certainly gave his politically active uncle help on the periodicals he edited, first *The Secularist* and later the *National Reformer*. This seems to have been his introduction to journalism; a more interesting and perhaps apposite apprenticeship may have been the time he spent in a solicitor's office where the managing clerk arranged the collection of a rate of his own invention from a number of City firms, although there is no suggestion Bottomley was involved in this fraud. After the police had put a stop to this, young Horatio moved on, first to another lawyer's office and then to work as a High Court shorthand writer. It is this that is given as his profession on the marriage certificate marking his wedding with young Eliza Norton in a Wandsworth chapel. He was twenty years old and about to exercise his first financier's muscles until he had developed into at least a mini-tycoon.

There were in various parts of London debating societies,

modelled on the methods and procedure of the House of Commons. Using his shorthand Bottomley began to report and publish the activities of these in a weekly called *The Debater* – charging a small fee in return for 'special attention'. From this first periodical he moved on, building up by the mid-Eighties a ramshackle publishing house named the Catherine Street Publishing Association. He brought out such journals as *The Furniture Gazette*, *Baby*, or *The Mother's Magazine*, *Youth* (which had Alfred Harmsworth, later Lord Northcliffe, as its sub-editor), *Draper's Record*, the then little known and unsuccessful *Financial Times* and a magazine called *The Municipal Review*, which in return for wide distribution in a selected borough would print a long and complimentary biography of its mayor.

With this as his base camp, Bottomley made his first attempt to scale the peaks; he went to see Osborne O'Hagan, a man still in his thirties but already famous in the City, with interests in collieries, breweries, cement and transport. O'Hagan, an easy, smiling man, but one not given to rashness, turned down Bottomley's request for financial backing. Catherine Street Publishing was too small for him as it stood, especially without printing facilities – had it had those, he pointed out, it could have handled all the printing for his other companies.

Two days later, Bottomley returned, with a printer named Douglas MacRae whose works had been running below capacity. O'Hagan, perhaps responding to this display of energetic initiative, added a small advertising agency and publishing house, Curtice & Co, to the package, founded MacRae, Curtice, underwrote half the 100,000 one-pound shares which were the new company's capital, and made Bottomley, at twenty-six, the chairman. Of the 50,000 shares that came on the market, only 231 were taken up; nevertheless MacRae, Curtice announced a 12 per cent dividend the following year and increased the share capital by another £20,000. For the first time Bottomley, at three meetings, let loose his oratorical powers and within a short time the new and the remaining shares had not only been sold, but doubled in value.

MacRae departed, taking with him, oddly, not the printing works he had brought, but the *Financial Times* and *Draper's Record*, always a profitable publication. Bottomley, now a printer, offered a number of large firms the opportunity of having all their printing done under one roof, instead of by several competing houses, and it says something about the increasing rationale of business that many of these took up an option on this offer. He also himself obtained an option on the printing of *Hansard*, the daily report of Parliamentary debates; with all this potential business in his hands, he went to O'Hagan again. This time, however, the canny financier refused to back his schemes – he thought Bottomley 'wanting in ballast' and 'unsuited to the paths of finance', as he put it, a verdict which suggests that he saw those paths as straighter than the routes Bottomley envisaged.

Despite this setback, the Hansard Publishing Union was founded, with a nominal capital of half a million pounds sterling. A month or so later, the Anglo-Austrian Printing and Publishing Union was founded, with the same capital issue and largely the same board of highly respectable directors. Indeed, at this time Bottomley must have seemed a highly respectable young man of great ability and unquestionable future; he had already stood for Parliament as a Liberal, halving the impregnable Tory majority in Hornsey and receiving a complimentary note from the aged Gladstone. He was the adopted candidate in the neighbouring constituency. There is therefore no need to be surprised at the calibre of his associates, who included a former Lord Mayor of London, nor at their endorsement of his ideas, which included the formation of a printing organisation with units active in both Britain and Europe, able to undercut opposition because of its size, able to switch work and seize opportunities – the kind of international firm, in fact, familiar today, although unknown among the fixed frontiers of those nationalistic final decades of the nineteenth century.

Bottomley travelled to Vienna and obtained options on thirteen Austrian publishing and printing firms, returning to ask his fellow-directors for an immediate sum of £75,000 as a deposit on the £600,000 the whole deal would cost. They paid up like the gentlemen they were, after which the record becomes a little obscure, although Bottomley did obtain three prolongations of the options. The directors voted him more money and themselves fees, and even went so far as to declare a dividend. This seems an odd way for reputable financiers to behave, but it was the way such people did behave when they were associated with Bottomley.

Early in 1891 a committee of shareholders finally stepped in and published a statement of accounts which, involving a total of £93,022, included the simple entry, 'Cash – to Mr Bottomley: £88,500'. The committee reported, not unexpectedly rather tartly, 'The Company has acquired no business in Vienna or elsewhere, has no property whatever, and its whole capital appears to be lost', adding that 'there are not sufficient funds to pay the expenses of printing this Report' – a sad enough remark, given the nature of the business which they were discussing.

The Hansard Publishing Union continued for a while, sustained more by the claims and promises of Bottomley than by the £500,000 which had been subscribed – there was to be expansion, new works were to be bought, the capital would be doubled. All this, however, came to an end when a Debenture Corporation, not receiving its expected dividend, put in a receiver. Bottomley struggled, issuing among other statements a 12,000-word *Manifesto to the Hansard Shareholders* which attacked everyone who had criticised or moved against him. It was all in vain and on 1 May 1891 he filed his first petition in bankruptcy.

The tale of early shipwreck does not end there, however; once the slackness with which the books were kept was revealed, the Board of Trade had to agree to a prosecution against him and his fellow-directors, on a charge of conspiring to obtain money from shareholders. As his trial approached he brought out a book of self-justification – *Horatio Bottomley, Hys Booke*. Perhaps because of his varied knowledge of the courts, he decided to conduct his own defence. He was by now, of course, a practised public speaker and seems, then as always, to have seen the courts as a platform from which he might spread his ideas and project his personality throughout the country. Sir Charles Russell had been going to defend Bottomley's co-defendant, Sir Henry Isaacs, but after a recent election found himself elevated to the Government as Attorney-General, so he led the prosecution, leaving Sir Henry to be defended by Sir Edward Clarke, the previous Attorney-General, who had originally intended to prosecute (a heart-warming and reassuring example of the professional flexibility of the Bar).

Russell's opening speech made a strong case – Bottomley had bought firms for the Hansard Union from his own nominees, who had earlier acquired them at a much lower figure; one of these nominees had been his own brother-in-law, who had simply endorsed the cheques with his name and paid them into the Bottomley account. Some £600,000, Russell said, had just disappeared. But Bottomley pleaded normal business procedures – nominees were nothing new, after all – and pointed out that he had gained the approval of his fellow-directors for what he had done without exerting any pressure on them. When one had said that the mill his brother-in-law had 'owned' seemed a poor investment, he himself had suggested they had better not buy it. He certainly had, as the prosecution charged, used the name Williams instead of his own –

did anyone doubt that if the sellers had had wind of the fact that Bottomley was buying, they would have raised their price? He established curiously cordial relations with a judge otherwise known to be hard on fraud offenders, and was given a great deal of latitude in his cross-examination of the Official Receiver – caught him out in a minor lie, forced him into contradiction, and left him a discredited witness and, incidentally, an enemy for life.

At a critical point the case was adjourned because of a juror's sickness. In the interval Russell left to serve with a Commission and was replaced by the Solicitor-General, a man unused to jury trials. He soon proved rather less at home, indeed, than Bottomley himself, and it seemed to observers that the bench shared the amusement this caused among Bottomley's followers. When the time for summing-up arrived, the judge announced himself quite unconvinced by the prosecution's case – he agreed that the directors had been neglectful, but neglect was not conspiracy. He thought the Official Receiver had shown bias against Bottomley. He said of Bottomley, 'He has a right to say, "I claim the right to be acquitted if you are satisfied"; that is the right every Englishman has!' Twenty-five minutes later the jury returned with a verdict of not guilty. 'Is that the verdict of you all?', asked the judge and, on being assured it was, said, 'In that case, there are thirteen of us.'

'His appearance at once arrested attention. Short and stout in person, he is relieved from insignificance by a massive head, a masterful power, and a certain geniality about the eyes and brow. ... Mr Bottomley represents the solid stuff out of which England's greatness has been woven.' Thus wrote an eye-witness at the time of the trial. 'The voice,' he added, 'is one of singular charm and power. Low, melodious and strong, it is an admirable instrument for an advocate.' One suspects this to be the view of a friend or hireling, but there is no doubt that this was the impression Bottomley made on thousands of the uncommitted over the years that followed. The eulogies he received were usually heartfelt and sincere. That head, that voice, were his natural weapons and, guided by his quick brain, they were deployed year after year to the delight and subsequent discomfiture of millions.

Not that he relied on these alone. He understood early that for the complexities of business as he conceived it (crudely enough, once examined, but camouflaged by the Bottomley rhetoric) and to further his ambitions as a Parliamentary candidate, he would need to have about him a few good men and true – good and true to him, in any case. He found them early, and he kept them long; most of this heterogeneous collection of smart operators never left him throughout his switchback and outrageous career. There was 'Tommy' Cox, an undersized ex-medical student, whose name appeared so often on the Bottomley prospectuses, circulars and company accounts he was known as 'Bottomley's rubber stamp'. There was a street-corner orator named John Harrison; he preferred to be called Perkins and because of the many times he set himself forth as 'a man of the people' he became known as 'The People's Perkins'. There was a furrier, Saul Cooper, who whisked usefully about the City; there was the brother-in-law, Dollman, already a bankrupt and now a veteran of the Hansard Union case; and there were others, in various gradations of sleaziness and criminality. And, glittering more visibly than this slightly down-at-heel, dog-eared little gang of semi-villains, one must not forget that bunch of city gentlemen, bedizened and accoladed, who for years moved profitably in step with Bottomley from one enterprise to another, lending him their respectability, obtaining from him in return, when they did not burn their fingers, their share of the long and pleasant proceeds of his frauds.

There was also, dimly, Mrs Bottomley. Eliza Norton had worked behind the counter in a dress-shop. Now, as Horatio's fortunes began to improve, she seems to have taken her changed situation with the dazed equanimity of the stupid. She lived on the periphery of her husband's life, never interfering in what he did, partly because she never really understood what that was. If asked to, in later years, she would travel abroad and live there, to come home obediently when told the time had come to do so. She seems not to have been extravagant and is, indeed, unlikely to have been given much opportunity to display such a propensity – Bottomley's generosity was always more a matter of gestures than hard cash. Once the early days of struggle and bargaining were over for him, and there was no longer any need for her to run his household and pinch those few pennies he allowed her, she never really had a function in his life. He had fathered a daughter, Florence, but showed her no more than the necessary affection; Horatio, it turned out, preferred chorus girls and the minor stars of musical comedy to anything he found at his own hearth. And now he discovered that more and more easily he could afford such simple luxuries as chorus girls and actresses, racehorses and their trainers, cases of champagne. In the gullibility of the British public there was a source of funds which must have seemed to him ceaseless and unplumbable. It was the tapping of this source that he now made his major ambition, the central activity of his energetic life.

The Hansard Union case had established him not only as a well-known figure, but by some paradox of public opinion as a successful man. Unquestionably he was honest – he had, after all, been acquitted. Thus the £600,000 which had disappeared had not, in fact, disappeared at all; and if the money had not disappeared, then naturally the companies had been a success. That no one except Bottomley (an honourable man, as the verdict proved) had made a profit could be explained by the admitted inefficiency of his underlings; while the bankruptcy had been forced by official malice, as the bringing of a baseless prosecution showed. If he had been given more time, if the bureaucracy had not been in so much of a hurry, doubtless everyone would have made a great deal of money. After all, Bottomley said so himself, constantly – and Bottomley, as the judge had demonstrated, was an honourable man. In some such way the shrewd, hard-headed, well-educated share-buying public of Britain, its eagle-eyed financiers at its head, urged themselves into a decision they were not to reverse for almost twenty years: for everyone to make a profit, you had to give Bottomley time – and, naturally, a little money. ... And, a little later, a little more time – and, naturally, a little more money....

In the meantime Bottomley still had to cope with the Hansard Union bankruptcy. This he proposed to do by putting all his property into the hands of the debtors and collecting the assets lying, ready to hand, in Vienna, kept there for the purposes of the Anglo-Austrian Printing & Publishing Union. Since he had only taken out options which he now did not have the money to take up, there were of course no assets in Vienna; nevertheless, despite the anguish of the Official Receiver, after a hearing dragging through two years Mr Justice Vaughan Williams accepted this scheme. The creditors, therefore, were finally paid off, not in solid coin gleaned from the sale of Viennese printing works, but in shares – The West Australian Loan & General Finance Corporation or Associated Gold Mines of West Australia had been floated in 1894 perhaps for this purpose. No planes, no intercontinental telephones, no radio – Australia was in all senses half a world away from London, a yellow desert haze, darkened by the memory of convict settlements – but now lit here and there by the glint of gold. It was romantic, it was far away, and this was the era of the gold rush: there were, after all, really lodes and nuggets in the Australian West and the Coolgardie and Calgoorlie fields were already being worked. No one worked them harder or gained more from them than Horatio Bottomley.

His methods were simple. He floated companies and people bought shares in them. Lake View South Gold Mines, Nil Desperandum Gold Mines, Waitekauri United Gold Mining Co., West Australian Joint Stock Founders, The Rubber Exploration Co. – the list is long and varied. In under ten years he launched companies which had a nominal capital between them of some £25 million. Every now and then – say, once a year or so – a Bottomley company would go into voluntary liquidation, thus becoming a candidate for one of his 'reconstructions'. This would be pushed through a shareholders' meeting packed with Bottomley men and meant that every public shareholder would then get a letter pointing out that there were enormous opportunities, that lack of capital had caused problems, that a new and enlarged company would now step forward into a glorious and profitable future, and that the fortunate shareholder was being given an opportunity to join in these triumphs to come. His original holding in the old company would be transferred to one worth double in the new – that is, if he held a £10 share now, he would hold a £20 share after the reconstruction. And yet he was not being asked to pay the full price for this magnificent opportunity; it was not an extra £10 he was being asked for, but only half that amount. At one stroke, he was assured, he would make himself a £5 profit. When the value of the shares rose, as it was bound to do, that profit would multiply – so hurry, hurry, hurry! And hurry they did, in their thousands, again and again, sending off their hopeful greedy cheques, their minds fixed on those teasingly elusive Antipodean profits.

If shareholders did not find this as attractive a programme as Bottomley hoped, they sometimes refused to play and asked for their money back. If they had small holdings, they would find the great man difficult to see and his underlings evasive. Threats of legal action sometimes squeezed out cash, although how often is not recorded. Holders of large blocks, however, were ushered respectfully into Bottomley's presence, there to sip champagne and find themselves interrupted by telephone calls clearly concerned with spectacular deals; an atmosphere of euphoria, of hopefulness, of energy, was evident. There were further horizons, newer projects – of course the visitor could have his money back, but did he not think that a wiser course would be to travel onwards to success? Another telephone call, talk of money, news from Australia, a second, a third glass of champagne – and the visitor would leave in the end, delighted to have been allowed to invest just a few more thousands in the spectacular schemes of Mr Bottomley. One only had to be with him for a short while, after all, to see how successful he was, how rich, how amiable, how far-sighted, how bound to succeed.

His life-style encouraged this view of him. He had a flat in Pall Mall and a number of places in the country, the most notable being at Upper Dicker, near Eastbourne. Here he had bought a cottage, which he slowly enlarged, with more sense of convenience than style, until it could take some thirty weekend guests; and here Mrs Bottomley lived, bemused, with Florence, an unexpectedly attractive child, while Bottomley played the squire, building new cottages for the villagers, planting trees on the recreation ground, presenting to the church a lectern and a Bible to read from it, giving employment to the men of the place, eight of them in the grounds alone. He spoke to everyone, found work for the workless and sometimes cancelled or paid their rent-arrears, gave sweets to the children and, when it was installed, invited everyone who needed it to use his telephone. The villagers accepted all this with a countryman's suspicion, but slowly came to like and appreciate him; the gentry, naturally, found him a bounder and his wife impossible.

All day he would drink champagne, dry for preference, beginning the day with a breakfast of kippers and champagne. From then on bottles were opened on every possible occasion and everyone who was with him shared them. He spent as much time as he could on the racecourse. In 1898 he bought his first horse; thereafter the Bottomley colours, vermilion-and-black jacket, white sleeves and cap, would often be seen on the courses of Britain, France and Belgium. His racing career was out of character with the rest of his life, not only because no one ever charged him with fixing a race, but also because of the wildness of his betting. His hasty and intemperate wagers, indeed, although they brought him some spectacular wins, might have given some of his associates cause to doubt his acumen in other areas – had it not been the display of that acumen which allowed him to bet on such a scale in the first place.

He was endlessly in quest of women – small and auburn-haired, for choice, but he was not over-choosey – almost all of whom were from the underpaid if high-spirited ranks of the chorus. But he was a strangely generous lover, in that he would want to meet the girl's family, offer a brother or father work, cable her constantly when she was out of town, sometimes put money into shows which offered her some opportunity to shine. (These last were almost uniformly disasters.) Sometimes Tommy Cox would find apartments for the girls; the lesser lights would have to accommodate Horatio in their own flats. He would run three or four such affairs at the same time, but even after the last poses of passion had been abandoned, he would often continue to take an interest in his ex-mistresses.

Thus he lived a life of wealthy unpretentiousness. He enjoyed simple things, but on a jovially gargantuan scale. He was vulgar, but only as the rich can afford to be. He never denied his origins, and he remained true to the proletarian pleasures which must once have seemed so desirable, seen from the bare tables and narrow cots of the Birmingham orphanage. As Julian Symons points out, 'All this is the poor man's dream come true. . . . By providing an incarnation of this dream in his own stout person, Bottomley took on the nature of a mythical fetish. Men and women willingly lost money in order that such a man should live the good life; it is customary to pay tribute to an idol.'

It was not quite as simple as that. At a meeting of the Hansard Union creditors, which Bottomley privately dubbed 'Hansard Day', he offered them a quarter of a million, a suggestion not surprisingly met with cheers. Some £100,000 was actually paid out – in gold shares. These were as always given a spurious value by Bottomley's unsupported but confident claims and many of the shareholders must have thought themselves fortunate when he stated, on one occasion, 'We found in one of our mines – one of those privately floated – there was practically in sight something like £4 million worth of gold.' When challenged about this at a shareholders' meeting, called when the shares had gone down to one-fifteenth of their face value, he repeated it – the gold was 'for all practical purposes in sight'. He was not, however, the chairman of the meeting, or the company, and the chairman took care to point out that 'the Board have no report . . . that there is four millions of gold in sight. . . . Mr Bottomley may have a report, but we have not.' In this way the company remained in the clear and the shareholders uncertain.

Bottomley's off-hand manner with criticism and his easy way of referring to vast sums always seems to have convinced his listeners that he had a clear conscience and an enormous fortune, both of which meant that they were themselves about to make a killing. When asked by a Mr Snow, a shareholder in Westralian Market Trust, why there was a disparity of some £700,000 in the figures and where that sum had gone, he is reported to have replied, 'In all sincerity and honesty, I have not the remotest idea'; at which there was laughter, which suggests something of the state of mindless euphoria into which he could manipulate his audiences.

By 1903, however, even those who had been rushing to fling themselves lemming-like to financial suicide over the cliffs Bottomley had provided were beginning to realise what was happening. Shareholders of the Associated Finance Corporation, which had been 'reconstructed' no less than eight times, insisted on a committee to examine the company's affairs – a step which Bottomley, adept at packing any gathering with well-wishers, was never to fear. The committee decided that the directors had, on the whole, been both incompetent and stupid – but exempted Bottomley himself from this verdict. There was one further reconstruction, creating the Joint Stock Trust & Finance Corporation and Selected Gold Mines of Australia, which has the distinction of being the last in the long line of Bottomley's gold-mining companies. Those mythical fields at the other end of the world were at last used up – hardly surprising when one realises that Bottomley had taken some £3 million in very real money out of them in under ten years.

In 1900 there had been the highly patriotic campaign of the Unionist party in what came to be known as the 'Khaki Election'. Summoning the fervour the Boer War had aroused, and channelling it to their cause, they had swept the country. Bottomley, however, standing as a Liberal in South Hackney, had only narrowly missed winning a seat, and had ever since been assiduously nursing it, speaking there often himself, while making sure that his minions, notably 'The People's Perkins', put in frequent appearances. He seems never to have been tempted to become a Conservative; his early Radical connections perhaps made this psychologically difficult, and in any case his *persona* was always that of an ordinary man. He never pretended to a culture or a background not his own; it was the platform and the respectability that being an MP would give him that he wanted, not the imitation gentility which would have been forced on him as an outsider in the Tory party's chilling embrace.

More to further the cause of self-advertisement, apparently, than anything else, he bought the London evening newspaper, the *Sun*, in 1903. In this he ran stories of scandals – he always found an attack on 'massage establishments' very good for readership – attacked the Unionist government, although always careful to give the Boer President Kruger the required number of whacks, and featured his own speeches and appearances with a somewhat disproportionate prominence. The editor of the *Sun*, Theodore Dahle, understood to a nicety the arts of sensationalist journalism and remained for over two decades in Bottomley's 'stable'.

In 1905 all this preparation was put to the test. It was time for a new election, time for all Bottomley's speeches, his lunches in local pubs, his opening of bazaars and his appearances as Father Christmas, to pay their required dividend. The Liberal party as such was rather disturbed by this tubby maverick and newspapers who supported their cause went so far as to ask the voters to ignore him. Bottomley, however, had no doubt. He couched his election propaganda in the language of the race track: 'Horatio, the favourite, continues to go strong. He is daily doing some excellent gallops, and yesterday went the full course of the constituency, pulling up sound and well.' As for his opponent, the sitting Member, Robertson, 'Apart from a marked disinclination to face the crowd, he has more than once shown a strong desire to bolt. He is probably stale, and requires rest.' It is perhaps no wonder that, in the event, Bottomley won the seat by well over three thousand votes.

'I heard his first speech in the House of Commons. . . . He spoke through icy silence: a silence cold and contemptuous, which could be felt. He made his little jokes and no one laughed. He made his eloquent periods and no one cheered.' Ironically, that account was left by C. F. G. Masterman, a politician then being spoken of as a coming Prime Minister, whom Bottomley later hounded virulently out of politics. The hostility against the new Member, based on suspicions of his honesty, did not last long; Bottomley was a man who accepted other people's low opinion of himself and turned it against them, usually as a joke: 'As the Chancellor would probably call me,' he said during one debate, 'his more or less honourable friend.' Men like Lloyd George, realists all, would find no difficulty in responding to his geniality, although balking at offering him any advancement in the Liberal Party. But for Bottomley the House of Commons was a place he could use, as he had the Law courts, in order to get himself more widely known. He sponsored for that purpose a number of Bills which had no hope of acceptance – at least not then, for it is a peculiarity of the measures he advocated that many of them, once thought outrageous, have since become the law of the land. He wanted to license bookmakers, to the horror of the Anglican establishment – but we now have taxpaying betting shops in Britain; he wanted public houses to open on Sundays – now they do; he asked for old age pensions for all those in need – now they get one.

In 1906 Bottomley, having sold the *Sun*, founded the paper which was to be the real fortress upon which the defences of his reputation would rest, the base from which he would launch his assault on the attention and the affection of the public. This was *John Bull*, a venture made possible by the investment of his financier friend, Hooley (the man whose transferred debts were almost to sink poor Daisy Warwick's foundering ship a few years later), and the business sense of Julius Elias, head of the printing firm of Odhams, then a business of medium size, but as a result of the *John Bull* connection to become one of the great printing and publishing houses of the world.

Despite its slogan, 'If You Read It In *John Bull*, It Is So', the paper from the beginning dealt in unsubstantiated scandal, hints of alcoholism and debauchery in high places – 'Who are the two Front Bench men who are in the habit of coming down to the House in an advanced state of alcoholic stimulation?' – and Open Letters to well-known men of the day, the first one of which was addressed to Edward VII himself: 'We have always believed that at heart Your Majesty is a Republican.' The tone of the paper was nationalistic and populist, strongly anti-foreign and against the – selectively chosen – rich and mighty of the land. The staff included Theodore Dahle, a man named Ernest Wray who always remained utterly devoted to Bottomley, and the vast assistant editor, George Wedlake, who wrote a great deal of the copy Horatio Bottomley signed. And there was also, writing a theatre column, reviewing books, composing leaders, the ubiquitous and scandalous Frank Harris, whose fortunes too were later to be intertwined, for a while, with those of the Countess of Warwick.

Bottomley had, naturally enough, his own office, reached through an antechamber and protected by a locked door. When unwelcome visitors arrived, as they inevitably did, he was able to rush out through the offices of his secretary, the impeccable Holland, of Wedlake, and of the 'Special Commissioner', who handled material dealing with the Services, finally to emerge, unruffled and far from embarrassment, through a side exit into Anne Street.

Apart from constantly raiding the cash box – Elias after two or three years took over the paper's financial control, which made only the petty cash available – Bottomley soon realised the value of *John Bull* as a source of revenue. He invited readers to take part in a Co-operative Partnership Scheme, issuing debenture shares to the sum of £25,000. He founded the *John Bull* Investment Trust, through which readers could route their stocks and shares business and in which some were especially invited to invest. No minutes were ever kept of any meeting of the Trust's board – perhaps with reason, since Bottomley was the sole director. More unpleasantly, *John Bull* began to run attacks on selected firms, suggesting that these were in financial difficulty, or even run on crooked lines. After a campaign of this sort had been featured for a while, it would come to an abrupt end – and another firm would take Mr Bottomley on its pay-roll as 'unofficial investigator' or 'complaints investigator' at a salary of £500 a year. It was different conduct, however, which in 1908 was making the House of Commons a little restive about the affairs of the amiable but suspect Member for South Hackney.

In 1906 the Joint Stock Trust & Finance Co. had gone into voluntary liquidation, but the percentage of votes over this decision was so much higher than normal that the Official Receiver thought he ought to take a closer look at the transfer and share registers. Unfortunately, after his officers had spent a day putting the transfers in order, they discovered them the next morning in mysterious disarray – and the next morning, and the next, and the one after that. Despite this, or perhaps because of it, enough evidence came to light to allow an application for the compulsory winding-up of the company to be granted. For two years the investigation dragged on, accompanied by thunderous and emotional appeals, denunciations and protests from Bottomley. Nevertheless the rumours multiplied that there had been a duplication of many thousands of shares. The Official Receiver, empowered by a judge's order, came to take away the company's books and found that details of share transfers under the letters B, C, H, M and S were missing. A year was spent on reconstructing share transfers from counterfoils and the remaining ledgers. It seemed clear that ten million extra shares had been issued, over and above the company's stated capital, and that hundreds of the happy and gullible now held them.

It was therefore a strong case that Horace Avory, KC, could present for the Crown. But he had never met a defendant like Bottomley, nor, indeed, a defending counsel, since he appeared for himself. Then one of Avory's principal witnesses, a one-time clerk of Bottomley's, practically admitted in the witness box that he had tried to blackmail Bottomley; there was confusion over whether the Official Receiver would be called and, when he was not called, it was made to seem that he could not be, because of the weakness of his evidence; Avory said it was a lie when Bottomley claimed he was being followed by detectives, and the next day had to admit it was the truth. In the face of Bottomley's urbane and apparently good-humoured heckling, Avory again and again lost his temper, in which condition he often said things strangely injudicious in a man destined to be a distinguished judge. The case was heard before three different Aldermen in succession, the first two having fallen ill, the last hearing only the final three days of a case which had taken twenty-eight altogether. Finally, and worst of all for Avory, many of the prosecution witnesses, defrauded though they were, gave evidence reluctantly, plainly wanting the heroic Bottomley to win his lonely fight. One said, 'I have always thought a great deal of you, Mr Bottomley,' and another, who held 27,000 shares, insisted that the charges against the defendant were 'absolutely unfounded'. Sir James Ritchie, the last of the Aldermanic judges, came to the conclusion that no jury ought to convict on the evidence that had been heard (but he had heard very little of it) and to the strains of 'For he's a jolly good fellow' Bottomley was carried in triumph from the court.

Yet there were some who could see through his flummery and rhetoric, and others who remained angry and in action. A righteous solicitor named Bell, whom Bottomley had tried to bribe and so made an enemy of instead, urged on one of Bottomley's archetypal victims to bring an action. This man, Platt, was so besotted with Bottomley that on one occasion he visited him with a furious demand for restitution, only to leave Pall Mall having handed over a further £4,000. Now things went the other way, for the law insisted that his unnumbered shares were worthless. A retired miller recovered £2,000 from the *John Bull* Investment Trust Agency. And yet it was at precisely this point in Bottomley's fortunes that the John Bull League was formed, without difficulty or any sense of paradox. For the inaugural meeting at the Albert Hall over sixty thousand ticket applications were received, and one hundred MPs joined in the optimistic festivities.

The League put on a non-Party face, a plain, John Bull face, standing for honesty in politics and a Business Government. It was never a power in the land, nor the alternative movement Bottomley must have hoped it might become. The idea of a Business Government always appealed to him, perhaps because it was the only one which might have accepted his services. Members were expected to buy a badge, which cost a shilling, and to make further contributions if they could. In return they received nothing, except whatever honour they thought it to wear a badge worth a shilling and belong to Bottomley's devoted. It served him, however, as a sounding board, a sort of platform; it gave him at least the appearance of having political leverage. He was, possibly, a decade or so before his time – by the early Thirties a German version of the John Bull League was doing rather nicely. (And certainly when in the 1910 election Bottomley was opposed by a Jew, that fact was used quite viciously in a *John Bull* article – effectively, too, since Bottomley held South Hackney in face of a Conservative landslide elsewhere in the country.)

In 1910, too, there was the Coronation of George V, marked by *John Bull's* erecting a stand of their own to overlook the royal procession, seats being allocated to 'the lucky persons' who had bought some of the 200,000 Readers' Shares. It turned out that what most of these 'lucky persons' saw was a view of St Mary-le-Strand, a pleasant enough church, but not the coronation procession, which passed by on the other side of the building. And those who might otherwise have caught a glimpse of the royal coach may have been a little disconcerted by the collapse of the stand at just about the moment it was due. Bottomley was both indignant and apologetic, throwing blame about as he always did, and nothing of the matter appeared in *John Bull*.

Much else did, however, and it is true that the paper, now with a half-million circulation, managed to play a certain crusading role. One scandal it took up was the cruelty then prevailing on the training ship *Akbar*; it was Masterman, the Under-Secretary of State at the Home Office, who produced a rather weak report which did its best to whitewash those in charge of the ship. There seems no question that Masterman, who had lost his small inheritance in one of Bottomley's ventures, was influenced to an extent by the credit that would go to *John Bull* if his report endorsed that paper's criticism. In any case, it was after this that Bottomley's journal began its vendetta, which was not called off until Masterman, with the aid of the 'stable', had been virtually driven out of politics.

Bottomley, however, often working hand-in-glove with Hooley, had now started out on the more dangerous course of fleecing particular victims in personal operations, confidence tricks of a much more conventional kind than the flamboyant company promotions of the past. As a result he found himself sailing through some very rocky waters, and often in danger of shipwreck. There were the Eyre brothers, for example, to whom he had sold shares in the London & South Western Canal, a thirty-three-mile strip of stagnant, weed-ridden water, and to whom he was forced to pay

£44,000 in restitution. This might have taught him that taking large sums off people he met face-to-face had its dangers in the long term, however complaisant and credulous they might be in the short. To quote Symons again, 'It is very much easier, in the way of ordinary business, to rob five hundred people of ten pounds each than it is to rob one person of five thousand pounds.'

The matter of Robert Edward Master, an old India hand who had lost his memory after an accident, is the most relevant case in point. Having burnt his fingers in Bottomley's West Australian mining ventures, Master received the standard letter: 'I have been going over the names of my old supporters and it struck me that I might now be able to do something for those people who have lost money in my companies. ...' Meetings followed, luncheons, dinners, much champagne – and the transfer of nearly £100,000 from Master to Bottomley, in return for the transfer of pleasantly printed but utterly worthless share certificates from Bottomley to Master. A little later Master died, happy to the end, one hopes, in his optimistic assessment of Bottomley's benevolence and financial standing. His executrix, a Mrs Curtis, took a different view. She issued a writ, having as evidence Master's own diary. A little later her solicitor's office was burgled and the diary stolen. Six months later the office was burgled again and a packet of Bottomley's letters to Master were removed. It was as well, at least for the prosecution, that all the documents had been copied. The case itself was made one-sided by Bottomley's refusal to go into the witness box; again he defended himself, but this time the court was less amused at all his little sallies. Prosecuting counsel called him 'the cleverest thief in the Empire' and the jury found him guilty. Damages were assessed at £50,000.

Bottomley declared his innocence in *John Bull*; the Court of Appeal was less certain and upheld the original verdict. Somehow, nevertheless, he prevailed on Mrs Curtis's solicitor, by means as yet unknown, to write to *The Times* pointing out that the Master prosecution had not been based on any misrepresentation of fact by Bottomley. He addressed twenty thousand people at a John Bull League gala. But he had enemies now and, in a sense, he had been flushed from cover over the preceding two years; the hunt was up, though not yet properly under way.

One of his enemies was the Prudential Insurance Company, against whom he had been conducting one of his *John Bull* campaigns. They retaliated, he sued them for libel – then, after the Master verdict, withdrew. By presenting him with a bill of costs, however, the 'Pru' made itself one of his creditors and pressed for his bankruptcy, which would involve a careful and, they hoped, unpleasant examination of his affairs. Bottomley had his own scheme for settling his affairs, which the 'Pru' turned down; Bottomley thereupon sent a man to tell them that unless they agreed, the attacks on them would start again. They promptly brought an action against him, for contempt of court, alleging blackmail and fraud as well. The judges – Mr Justice Darling, a favourite of Bottomley's, was one – thought these allegations extravagant, but fined Bottomley £100. And, in February 1912, Bottomley faced his examination in the Bankruptcy Court, four days of which were taken up by the questions of Astbury, the Prudential's counsel. By then Bottomley must have wished he had taken out some form of insurance against the risks of attacking a large insurance company.

Astbury took him systematically through the frauds and deceits and petty blackmailings in which he had been active over the previous three or four years. The Eyre brothers were mentioned again, Master, the John Bull Investment Trust (which Bottomley had removed to Guernsey in an effort to wind it up without fuss but was foiled by the vengeful Bell), the Bennet brothers, known rogues who had covered some of their activities by the use of pseudonyms, and other such matters. In vain Bottomley threatened to 'run down to the House and introduce a Bill to curtail the privilege of counsel'. By the time Astbury had done, Bottomley was left with little in the way of credit. He made a last speech in the Commons – typically, it was to insist that the privileges of working-men's clubs should be no less than those permitted in the richer establishments of London's West End – and then resigned.

He was, however, by no means finished – on the contrary, he claimed at a meeting in the Queen's Hall that it was the House of Commons which was played out. As for him, he heard a call, faint yet, but growing throughout the country: 'Wanted – a Man!' He established relations with yet another musical comedy actress, a girl named, felicitously, Peggy Primrose, and was attacked for it by her husband. For once the relationship struck roots and grew and developed. Peggy Primrose was from this time on his most notable, and his only constant, female companion. His wife, renamed Alyse and now a redhead, lived in Nice; the chorus girls still came and went; it was Peggy Primrose who remained faithful to him through the zig-zags, the climbs and drops his life was still to take. In the meantime, sustained by the tolerant adulation of the thousands who had formed the now-moribund League, by the wider public he could still reach through the columns of *John Bull*, and by the systematic redistribution of his threatened property to various nominees and stooges, Bottomley lived as he had always done, bankrupt or not, sipping champagne, watching his horses race, striking his poses and sending forth reams of his – often ghost-written – rodomontade.

It was to *John Bull* and its readership that he now turned in an effort to make another fortune. He ran competitions, which seemed straightforward enough until the periodical *Truth* began to look a little more closely at their winners. In one case readers had been asked to forecast the results of twenty football matches; four winners were announced, with addresses in Torquay, Leicester, Manchester and Brighton. The first three, however, had only made brief stays in those cities; the fourth was, apparently, too ill to see anyone. *Truth* thought the odds rather high against the chance of the right results 'being picked out by men who all depart from London at the same time to spend a few days respectively in lodgings or hotels at Torquay, Leicester and Manchester'. Ten days later *John Bull* agreed, noisily alleging a conspiracy, the details of which remained conveniently vague.

At this time sweepstakes on horse-racing, illegal in Britain, were being run by certain firms in Switzerland, which did rather well out of them since it was not against the law for British citizens to enter a foreign sweepstake. A *John Bull* investigation discovered one or two firms whose probity they recommended, dubbing the rest 'Dirty Derby Diddlers'. One of those praised was a certain newcomer named, apparently, Patrick O'Brian, and under his auspices *John Bull* arranged its own Derby Sweep. Hundreds of thousands of tickets were sold, at ten for £1. This was followed by a final offer of twelve for the same price, these tickets being a different colour from the first issue. A useful distinction – the money which they brought in went straight into Horatio's pocket, or, more accurately, into the large wicker baskets which, full of postal orders, bank notes and coins, were carried unopened again and again through Customs on his journeys to Switzerland and back. Whether the actual draw was fair, after all this, remains a purely academic question. Two of the witnesses were ex-convicts, but this need not diminish their accuracy of observation, and as Bottomley pointed out, the Press was represented – even if it was only in the person of the *John Bull* reporter. In any case, £15,000 in prizes was paid out, whether to selected nominees or not; some £270,000 had been received.

Even after the heavy overheads had been deducted, this represented a profit interesting enough even for Patrick O'Brian – who, it turned out, was the ex-convict among the same Bennet brothers about whom Astbury had asked during his examination of Bottomley the year before. The Bottomley organisation, therefore, now threw itself into the business of sweepstakes and lotteries, with *John Bull* as their medium for publicity. They tried to be as efficient as possible, but sometimes they slipped up. Tickets for every reasonable chance in the 1914 Grand National were passed to members of the Bottomley 'stable' – but an outsider won, a horse called Sunloch no one had considered, and the holder of its ticket, an electrician named Tibbs, proved so uncooperative that he even refused a parcel of Bottomley's valuable shares in lieu of money.

For the Derby Sweepstake of the same year, Bottomley took fewer chances. Guaranteed by a £50,000 cheque, deposited in the London, City & Midland Bank with photographs and much publicity (but withdrawn rather less noisily seven days later), the sweepstake proved very popular. Bottomley held the draw in the middle of Lake Geneva three miles from the shore; there had been concern at the attention he and the sweepstake firm were getting from the Swiss police. The winner was a certain Helene Gluckman, billed in *John Bull* as 'the blind widow of Toulouse', but discovered by *Truth* to be a stranger to that town, who had been there only a short while just before and after the Derby – and who was the sister-in-law of Saul Cooper, the furrier who had always been so busy round and about the City in the interests of the Bottomley 'stable'. As Bottomley pointed out, there was no reason why Cooper's sister-in-law should not have won the sweepstake as well as anyone else – though there may have been some for her not endorsing the £25,000 cheque she received from *John Bull*, pocketing £250 for herself and letting the rest drift back into Bottomley's own account. Thereafter, most of *John Bull*'s prize-lists consisted merely of rows of winning numbers, which made for fewer complications and seems to have done little to dampen the enthusiasm of the punters.

The sweepstakes were not, of course, either Bottomley's or *John Bull*'s only activity. In the paper the revelations, the inaccurate predictions, the fight for lost and, sometimes genuinely deserving causes, continued. Bottomley changed the name of the John Bull League, reviving it as the Business Government League. To publicise it, himself and the paper, he travelled the country, speaking everywhere to packed audiences for fat fees. His own column unerringly mistook the currents and cross-currents of politics, but neither his popularity nor, apparently, credibility, ever diminished with those who read him or came to hear him. This was partly due to his adroit use of advance information – he would press for something which he knew the Government was about to enact, then take credit for it when the announcement or concession was made. He was, however, still in the wilderness, well known, but powerless, a proven fraud, an undischarged bankrupt – to those truly in the seats of power, doubtless something of a joke.

The outbreak of war altered all this. It provided the atmosphere of mindless fervour and hysteria in which his brand of sloganising chauvinism could flourish. Within a fortnight of the war's beginning, Bottomley was advocating that 'Germany must be wiped off the face of Europe', and in that same rabble-rousing mood, he turned the attention of *John Bull*'s readers to everyone in or near public life whose name hinted at German origins – German here being interpreted to mean almost anything foreign. Major-General von Donop, Captain Sueter, A. A. Worzel, Sir Claud Schuster – who were these men in public office? Were they undermining the fibre of the nation, tunnelling secretly from within? All German property was to be confiscated, all Germans put in prison, and those with the foresight to have got themselves naturalised were to wear a special badge.

At the same time, more usefully, *John Bull* started its column of complaints from servicemen. Entitled 'Tommy and Jack', this was strictly against wartime law, but the Government eventually decided that its existence was doing more good than harm, and indeed some of the grievances it brought to light were remedied. Bottomley himself, during these years, began his weekly column in the *Sunday Pictorial*, part of that Northcliffe Press created by the pale young man who had once been Bottomley's sub-editor on *Youth*. For this he received almost £8,000 a year, an enormous sum by contemporary standards. It was, however, as a recruiting orator that Bottomley made his greatest impact. His first venture in this field was at the London Opera House, six weeks after the war had begun. Twenty-five thousand people milled in the streets outside, trying to get in. When he spoke at the Albert Hall, crowd control, more than adequate for a meeting a few weeks earlier addressed by Lloyd George, Asquith and Winston Churchill, broke down almost completely. He spoke as part of the general entertainment at the Empire, Leicester Square (where at other times Marie Lloyd reigned), charging £100 for a performance. For a week's speaking in Glasgow, he received £1000 – none of which, he told the audience, would come to him, since it went into a fund to help the dependants of volunteers. But he haggled for every penny and always made sure he was paid. As he said once, 'I'm an oratorical courtesan. I sell myself to the man with the most money.' He helped avert a shipyard strike on Clydeside with his speeches, he went on lecture tours at which he played both prosecuting counsel and judge in the case against the Kaiser (for around 75 per cent of the gate), he visited the Front. Everywhere he went, he struck a note of optimism – the war would soon be over, the Hun was already on the run. Only the end of the war caught him unprepared with an appropriate prophecy.

At the same time he used his new-found influence to promote himself. He seems genuinely to have thought that there would be a call for a Leader, and that it would be to him. He supported certain candidates and opposed others, and everywhere his intervention had an effect. His patriotism had papered over the cracks in his reputation, and prominent men were not ashamed to share a platform with him. *John Bull* had become known as 'Tommy's Bible', so popular was it with the troops. Small wonder that its owner felt increasingly the temptation to play God. To do so effectively, however, meant that he had to return to Parliament. The first postwar election was held in December 1918 and, just in time, three companies agreed to take up his debts at a heavy discount, so discharging him from bankruptcy and allowing him to stand again for South Hackney. Perhaps because of his wartime efforts, no one took much notice of the fact that these were all firms controlled by Bottomley associates. By the end of the year he was back in the Commons with a majority of some nine thousand.

He must in the following two years have thought that nothing would ever again go wrong for him. His call for a Business Government had its hearers, and there was established in Parliament a loose association of some half-dozen MPs who, while never a party, more or less looked to him for a lead (one of them, ironically, was Sueter, the man he had attacked as a potential enemy during the war). At the same time, he had begun the last and greatest of his financial schemes, his Victory Bond Club.

Victory Bonds had been issued by the new Government in an effort to use the nation's savings for revitalising the economy. They came in £5 units and the Victory Bond Club's minimum subscription was £1, which gave one a fifth-share in a government

Sir Robert Baden-Powell (1857–1941) with his wife Olave at the
christening of their son in February 1914. Below, June 1914

Horatio Bottomley 1860–1933

Sir Arthur Conan Doyle 1859–1930

Marie Lloyd 1870–1922

bond. The money sent in would be used to buy bonds and a draw would be made to distribute the interest. Soon it took a staff of a dozen to cope with the flow of money that came into the *John Bull* offices; people queued for hours to hand their savings to the minions of Bottomley, the super-patriot. Inside, the great man would interrupt bouts of drinking his habitual champagne with periodic raids on the postbags, removing any ready money he could get his hands on.

Everything was run on the most confused lines, a confusion perhaps deliberate, given Bottomley's experience with the law. After six months the Victory Bond Club went through a Bottomley reconstruction. The Thrift Prize Bond Club appeared, with headquarters in Paris, and subscribers were given the opportunity to become holders of French Credit National Bonds provided they sent in just a little more money. Many people agreed; many more began to send their money to the new Paris office, others, the suspicious or the cautious, asked for their original subscription back. The confusion was by now hardly to be unravelled; yet Bottomley travelled once or twice a week to Paris, returning untroubled by Customs with a suitcase full of money. In Paris, meanwhile, French £15 Bonds were selling at £9, so that on every one the Club acquired, Bottomley in any case made a profit of £6. With his customary generosity, he now offered every holder of such a bond the chance of buying another for only £12, thus halving his automatic profit.

Truth, a periodical which had caused him trouble in the past, seized on this and other matters, and week by week attacked the Club and Bottomley. He threatened libel suits and issued writs, but he knew, and *Truth* knew, that he would never take the cases to court, and for nearly two years they persisted in their attacks. At the point of the highest confusion, Bottomley did what he had done so often before – he called in the Receiver. He sent a letter to the subscribers, admitting that affairs had become confused and offering help in formulating claims. *Truth* wrote, 'We have no hesitation in saying that Mr Bottomley, or any representative of Mr Bottomley, is the last person from whom subscribers in the Club should seek help.'

Bottomley's world was now falling apart. There were hecklers at his meetings, a subscriber to the Club sued him and won £468 and, worst of all, Odhams, which had all this time stolidly accepted the vicissitudes of his career, now insisted that the life-editorship of *John Bull* they had granted him fourteen years before must after all be terminated. They paid him £25,000 and took from him his most powerful platform.

On the streets of Britain's cities, meanwhile, a pamphlet had appeared, issued by a one-time colleague of Bottomley's, Reuben Bigland, a man who had had a long love-hate relationship with Bottomley, which, over years of disappointment and off-hand treatment, had curdled into hatred. So virulent and pertinent was this pamphlet, that Bottomley, still an MP and a public man, had no alternative but to sue for libel. He also charged Bigland, however, with trying to obtain money by menaces. If the courts could be induced to concentrate on that charge, the evidence of dark dealing which Bigland undoubtedly possessed and would use to justify his attacks might never come to light. Bottomley went to the magistrate's court to discredit Bigland, and he failed. Bigland said he had been offered up to £20,000 to write an agreed apology and so halt the case against him. Bottomley said this was a lie – but Elias, for so long Bottomley's partner and still head of Odhams, agreed that it was true. From this moment, Bottomley's run was over.

When the libel case was heard at the Old Bailey, the prosecution, under the lofty pretence of not wanting to help Bigland by letting him read his plea of justification, offered no evidence. Bigland was discharged, his case against Bottomley still publicly unheard – to his own intense chagrin, but to Bottomley's discomfiture as well, since everyone knew that this had been no more than a desperate court-room manoeuvre. The money-with-menaces case still remained to be heard, and this at last gave Bigland his opportunity. His detestation of Bottomley had reached such a pitch he had no hesitation in condemning himself, if at the same time he could condemn the financier. He told from the witness box of the many 'services' he had rendered Bottomley – of Duos, once a *John Bull* employee and a potential witness in an action against Bottomley, whom he had spirited away and bribed; of the arrangement he had made with a printer to bring out a scurrilous pamphlet against Bottomley, so that Bottomley could sue the printer and not the real author, who knew too much; of deals arranged and lottery prizes rigged. Mr Justice Darling, once the man Bottomley preferred to judge his cases, summed up with a destructive clarity: 'Bigland's story has been supported by documents and not contradicted in one single particular, not by one word, from the man who can contradict it.' Bigland, after the jury had retired a mere three minutes, was found 'Not Guilty', and to all intents and purposes Bottomley's career was over.

At his inevitable trial for fraud he made a moving speech, as he usually did. But the prosecuting counsel, Travers Humphreys, was an accountant as well as a lawyer, and he took the jury, and the defendant, step by step through such of his misappropriations as could be traced. And many could be traced, not through Bottomley's own muddled accounts and half-kept books, but through the records of his banks. Perhaps the most damaging admission, if not with the jury then with the country as a whole, was Bottomley's revelation that he had received £27,000 for his speeches during the war. The great patriot, the rouser of martial fervour, the optimist, the rhetorician – revealed at last as no more than 'an oratorical courtesan'! It was the last straw.

For the court it was the accumulation of evidence, the contradictions, the outright lies, which did the damage. After only twenty-eight minutes the jury brought in a verdict of guilty. In passing sentence, Mr Justice Salter said, 'Your crime is aggravated by your high position, the number and poverty of your victims, by the trust which they reposed in you and which you abused. . . . The sentence of this court upon you is that you be kept in penal servitude for seven years.'

Bottomley was a mixture, an outrageous oddity. There is a mystery about him, lying in that quality which enabled him to hoodwink so many for so long. What makes him so strange, so baffling, was his refusal to accept the basic social logic which leads us to expect that those who have been exposed as blackmailers, thieves and liars, will retire, confess, perhaps atone. Bottomley, throughout the great days of his career, never did any of this. He challenged the verdicts that had gone against him, he appealed, over the heads of those who had judged him, direct to the people, using the most outrageous lies to do so, and I think that it was this refusal to accept his guilt which always confounded and confused the straight and the conventional. Few could remain neutral in face of this attack on the implicit structure of their world. Some reacted by a violent hatred, others by an irrational conviction of Bottomley's innocence. Most of the former found only frustration, most of the latter lost a great deal of money. Somewhere locked within him, however, was another Bottomley, a much more dangerous man, a great populist leader whose policies, mixed from equal quantities of common sense, working-class radicalism and extreme nationalism, might if more energetically directed have had extraordinary consequences on the twentieth-century history of Britain.

Towards the end, in the last days before his trial, he may have been a little mad, withdrawing from reality – he said that he would shortly become Prime Minister and offered Odhams's business manager a post as his secretary, and a title to go with it. Certainly the Napoleonic, messianic streak in him, although always disorganised, grew stronger and stronger as the years of facile success fed his vanity. But his disintegration was already discernible in his beginnings. He was, finally and always – perhaps helplessly – a cheat, even laying out his tennis court at The Dicker in a way which much increased his own chances of winning. He was a man who enjoyed the instant gesture, the immediate response; it was this need for winning there and then which made him much less of a shark than he might have been had he been able to add patience and long-term planning to his armoury.

Yet he had charm and magnetism, which hardly ever let him down in a crisis. The heavyweight champion, Jack Johnson, once arrived furious at the *John Bull* offices, bent on revenge for an attack on him which the paper had run. He slammed into Bottomley's sanctum, there was a period of silence – then boxer and editor emerged, arm-in-arm and beaming. A result of this trait was his ability always to elicit loyalty, both from vast crowds of strangers and from those who worked most closely with him. Some of this survived even his prison sentence; Peggy Primrose was with him until he died. He was an amiable man, one who liked to be liked, who enjoyed a laugh and hardly cared if it was at his own expense: he had, after all, few pretensions. His own most famous quip illustrates both this and his unquenchable humour; a visitor to Wormwood Scrubs prison saw him one day, busy over the obligatory mailbags. 'Ah, Bottomley,' he said. 'Sewing?' 'No,' replied Bottomley, 'reaping.'

Conan Doyle

ARTHUR CONAN DOYLE might have been destined for a different art, since his grandfather was a noted caricaturist and his uncle, Richard Doyle, an illustrator who was one of the most prominent contributors of his day to *Punch*. His father, Charles Doyle, an architect with the Office of Works in Edinburgh, was also a painter, with an imaginative eye for the fantastic, producing works that seem to link his sensibility with that of the Pre-Raphaelites. Perhaps the important creative elements in Conan Doyle's inheritance came to him through his mother, Mary, circuitously descended from the Percys (great Border barons who had for centuries fought and raided against the Scots and who were themselves descendants of the Plantagenet kings); even more relevant, she was a distant connection of the novelist, Sir Walter Scott.

The first son and the second child of the marriage, Arthur Conan Doyle owed one name to his art-critic godfather, Michael Conan, and the other to that king of legend, Arthur of the Round Table, so often the cause of chivalry in others. If one adds to this his mother's interest in heraldry, it is no surprise to discover that Conan Doyle himself always thought his historical novels the best of his work. He was born in 1859, in Edinburgh, and his first school was one of those dreary educational mills, supervised by a sadistic dominie, typical of the Scotland of that period. In 1868 he entered Hodder, the preparatory school for the Catholic public school, Stonyhurst: the Jesuits offered the boy free tuition if his mother would in return bind him to a career in the Church, an arrangement not surprisingly rejected by a lady who, some years later, was to see her son off to take up a post away from home with the advice, 'Wear flannel next to your skin, my boy, and never believe in eternal punishment.'

Conan Doyle seems to have accepted life at Stonyhurst more with stoicism than delight. The chief instrument of discipline was the tolley, a flat piece of rubber with which the pupils would be beaten on the hands: as a boy of spirit, he often suffered the swollen and bruised fingers this caused. He always worked hard, however, and he discovered cricket, a game at which he became captain of the school Eleven. But he also found in himself another ability – that for writing poetry, in many adolescents the first manifestation of some literary talent. In 1875 he took his matriculation exam, and passed with 75 per cent. Encouraged by this, and recognising in him some special potential, the Brothers suggested that he spend a further year at the Jesuit school in Feldkirch in the Austrian Tyrol.

There he wrote for the school newspaper, produced more poetry and played in the school band. At the year's end, however, with his father ill, it became necessary for him to make some hard choices about his career. It was his mother – 'Ma'am', he called her – who seems to have suggested medicine. The Faculty of Medicine at Edinburgh was one of the finest in the world and within reach of his home, and they were supported in their choice by Dr Waller, a friend of the family's, who coached him for the bursary examination of 1876. This he passed, but lost the bursary through a clerical confusion. Nevertheless he entered medical school and spent the next five years in a state of hard-working boredom. He helped pay for his studies by working during the vacations as assistant to doctors already in practice. In 1880, however, he travelled a little further afield – to the Arctic, signing on the whaler *Hope* as a regular hand, with his medical knowledge as an extra. It was while he was a student, too, that he began to write more seriously, one or two of his stories appearing anonymously in print.

In 1881 he took his MB degree and then spent three months as a doctor on the *Mayumba*, a liner on the Africa run. He fell ill in Lagos and the ship burst into flames on the way home; possibly this left him a little disillusioned with what he might at first have thought the glamorous life of a sea-going medical officer. Yet he had to find work, for his father was now in a nursing home, leaving him as the effective head of the family and the main support of his mother and her six other children. His Doyle uncles and aunts called a family conference in London. They had useful connections in Catholic communities, they told him, and they would be delighted to use all their influence on his behalf. If he would just tell them where he would like to set up his practice, they would send out the word. Conan Doyle refused – he said he had lost his Catholic faith; it was impossible for him, therefore, to trade on his Catholic background. In this conscientious stubbornness, which resisted all arguments, he resembles his uncle Richard Doyle, who years before had resigned from *Punch* over an anti-Papist campaign the magazine had been running.

The breach this made between him and his relations was final and not even the long years of his success were ever to repair it. It left him, however, still without work and quite unsupported in the world. What he needed was an opportunity, and this seemed unexpectedly to appear when he received a cable from Plymouth, 'Started here last June. Colossal success. Come down by next train if possible. Plenty of room for you. Splendid opening.' It was signed

by a man named Budd, a fellow-student of Conan Doyle's at Edinburgh, who had had a reputation for brilliance marred by eccentricity. Budd had the charisma and the instability of the gifted
charlatan, half-hypnotising his patients, who became more his followers than people coming to be cured.

Conan Doyle, however, with no knowledge of this and no other
opening to beckon him, travelled down to Plymouth, where Budd
had his surgery, there to put up his plate next to his colleague's.
Always a correct and punctilious man himself, he must soon have
had his doubts as he watched Budd make his patients swear to stop
drinking tea, using for the purpose a great volume which he said
was the Bible, but which Doyle could see was a Medical Jur-
isprudence; or as Budd marched through the main streets of the
town, displaying in a canvas bag his day's takings, to the chagrin
and fury of Plymouth's less successful doctors. His mother never
questioned that Budd was a charlatan, and said so in a succession of
letters. Some of these Budd saw, and so the association came to an
unpleasant end, Conan Doyle, a big, athletic man, signalling the
break by wrenching his brass plate off the door with one muscular
heave.

Conan Doyle then opened a practice of his own, renting a house
in Southsea. When he walked through these new rooms of his, he
did a little dance in every one, but when his waiting room had been
respectably furnished he found himself with only £2 in the world.
His young brother Innes came to live with and help him – 'We
have made three bob this week,' he wrote to Ma'am. 'We have
vaxenated a baby and got hold of a man with consumtion....'
During his first year in Southsea, Conan Doyle earned £154; at one
time he was having to live on less than a shilling a day, and planning how to cut even that pittance down. He returned a tax-form
with no taxable income entered. 'Most unsatisfactory,' wrote the
Inspector of Taxes in the margin, sending it back. 'I entirely agree,'
put Conan Doyle, and sent it in again unchanged. But within two
or three years he had doubled his income and in those days £300 a
year, although no fortune, was a sum a man could live on.

In 1883, one of the leading literary magazines in England, the
Cornhill, accepted one of his short stories, and from that time on he
must have thought of literature as a possible alternative to medicine. However, it was still as a doctor that he married; indeed, it
was because he was a doctor that he met his wife. One day a small
boy named Jack Hawkins was brought to his house suffering from
cerebral meningitis and in need of day-and-night attention; despite

everything that Doyle could do, the small boy died a few days later. It was in this confusion of suffering and grief that he met Louise, the boy's sister; they fell in love and in August 1885 they were married.

It was in 1886 that Conan Doyle fashioned the giant whose shadow was to overhang all those creations which he himself preferred but which, despite all their popularity, were never to outgrow that one enormous and immortal character. He wrote A *Study in Scarlet*, in which John H. Watson, MD, back from the Afghan War, agrees to share rooms with a man only recently moved into lodgings at 221B, Baker Street: Sherlock Holmes.

So far as Conan Doyle was concerned, there were two ancestors from whom Sherlock Holmes descended, one literary and the other existing and observed. The former was Chevalier Dupin, Edgar Allan Poe's intellectual detective – on the first notes which young Dr Doyle wrote for A *Study in Scarlet*, we find the words: 'Dupin was decidedly smart – his trick of following a train of thought was more sensational than clever but still he had analytical genius.' The man Doyle had actually met and studied at close hand was Dr Joseph Bell, professor of medicine at Edinburgh University. Conan Doyle later wrote of him that 'he often learned more of the patient by a few quick glances than I had done by my questions', and then he quotes a little conversation between Bell and a patient which will strike a familiar note with readers of the Sherlock Holmes canon.

'Well, my man, you've served in the army.'

'Aye, sir.'

'Not long discharged?'

'No, sir.'

'A Highland regiment?'

'Aye, sir.'

'A non-com officer?'

'Aye, sir.'

'Stationed at Barbados?'

'Aye, sir.'

And then, Doyle tells us, Bell explained that 'the man was respectful but did not remove his hat. They do not in the Army, but he would have learned civilian ways had he been long discharged. He had an air of authority and he was obviously Scottish. As to Barbados, his complaint is elephantiasis, which is West Indian and not British.' The method, and the tone, is strictly Holmesian. Yet without question Conan Doyle himself merged into the character of Holmes, not only forced into the role later by an adoring reading public, but, consciously or not, emphasising the connection from the beginning by the syllabic structure of the two names. Indeed, the character's original name was to be Sherrinford Holmes, but Conan Doyle felt impelled to change it.

A *Study in Scarlet* was turned down by *Cornhill Magazine*, then by the publishers, Arrowsmith, then by Fredrick Warne & Co. Finally Ward, Lock bought the story outright for £25 and published it in their *Beeton's Christmas Annual*, where neither it nor its extraordinary detective seemed to attract the slightest attention from anyone. Conan Doyle meanwhile was intent on finishing *Micah Clarke*, a novel which centres on the Monmouth rebellion. He had no thoughts of Sherlock Holmes, or any idea that that self-possessed polymath had any future at all, when he wrote to his mother: 'We must try and retain the copyright of *Micah Clarke*. It should be an income in itself.' The book appeared in 1889, and had an immediate success. The author, delighted and perhaps remembering his connection with Scott, his mother's fascination with heraldry, her Border-baron ancestors, at once set about the writing of his great romance of Middle Ages chivalry, *The White Company*. In the same year his daughter, Mary Louise, was born – and Holmes once more reared his head.

Someone had, after all, read *A Study in Scarlet*. A man named Stoddart, agent in London for the American *Lippincott's Magazine*, invited Conan Doyle to London – he had retreated to the New Forest in order to be closer to the England of his knights and armour-clad villains – and there commissioned him to write another Sherlock Holmes adventure. The story Doyle wrote as a result, *The Sign of Four*, was completed very quickly. He wanted to return as soon as possible to *The White Company*, a work, he always felt, of real consequence. When at last he finished it, 'I felt a wave of exultation and with a cry of "That's done it!" I hurled my inky pen across the room, where it left a black smudge upon the duck's egg wallpaper. I knew in my heart that the book would live and that it would illuminate our national traditions.'

Cornhill accepted *The White Company* for serialisation in 1890 and in the same year *The Sign of Four* was published on both sides of the Atlantic. The following year Conan Doyle, now specialising as a consulting oculist, rented a flat in Bloomsbury, put up his plate in fashionable Devonshire Place, and waited for patients. 'Every morning I walked from the lodgings at Montague Place, reached my consulting rooms at ten and sat there until three or four, with never a ring to disturb my serenity.' He might have sat there for a long time, out of a sense of duty, an obligation, perhaps, to the ambitions of his student days, but for an attack of influenza which kept him in bed or convalescing for several weeks. During that time he decided to commit himself totally to writing.

The *Strand Magazine*, which was to last for sixty years, had recently been started by George Newnes, and in many ways Conan Doyle was to be the writer most closely associated with it. Sherlock Holmes is the character everyone still thinks of when the periodical is mentioned. It was in 1891 that the first of six new Sherlock Holmes stories appeared there – *A Scandal in Bohemia*, concerning the consequences of an amatory indiscretion by the highest in that distant land. Yet as these stories unfolded, to wider and wider acclaim, their author continued to concern himself with his other fiction, the works he thought of as central to his literary life. He wrote *Beyond the City*, a realistic novel, as he considered, set in suburbia, and he started a long novel about the Huguenots, *The Refugees*. But Holmes would not let him alone. The *Strand Magazine* wanted more adventures, and Doyle wrote another twelve for £50 each, this collection including some of the best-known he was ever to produce: *The Speckled Band*, *The Naval Treaty* and *The Greek Interpreter*, which for the first time introduced to the amazed Watson Holmes's even more remarkable brother, Mycroft. But as the series progressed Conan Doyle was contemplating murder. He wrote to his mother, 'I think of slaying Holmes. . . . He takes my mind from better things.' In *The Final Problem*, he did so, Watson turning as he walked, seeing that figure in the distance, the fatal struggle yet to come, 'the last I was ever to see of him in this world'.

In 1892 Conan Doyle's son, Alleyne Kingsley, was born, but in the following year Doyle's father died, after fifteen years in a nursing home. Tragedy approached even nearer, for his wife, Louise, had developed tuberculosis and was now given only a few months to live by specialists. Conan Doyle refused to accept this medical prophecy and for the next three years took his wife on a series of journeys to climates which restrained her disease. As a result, she survived for many more years.

It was on these travels that he wrote *The Stark Munro Letters*, basing the novel on his experiences with the outrageous Dr Budd of Plymouth. He also produced many short stories and he wrote a new historical novel, *Rodney Stone*. Perhaps quite incidentally he did the world another service, introducing the 'snow-shoe' into

Switzerland – as he wrote to his mother, 'Yesterday I performed a small feat by crossing a chain of mountains on snow-shoes (Norwegian Ski) and coming down to Arosa ... It has created quite a little excitement.'

In 1894 the first of his plays, *Waterloo*, was performed at Bristol and a year later formed part of a double-bill with that famous piece, *The Bells*, both plays becoming inseparable from the memory of Henry Irving and his Lyceum Theatre. Conan Doyle wrote in his diary, 'New play enormous success. H.I. fine and great. All laughed and wept. ... Eight calls at end.' In the autumn of the same year he made his first visit to the United States, the country which had after all been mainly responsible in the beginning for dragging Sherlock Holmes out of oblivion. He found himself caught up at once in that exhausting if hospitable circus with which America greets visiting celebrities, and, as most people do, found it both tiring and exhilarating. For Conan Doyle, this was not only a personal triumph, but an affirmation of what he thought of as an essential cousinship between the Americans and the British. However he recognised that a change had already occurred – 'The centre of gravity of the race is over here,' he wrote, 'and we have got to readjust ourselves.' It was while he was in America, too, that he met Kipling for the first time, at a Thanksgiving dinner in Vermont. They stayed together two days and 'had a great time and golf and much high converse. He is a wonderful chap'.

Returning to Switzerland, Conan Doyle began the stories about the Napoleonic wars which were to be published by *Strand Magazine* under the title of *The Exploits of Brigadier Gerard*. In the autumn of 1895 he was in Egypt – 'of all things on this earth the last I should ever have prophesied is that I should ride on the Sahara desert on an Arab stallion' – and so settled on the subject for another novel, *The Tragedy of Korosko*. When he learned that Kitchener was on his way to retake the Sudan, he left his wife and his sister in Cairo and getting himself appointed war correspondent by *The Westminister Gazette*, set off across the desert by camel. At Wadi Halfa, however, he found that there was to be no action for several weeks and, with the summer coming to threaten his still-delicate wife, he could not stay and wait for it.

In October 1896 Conan Doyle moved his family into a new house which he had had built at Hindhead. Called Undershaw, it gave a new centre to his life and was a haven for Louise, still ailing and over the years to weaken further. The next decade was to be an ordeal in many different ways for him: not only was he to watch over Louise's slow death but his concern for her was to be made ambivalent by his having met and fallen in love with a slim, fair-haired girl named Jean Leckie. There seems no question that while Louise was alive Conan Doyle never allowed this affair to move past a mutual and desperate yearning. He was in this, perhaps, more Victorian than Edwardian; certainly his sense of duty and even of chivalry and honour, those qualities he admired so much in his own heroes, permitted him no more than an open awareness of his feelings, never to be translated while Louise lived into a sexual, a physical, reality.

The complaints of the *Uitlanders*, the Jameson raid, the fury of Britain, the Kruger ultimatum – thus Britain drifted into the Boer War. Conan Doyle, not only a patriot but a race-patriot, concerned about Anglo-Saxons everywhere, quite naturally volunteered, despite the protests of his mother and the fact that he was now forty. He made the journey to South Africa as a medical man. A friend of his, the philanthropist John Langman, had assembled a field hospital and it was in charge of this that Conan Doyle arrived at Bloemfontein in April 1900. He settled his forty tons of equipment on a cricket field, and when he had organised his hospital, it had a capacity of 160 patients. But Christian de Wet, whose trail Baden-Powell was to cross and recross in his efforts to catch the Boer leader and his commando column, had captured Bloemfontein's water-supply. Within weeks Doyle's hospital was swamped with hundreds of victims of enteric fever. The senior doctors with him seem to have broken under the strain, one going home and the other taking to the bottle. Conan Doyle, two junior surgeons and a staff of forty-five fought on; one by one, they too came down with the sickness which the flies carried about the town in their deadly squadrons. Thousands of the patients died. Although there was a desperate need for more beds, the authorities refused to open empty private houses for the purpose. Wearily the three-quarters of the staff left on their feet struggled to cope, as medicines ran out and the dead were buried in the rough ditches of a mass grave. Later, there was to be criticism of the medical attention that had been available and offered in the epidemic, until Doyle silenced that with a letter in the *British Medical Journal* pointing out what the situation had actually been.

By this time, Conan Doyle had begun to take himself very seriously indeed as the possessor of a public voice to which people, and especially the young, seemed prepared to pay attention; he saw himself and Kipling as the two great inspirers of the future nation. It was no surprise when on his return from South Africa he stood for Parliament. As he wrote in his Journal, 'I am 41. If I miss this election the chances are that it will be seven years before another. ... So it is now or never.' He contested Central Edinburgh and for a while his campaign, rather against expectations, seemed to be going very well. On polling-day, however, the district was placarded with virulently anti-Catholic posters – a move which, directed against a man who had long given up his religion, has its own irony. It may have swayed impressionable Protestant voters; in any case, although the Unionist vote had been increased by 1500, it still fell 600 short of the number necessary to send Conan Doyle to the House of Commons.

In the meantime the Boer War itself, and the lessons that might be derived from it, still exercised him. In A History of the War he covered not only the origins and conduct of the conflict, but went on to suggest what might be done in the future – 'the making of political martyrs is the last insanity of statesmanship,' he wrote, advocating amnesty – and how the British Army might be strengthened and reformed after its South African experiences. He was one of the first and most influential advocates of the kind of highly professional army Britain has today. He wanted this supported by something like the Swiss system, in which every able-bodied man was to learn at least how to shoot, in order that there should always be available a kind of nation-wide volunteer defence force. To further this, he founded and financed Britain's first civilian rifle-range, setting it up in his own grounds.

In Europe, in the meantime, there had long been conducted a propaganda campaign, the effects of which have not disappeared to this day, about the 'atrocities' of which the British forces were alleged to be guilty. That there were some seems undeniable; the war was fought against a fundamentally civilian army, not wearing uniforms, highly mobile, able to appear and disappear into the surrounding countryside and population as it pleased. Houses were burned, whole families rounded up, hostages taken. But the accusations of dreadful cruelty which were levelled at the British troops were based more on the natural sympathy felt for the Boers by the Germans and the Dutch than on the actual events. Conan Doyle set himself to redress the propaganda balance and in 1902 published a 'pamphlet' of 60,000 words, setting out a reasoned and objective account of what had really happened, accepting some blame, but clearing the British Army of the worst of the indictment. He did so with clarity and the presentation of detail perhaps only possible to a man who was both a writer and an eye-witness of the events he described. Each copy of the paper-bound *The War in South Africa: its Cause and Conduct* was to cost six-pence, one penny of which went into a special fund to finance translations of the book. In six weeks not only had three hundred thousand copies of the book been sold, many people had also sent donations to support Conan Doyle's effort; Edward VII made a personal contribution of £500.

As a result of all these services, Conan Doyle was knighted in 1902. He had struggled against accepting the honour. 'All my work for the State would seem tainted if I took a so-called "reward",' he wrote to his mother; but Ma'am was firm – to refuse the knight-hood would be an insult to the king. This chivalric reasoning went straight to Doyle's heart, and in August he became Sir Arthur. But his conscience was never easy about it, and in a story published more than twenty years later his *alter ego*, Sherlock Holmes, was shown to have refused a knighthood 'shortly after the conclusion of the South African War', offered for 'services which may perhaps some day be described'.

In 1902 there also appeared the first sign that the dam Conan Doyle had built against the continuing pressure of public demand for the resurrection of Sherlock Holmes was beginning to show signs of wear. Through a crack there came one intense spurt of inspiration, *The Hound of the Baskervilles*. He insisted that this was a tale, gone unrecorded, of the great investigator's heyday, before he had gone plunging down into the Reichenbach abyss locked in the arms of his arch-enemy. The public, however, knew better – the ghost walked, his careful footsteps echoed softly in Doyle's brain and would not after all be stilled. Pressure on him increased – at the Lyceum, the American actor William Gillette repeated before enthusiastic audiences the success he had already had in New York with a play called, simply, *Sherlock Holmes*. Then, in 1903, Conan Doyle was approached by an American pub-lisher, who offered to pay $5000 each for a minimum of six short stories in which Sherlock Holmes was to be plausibly resurrected and set once more about his keen-eyed adventuring. George Newnes agreed to pay the equivalent of half this amount for the right to publish these stories in the *Strand Magazine*. Conan Doyle was only human. 'Very well. A.C.D.' he wrote on a postcard to his agent, and within months readers on both sides of the Atlantic could gape as Dr Watson, confronted by the transformation of an elderly and irritable stranger into the smiling, reborn Sherlock Holmes, fainted for the first time in his life.

Thus Conan Doyle could reap the benefit of that strange, myth-like last scene in what he had, perhaps optimistically, named *The Final Problem*. Had Holmes been seen to die, had his corpse been laid out, mourned, the brain dissected, it would have been hard to give a new life to the great detective. But the end had been left ambiguous. Now that he was back, his adventures continued to excite and entrance millions of people on both sides of the Atlantic, and very soon much further afield – as they always excited and entranced Doyle himself, however much he resented the fact and however much he insisted that his best and lasting work lay else-where. The queues formed at the bookstalls – 'worse than anything I ever saw at a bargain sale', an eyewitness wrote – and Conan Doyle took up again the stories which would, after all, be the ones to give him immortality.

In 1906 Louise finally died, more than a decade after the doctors had given her only months to live. For him it must have been in many ways a release, honestly and conscientiously though he had looked after her, and it left him free to discover that happiness he had forced into abeyance: late in 1907 he finally married Jean Leckie. By then he had stood again for Parliament, this time for the Scottish border constituency of Hawick, and had again lost. He never stood for office again, although always remaining aware that he could, and even should, make his contribution to public debates. Indeed, there were a number of causes in which he was always prominent: his concern for close ties with the United States; his notion of a trained reserve of men for home defence; divorce reform, ensuring that women should have equality before the law instead of finding divorce legislation weighted, as it was then, heavily in favour of men. He was a strong advocate of the *entente* with France and among those well aware that the jealousies and militarism of Kaiser Wilhelm's Germany threatened European peace in general and British equanimity in particular. In addition to these public concerns, he also carried on, with increasing fervour, a private struggle for justice. Not the social justice which had brought the Labour Party into being, but justice for the individual denied it by the mismanagement of bureaucracy, by police bias, or by political pressure. This was certainly in part due to his role as Sherlock Holmes's creator. There are several anecdotes, some more substantiated than others, which suggest that from around the turn of the century people had been coming to him with problems very similar to those which, in his stories, prospective clients brought to Holmes.

The first case in which Conan Doyle intervened decisively was probably the Edalji affair. The elder Edalji was a Parsee who had become an Anglican. He had for many years been the vicar of Great Wryley, a mining village near Birmingham, although never fully accepted by an insular congregation. He had a son, George, who in 1903 was a law student. It was in that year that a young miner came across the dying carcass of a pit pony. Blood seeped from a long slit in its belly. This was one in a long sequence of such incidents in which sheep, cattle and horses had had their stomachs ripped open. This maniacal butchery had been accompanied by a series of anonymous letters to various village worthies, denouncing George Edalji as one of an organised gang of cattle killers. The existence of these letters had revived police memories of a previous series of anonymous notes, full of hatred of the Edaljis and threats against George, accompanied then by newspaper advertisements purporting to have been signed by him, and also by the strewing of the vicar's lawn with garbage; one day, the key of Walsall Grammar School had even been found lying on their doorstep. At that time, the police, without much evidence and certainly without giving the boy any kind of hearing, had convinced themselves that young George was guilty of these extraordinary acts. The Chief Constable had gone so far as to write to the Reverend Edalji to tell him that he would not believe the boy's innocence, however much he protested it. Now, therefore, with the discovery of the dying pony, the police went at once to the nearby vicarage and searched George's room, George himself having gone to work in Birmingham. They then arrested him. They had, they said, had their eye on him for some time and they had no doubt that he was the guilty man.

In searching the room, the police had found a set of razors suspiciously stained with what they said was blood. They had found a boot which, they testified, matched prints found near the dead pony. They had found a jacket, which was damp, had a few horsehairs clinging to it, and the stains on which, they said, had almost certainly been caused by blood. They found trousers stained with still-damp mud. George Edalji, in his defence, said that the evening before he had made some calls in the neighbourhood, come home, had his supper and then, at about half past nine, gone to bed. His father testified that his son had not left the house after that time – they shared a bedroom, he was a light sleeper and had, in any case, as always locked the door of the room. If George had slashed the pony before he came home, it would not still have been alive when found in the morning; to have gone out unobserved later, he would have had to evade not only his admittedly sleeping father, but the half-dozen policemen who were surreptitiously watching the house. This is nevertheless what the prosecution contended – he had slipped out some little time before three o'clock in the morning, walked half a mile, crossed a railway line, slashed the pony and then returned, all this time evading the vigilance of the assembled constabulary. On this evidence, George Edalji was convicted to seven years' penal servitude. What the plain statement of verdict and sentence conceals is the feeling against the young man, the hysteria which his case had aroused and which rose to such a pitch that a crowd tried to drag him from the cab which was taking him to the trial.

Once the trial was over, however, and cooler sense had a chance to assert itself, it became plain that the case against George Edalji had been a thin one – and it was made no more substantial by the fact that the animal slashings continued (the police explained that this was the work of the guilty man's accomplices, who were trying to convince people of his innocence). A petition was organised and signed by 100,000 people, many of them in the legal profession, but the Home Office would not budge. A young man confessed to the crimes, and emigrated to South Africa. Again, no response came from the Home Office: there was, they said, no way in which the case could be reopened. Yet, after having served three years of his sentence, George Edalji was mysteriously freed. He was given neither explanation, compensation nor pardon; he was simply allowed to go.

When George Edalji's case came to Conan Doyle's notice, it caught the writer in a mood of despondency. Louise had died not long before, he had written nothing for some months and he had failed in what he knew would be his last Parliamentary campaign. It was therefore with enthusiasm that he accepted the challenge posed by it – and under the scrutiny of his logic the case against Edalji weakened, withered and died. The stains on the razor, chemical analysis had shown, had been rust, there had been no bloodstains at all. The coat had been wet, certainly; but Edalji agreed he had been out the evening before, when it had rained. There had been stains on the jacket – but if they had been blood spattered over the cloth at the same time as the rain, then they too would still have been wet! Besides, these stains had dwindled in the testimony until they were only two patches, each the size of a small coin, on the cuff of the right sleeve – 'the most adept operator who ever lived would not rip up a horse with a razor upon a dark night and have only two threepenny-bit spots of blood to show for it'. As for the horsehairs, they had not been on the clothing at all when the police took it; if they had been picked up on the jacket when the cut was made, they would have been short and soft, like the hair that grows on the belly of a horse. But they had been long and coarse, which had indeed seemed damning evidence, since they corresponded exactly with the hair taken from a piece of the horse's hide thoughtfully taken away by the police – at the same time as the jacket! They must therefore, Doyle concluded, 'have been transferred ... from that particular piece of skin'. There had, as the police testified, been mud on the cuffs of Edalji's trousers – but it had been black mud, not the reddish clay and sand of the soil where the pony was found. As for the footprint, that had been tested long after a multitude of investigators had trampled any possible evidence into oblivion.

Herbert Gladstone, the Home Secretary, faced with this demolition of the police case, appointed a Commission of Inquiry which, as is often the way with such commissions, in 1907 brought out a report agreeing with everybody. No, Edalji had not slashed the pony, therefore the verdict against him had been wrong; but, yes, he had written the self-incriminatory and anonymous letters, therefore to be let out after three years was about what he deserved. Conan Doyle was not to be dissuaded; he began to try and establish a connection between the earlier series of anonymous letters and those for which Edalji had been condemned. They had been signed by the name 'Greatorex' and there had been a young man of that name in the neighbourhood who, although he himself could not have written the letters, had been a pupil at Walsall Grammar School. It was the key of this establishment which had been one of the objects found outside Edalji's house; the letters had been posted in Walsall. The connection, therefore, was that town and, in particular, that school. His suspicions soon fell on three brothers named Sharp and in particular one of them, Royden Sharp. He had been at the school, where he had acquired an unpleasant reputation, he had known Greatorex, he had known George Edalji. He had been apprenticed to a butcher, then served on a cattle boat. During the period when there had been no anonymous letters, he had been absent from the country. When the letters had started again, they had contained several references to the sea-going life, and one at least had been posted at Blackpool, a seaside resort very convenient to the port of Liverpool and thus popular with sailors on leave. Then Conan Doyle considered the nature of the actual slashes which had been inflicted – 'In every case there was a shallow incision; it had cut through skin and muscles, but had not penetrated the gut.' He concluded that these cuts must have been made with a horse-lancet – and Mrs Greatorex herself testified that Royden Sharp had shown her one and told her that the criminal must have used such an instrument. Nothing, however, could move the Home Office. The Commission's verdict on the Edalji case stood. Conan Doyle wrote letters and used what leverage he could, but all in vain; he demonstrated what he felt about the young man, however, by inviting him to be one of the few guests at his quiet wedding to Jean Leckie late in 1907.

Two years later, his concern for justice and for the rights of other races found expression in his struggle to publicise the appalling conditions in King Leopold's Belgian Congo. This so-called Free State had, by a series of loans and the imposition of duties, been turned into a colony which for a long time seemed almost the Belgian king's personal property. The Congolese were deprived of the right to trade or to farm their own land. Standards of production were imposed on them, sometimes impossibly high ones, and if these were not met violence and mutilation resulted. Peasants and workers were terrorised, until the whole country seemed nothing more than a gigantic labour camp. When Roger Casement became British consul at Kinchassa, he began to investigate conditions in the Belgian colony. With a shipping agent named Morel he founded the Congo Reform Association and, by the time he returned to London in 1903, he had sent forty-three long reports to the Foreign Office which described torture, mutilation, summary executions and told of men, women and children who worked and often died chained together night and day. The Foreign Office published a report themselves, while Casement began to raise support among writers of influence – Anthony Hope, Joseph Conrad, Conan Doyle.

Of these, it was Doyle who took the most effective and vigorous action. He attacked the problem, as he always did those which seized his interest, with an unremitting energy which seemed to assault it from all angles. He published a 60,000-word book, *The Crime of the Congo*, and he travelled up and down the country – Hull, Liverpool, Edinburgh, Plymouth – giving a series of telling lectures on the subject. He sent copies of his book to influential people – President Roosevelt, the Kaiser, Winston Churchill. He sent a circular letter to sixty American newspapers. He arranged for his book to appear in French and German. But as Morel wrote later, 'Conan Doyle's intervention at that time exercised a decisive influence on the course of events. ... Yet it was not his book – excellent as it was – nor his manly eloquence on the platform, nor the influence he wielded in rallying influential men to our cause, which helped us most. It was just the fact that he was – Conan Doyle; and that he was with us.'

International pressure, whipped up by Casement, Morel, Doyle and Governments with interests in Africa, slowly forced the Belgian king and, later, the Belgian Government, to modify and improve the conditions of those over whom they had made themselves responsible. By this time, however, Conan Doyle was engaged in another of those crusades which make the identification between him and Sherlock Holmes so easy. This was the case of Oscar Slater, a man who became the victim of a judicial system which has never, whatever its blunders, ceased to preen itself on its impartiality and effectiveness. Slater was a man who might have been made to be the victim of British chauvinism, prejudice and hypocrisy. He was foreign, a Jew, certainly a gambler, probably a pimp, and living 'in sin' with a lady who was not only not his wife, but had compounded this viciousness by the folly of being French. In December 1908 a certain Miss Gilchrist, an old spinster living in a small apartment in Glasgow, was found by her servant, Helen Lambie, who had been out for a few minutes, battered to death in her own dining-room. A diamond brooch was stolen, although other jewellery had not been touched, and a box containing Miss Gilchrist's papers broken into. A neighbour named Adams, who had heard suspicious sounds but been unable to get into the flat, saw Helen Lambie return from her errand and also noticed a man come out of the flat's bedroom and walk out of the house. Outside the house a fourteen-year-old girl, Mary Barrowman, was bumped into by a man leaving the house at about this time. Her description of this stranger, however, did not then match the description given by Adams.

Four days later, the police discovered that Oscar Slater had pawned a diamond brooch, crescent-shaped like the one which had been stolen, that he had immediately left for Liverpool and from there set out in the *Lusitania* for the United States. From that moment on, the police decided that Slater was their man – he had a record of immorality, he was a frequenter of racecourses and he had been born Joseph Leschnizer: it was enough for them. No fact, no illogicality, no improbability was to shake their case. They based themselves on identification – and they made absolutely certain that they would have identification. All the witnesses they called had been primed beforehand by long study of Slater's photograph; for the extradition proceedings in New York, they even made certain that Helen Lambie and Mary Barrowman saw Oscar Slater in the custody of two policemen just before the hearing, so that no mistake would be made in the courtroom. Later, in Edinburgh, the police made certain that they had identification parades in which the foreign and admittedly rather shifty-looking Slater would stand out like a sore thumb. They found a hammer in his belongings, which according to medical evidence was almost certainly too light to have been used in the murder and which showed no trace of blood, skin or hair. They suppressed the medical testimony and entered the hammer as the weapon. Helen Lambie gave them the name – never revealed – of the man who had been in the apartment; they persuaded her to say no more about it. They had their man, after all.

Slater's defence was that he had been dining with his mistress at the time of the murder, a fact which she confirmed. But who would believe such shady characters as these? The prosecution made a great deal of the fact that Slater had left Glasgow so soon after the murder – omitting to mention that his apartment had been let and his passage to America booked several weeks earlier. They did not establish how Slater had ever even heard of Miss Gilchrist, nor why, if he had murdered her, he had taken only one piece of jewellery. And no one was able to explain, nor did the lack of explanation seem to make any difference, how it was that Slater had been able to pawn the diamond brooch almost a month before the murder; it was not, of course, the same brooch at all. In the hysteria which shook Britain, however, these gaps in the case went unobserved. Slater was a villain of unpleasant habits, therefore he had murdered Miss Gilchrist – the logic was no more sophisticated than that. As the judge, Lord Guthrie, put it in his summing-up, 'Up to yesterday afternoon I should have thought that there was one serious difficulty which confronted you – the difficulty of conceiving that there was in existence a human being capable of doing such a dastardly deed. Gentlemen, that difficulty, I think, was removed when we heard from the lips of one who seemingly knew the prisoner better than anyone else, that he had followed a life which descends to the very lowest depths of human degradation.'

So Lord Guthrie admitted into his court, and recommended to the attention of his jurors, a piece of hearsay evidence he should have been the first to throw out. It says something for the honesty of juries that there was no unanimity in its verdict of guilty, but under Scottish law a majority was sufficient, and it was doubtless with a great deal of pleasure that Guthrie pronounced the death sentence.

However, there were consciences stirring. A petition was organised and signed by 20,000 people and as a result, two days before he was due to hang, Slater had his sentence commuted to life imprisonment. A Press campaign began to build up, most of it insisting that the verdict had been incorrect. The Establishment stood firm; the law must prevail over justice. It was at this point that Conan Doyle, who had been made aware of these facts by those who championed the condemned man's cause, published his eighty-page *The Case of Oscar Slater*. It was in this that he, in the Holmesian manner, put his finger on what others had missed – that the object of the crime had probably not been the jewellery, but something among the old lady's private papers. If it was a will, then that might have been of interest to someone in her family or who knew her, and this was consistent with the door's not having been forced. When the neighbour, Adams, tried to get in, he had found it locked; therefore the cautious Miss Gilchrist must have opened it herself and led her visitor to the dining-room, a thing she would not have done for a stranger. Officialdom, however, gave no hint of having digested, or even heard, these objections. Questions were asked in Parliament; the reply was that the affair was closed. In 1914 a Glasgow policeman, a detective named Trench, revealed through a lawyer, David Cooke, that on the night of the murder Helen Lambie had told him who it was she had seen leaving Miss Gilchrist's flat. The authorities relented, at least to the extent of ordering an inquiry, the hearings of which were held in secret, the witnesses to which were not on oath, and at which Oscar Slater was in no way represented. It is no surprise that nothing they said persuaded the Secretary of State for Scotland to take any further action in the matter. Not, in any case, on behalf of Slater; the matter of Trench, on the other hand, was most vigorously pursued. After twenty-one years in the police, during which he had won the King's Medal, he was dismissed and, in 1915, he and Cooke were both arrested on a trumped-up charge and held three months in prison before the case against them was thrown out by the trial judge.

All this while, Slater remained in prison. The War came and went. The fifteen years a 'lifer' usually served passed. Still Slater sat behind the walls of Peterhead jail. In 1925 a released fellow-prisoner of his smuggled out a message from him, carrying it in a hollow tooth. Slater had asked him to see Conan Doyle and this he did, travelling to Doyle's house in Sussex. So, after all this time, the campaign to release Slater started once more. The authorities were still adamant, but now the Press began a hue-and-cry of their own. They discovered Helen Lambie, married now and in America; she admitted having given the Glasgow police a name, but of having then allowed herself to be dissuaded from standing by her first statement. They found Mary Barrowman in Glasgow, and she told them that the police had practically dictated her statement. In 1927 Slater was at last released; at a rehearing of his case in the summer of 1928 he was finally – though reluctantly, almost on a technicality – cleared of his guilt. Conan Doyle advanced Slater £1000 to cover the expenses of the case; he never had his money back, but he did receive Slater's gratitude: 'Sir Conan Doyle, you breaker of my shackles, you lover of truth for justice sake, I thank you from the bottom of my heart for the goodness you have shown towards me.'

By then, however, the First World War had altered the history and geography of Europe. Conan Doyle, a Unionist in politics, a patriot in the Boer War, played his part as might have been expected. He volunteered to fight, but was turned down. Instead, he gave to his country his talents as a writer. But he valued his independence too much to do so in any official capacity; he was offered the directorship of an official propaganda department, and refused it. None the less, the articles he wrote early in the war were officially approved and one, *The Outlook on the War*, was circulated among neutral countries by the orders of the Director of Propaganda (C. F. Masterman, the politician later so relentlessly pursued by Horatio Bottomley).

His main effort was directed towards writing a history of the conflict, basing it on the documents and diaries of those who were taking part in it. At the same time he continued to offer a fund of suggestions, new ideas, predictions and inventions. In a story and an article published just before the war he had prophesied the menace to Britain which the submarine could represent. In 1915 the German Naval Secretary pointed out triumphantly during a speech in the *Reichstag*, 'The German people can thank the British Admiralty for disregarding the warning on U-boat warfare given by Sir Arthur Conan Doyle.' He organised the manufacture of an inflatable collar to be issued to all sailors, a sort of precursor of the Mae West; he advocated the installation of inflatable lifeboats on warships, forerunners of today's life rafts. He was among those who pressed for the British soldiers to be issued with steel helmets, like the French. He saw immediately the advantages of the tank. He asked for the provision of some kind of body-armour, a waistcoat similar to the 'flak-jacket' the Army often wears in action today. He tried to perfect a system of protection for ships against the torpedo. He visited the fronts and brought back from them impressions which extended by the stretch of his novelist's imagination the British public's realisation of what conditions were actually like in the trenches.

In the middle of all this patriotic effort he did not forget his primary idealism, and in 1916 he was foremost among the handful of intellectuals who tried, by argument and petition, to save the life of Roger Casement. For him in particular this was an unexpected cause to fight in. Casement, a man knighted by the King for his services overseas, had revealed himself at the start of the war as an Irish nationalist, a revolutionary, a Sinn Feiner. Yet Conan Doyle was a Unionist – that is, it was central to his political beliefs that Ireland should remain a part of the United Kingdom. That had been his platform in two elections. Nevertheless when Casement was arrested in Ireland and tried and convicted for treason, having been sent there by the Germans to help foment the Easter Rising of 1916, Conan Doyle was one of the first to protest against the sentence of death that was passed. His ostensible reason was straightforward enough. Casement would become a martyr. As a homosexual and an ineffective recruiter of an Irish Nationalist Army, he had become something of an embarrassment to the Germans; as an Irish martyr he would be of great benefit to them, rallying waverers to the Sinn Fein movement. It was Conan Doyle who wrote the petition for clemency which was signed by, among others, Sir James Frazer, the Webbs, Robert Blatchford (Daisy Warwick's mentor in Socialism), Arnold Bennett, G. K. Chesterton, John Galsworthy, Jerome K. Jerome and John Masefield.

The Establishment remained inflexible and unimaginative; they circulated the 'Black Diaries', Casement's own record of his homosexual adventures, as though these in some way justified an execution. The diaries caused Doyle no consternation – he thought homosexuality a mental aberration and had made Casement's possible mental instability one ground of his appeal in any case. Apart from this, he thought Casement's attempts to recruit Irish prisoners-of-war for the Kaiser's armies far more heinous than his sexual exploits.

The appeal failed, Casement died and duly became, as Conan Doyle had warned, a martyr and a fount of inspiration for Irish Nationalists until the foundation of the Republic. But there is a possibility that Doyle had had another reason for his petition – the suspicion that Casement had after all gone to Berlin not in the German interest, but in the British. Casement was an acquaintance of the Count Blücher and his English wife, and there is a suggestion that Blücher or his wife were in contact with British espionage circles throughout the war. Whatever Casement's motives, there is no question that he had worked long and hard for the Foreign Office in the previous dozen years or more and that with more imaginative people in power and a less hysterical atmosphere about them, Conan Doyle's appeal might have had more effect.

The last and, for him, perhaps the most important cause Conan Doyle ever took up was that of Spiritualism. Although he had lost his Catholic faith, he had never failed to believe in God. Indeed, not only was atheism unthinkable to him, so was religion as a static system, a communication between man and God in which the last important word had already been said. In *The Stark Munro Letters*, that autobiographical novel published in 1895, there is already apparent his lifelong concern with the problem of religion; correspondence published eight years earlier in the magazine *Light* suggests that even at that time he was among the many who then took a deep and serious interest in the activities and possible powers of mediums. In a letter, written in 1910, he said of Spiritualism, 'I . . . cannot easily dismiss it, in spite of the presence of frauds.'

Whatever experiences prompted it, there is no question that he went through a full conversion to Spiritualism in the course of the First World War. In a letter written in May 1915 he said, 'You know what I think of death. It is a most glorious improvement upon life, a shedding of all that is troublous and painful and a gaining of grand new powers. . . .' By 1917 he was lecturing audiences on what he called 'the new revelation'. As the war came to an end, he was working on two books on the subject, *The New Revelation* and *The Vital Message*. From then on he spent a great deal of his time and energy in lecturing throughout Britain, Australia, the United States, Canada and Europe. Perhaps the deaths in the war of his brother, Innes, once the small page at the door of his surgery, and of his son, Kingsley, gave his beliefs a decisive and personal impetus.

He recognised a failure which in this century has become increasingly apparent – that of the traditional churches to answer the spiritual needs of the more and more highly educated, more and more materialist (in both the popular and the philosophical sense) people of the Western, developed nations. He wanted to develop a new religion, compatible with the notion of human progress upon which he, in common with most of the middle classes born during Victoria's reign, predicated all his ideas about man's condition. For what was different in his case was that he included religion in that notion of progress, instead of opposing the two as the scientific materialists did. This naturally involved an altered notion of religion – in his belief, it should be a religion based upon the certainty of an individual future in another world. This in turn meant that the ancient sanctions of heaven and hell were to be done away with; such a conclusion might, even after all those years, have come as a relief to one who had been brought up under the stern discipline of Jesuits. This led him to formulate a new morality, based on the realisation 'not as a belief or a faith, but as a fact which is as tangible as the streets of London, that we are moving on soon to another life, that we will be very happy there, and that the only possible way in which that happiness can be marred or deferred is by folly and selfishness in these few fleeting years'.

It was this message that he preached up and down the world during most of the Twenties. In 1928 he travelled through South Africa, Rhodesia and Kenya, in the following year through Holland and the Scandinavian countries. He came home from Sweden on a stretcher, having had a mild heart attack. Soon after he spoke again, at an Armistice commemoration. As a result, he had a second, more severe attack. Perhaps, like all big men who have once been very strong and fit, who have always exercised and carried themselves well, he could not believe that he was really ailing. On the other hand, it may be that, secure in his beliefs, he remained unconcerned. Early in July 1930 he had another heart attack and died, upright in his armchair, at half past eight the following morning.

Conan Doyle made an enormous mark on his own times, in many different ways and many different areas. He believed in tolerance – perhaps because as a Catholic he could identify with those who suffered persecution. The people he championed – a Parsee, a German Jew, a homosexual Irish nationalist – were not friends, men for whom he felt an instinctive sympathy. They seemed to him simply unfortunates in need of a champion and so he rode forth to do battle. Indeed, there is a sense in which their need, their very unpopularity, may have made their cause attractive to him – the tales of chivalry had been an important part of his childhood; he had not, perhaps, been named Arthur for nothing. Yet there is an irony in the nature of his immortality: at least immortality as we understand it, this side of the grave. For Conan Doyle is remembered for what he must always have thought the most forgettable work he ever did – the strange yet trivial mysteries with which he faced Sherlock Holmes, and that great character's fascinating ways of solving them. Those stories, while never a drudgery for him, were always a distraction. Thus, if his other world exists he must now and then glance back at this one in some bafflement. Can it really be that all he thought his finest work – *The White Company, Sir Nigel, Micah Clarke* and the rest – although still read, has really faded into a relative insignificance, while that preposterous, cocaine-sniffing, violin-playing, boxing bachelor of a detective still stalks the languages of the world, as alive as ever he was? It would be hard for him to accept but, as Sherlock Holmes himself has told us, 'It is an old maxim of mine that when you have excluded the impossible, whatever remains, however improbable, must be the truth.'

Marie Lloyd

THERE WAS the Canterbury, by tradition the oldest of them all; and then the Bedford, the South London, Collins's (to burn down after a hundred years), the Metropolitan, Gatti's at Westminster Bridge Road, the Victoria Palace, all built in the 1860s; and the Alhambra, the Clapham Grand Hall, the Albert, the Hippodrome, the London Pavilion, the Cambridge, the Foresters', Gatti's at Charing Cross, the Star, the Tivoli; and then all the Empire's – the one resplendent in Leicester Square, the Eastern, the Holloway, the New Cross, the Stratford; and all the Palaces – the Brixton Empress Palace, the Victoria Coffee Palace, the Hammersmith Palace, the Camberwell Palace and in the West End, the Palace *tout court*; and there were the Oxford and the Paragon and the Royal and the London and the Middlesex and the Marylebone; and at Euston the Varieties, and at Kilburn the Varieties, and at Hoxton the Varieties; and at Poplar the Queen's, and at Greenwich the Parthenon, and at Walham Green the Granville; the music halls, all packed, the crowds agog, their balcony seats a shilling each, their programmes twopence, the bitters in their hands twopence a pint, and on the gas-lit stages the jaunty, bouncy, raucous, perky, lugubrious, uproarious, dressed-up or transvestite performers, prancing and carolling their way into the hearts and fantasies of whole generations together, there to become the stuff of legend, lay figures for the heroes and heroines, gigantic and dazzling, which out of their memories those who had seen them were to create for us in their own old age.

Those legends, those memories – can we really believe them? Was there really a golden age which those who say they witnessed it were blessed to live through? It is hard to say now: I saw Robey when he was an old man, a tired comedian with grey hair stepping with the slight unsteadiness of age out on the dusty stage of a factory canteen. I was a child and for me the jokes fell flat; I felt disappointed and, I think now, a little sad for him. But I can still see his figure, fuller than in the pictures of the best years, soberly suited in grey, those eyebrows hardly emphasised, standing spotlit above the overalled crowd which had come to take a lunchtime's rest from fuelling the war – the impression was made, the impact was there; I remember none of the others on the bill. Perhaps presence was the secret, that mystery 'personality'; not craft at all. What is certain is that we remember them: Robey himself, and Dan Leno, Harry Champion, Vesta Tilly, Little Tich, Harry Lauder, Gus Elen, Albert Chevalier – their names seem as solidly a part of English history as Agincourt or the Spanish Armada. Their decades of conquest were between the 1870s and the First World War, their heyday probably the Edwardian era, the first ten years of the century. In 1900 there were over fifty music halls in London, well over two hundred in the rest of the country. Birmingham, Liverpool and Glasgow had six each. Sheffield had five, Leeds three.

The history of music halls began in the public houses, and most of them always had about them the mood, the free-and-easy, slightly raffish, noisy, indefinably dangerous mood of a successful, overcrowded public bar. Because of these origins, which they never betrayed by charging beyond the pockets of those who had made them famous, the working classes felt no awe of them. They were not alien, as were the theatres where Henry Irving or Beerbohm Tree ranted; they smelled of sweat and beer and tobacco smoke. The performers on their stages had accents like the people who watched them, and the songs they sang were about things that those people knew about, things they could laugh at or, on occasion, companionably weep over, or patriotically cheer.

For the dispossessed, the struggling, the millions of the poor and underpaid who felt the full weight of a too-swiftly urbanised country on their shoulders, whose own culture and sense of self and place had been disrupted as industrialisation tore up the roots of a people until then settled on the land, the music hall became not only a place of resort and recreation, it became a way of escape. Those who knew or imagined that they had some talent, the ghost of a singing voice, a dancer's litheness, perhaps no more than an ingratiating manner, saw 'going on the halls' as perhaps their only chance of fame and even, given a little luck, of fortune. Even the most bedraggled and desperate performers must have appeared in some way magical. The lights, the music, the attention of an expectant public must have made them seem members of a brotherhood set apart and above the ordinary.

Yet, from the biographies which everybody knew, it was clear that in the past these compelling personages had been ordinary men and women, indistinguishable from everybody else. Then, one day, they had stepped out before their fellow beings, they had sung a song, told a story, juggled, twirled into a dance – and been translated into demi-gods. It was a marvellous transformation, yet one which might be just around the corner for anybody. Well beyond the glare and rumpus of the music hall proper, therefore, a thousand little pubs and sad, extemporised stages gave their first chances to unknown numbers of would-be performers, most of whom went through their clumsy motions, bowed to the thin applause (three friends, a parent, an aunt or so), took their shillings or half-crowns and stepped away into the darkness, never to be heard of again.

Some went further; managers from the smaller halls saw them, for these were the places where they fished for likely minnows. On their own stages they fattened them, if they were amenable to growth; when they had become too big, they would float off – the Tivoli, the Empire, Leicester Square; Paris, later, even America.

In 1885, on the first step of such a journey, a fifteen-year-old girl, Bella Delmore, stands on the stage of The Grecian, next to the Eagle in the City Road. She sings, she smiles, she nods at the audience; when she winks at them, they stir a little. Her nose is not straight, her teeth protrude somewhat, her chin is firm, almost aggressive. Yet they stir when she winks, their heads move when she sings, they smile. When she comes to the end of her act, their applause is warm.

Some stars struggle to the top. They have a quality few people can detect. Sometimes they are the only ones to know it is there, and even they must often be unsure. Others appear ready-made; they do not seem to doubt themselves, to question their ability or what their destiny will be. They stand on a stage, doing what a hundred others can do as well or better, and an excitement passes through those watching; they are in the presence of a different reality, they can sense and are delighted by an indefinable yet powerful attraction. Even at fifteen, Bella Delmore must have had this quality. A manager – perhaps of The Grecian, perhaps of one of the other halls she played – took her aside and told her he disliked her name. Her real name, she thought, was worse: Matilda Alice Victoria (known as Tilly) Wood. You couldn't, she felt, stand on a stage with the name Tilly Wood to weigh you down. The manager, who knew a thing or two, agreed – but Bella Delmore, with all its childish pseudo-sophistication, wouldn't do either. Something else would have to be found.

With the first name Bella, or Tilly, had no problem. All her life she had insisted on being called Marie, with the *a* long, as in 'jar'. But the surname defeated her. It should be short, the manager said. It should be easy to say and to remember. Bella, or Tilly – or, now, Marie – agreed; but no thoughts came and stayed as to what it should be. Yet all the time it was around her, seen everyday, enormous and peremptory: an old man, kindly, but stern, admonishing passers-by from where he sat hugely on a hoarding – a poster, captioned 'The Family Oracle', for *Lloyds Weekly News*. When, a little later, Bella Delmore agreed to play The Star, Bermondsey, at fifteen shillings a week, it was under her new name: Marie Lloyd.

Tilly Wood was born early in 1870 in Hoxton, once rather a splendid suburb at the north-eastern edge of London but which had long before been overtaken by urban sprawl. Now the poor lived there, spending their underpaid working lives in the factories which had opened in the mean streets, small fountains of noise and grime among the shabby houses. For all that, a tiny touch of prophecy lit Tilly's birth – the house she was born in stood on a street called Peerless. She was the first child of a couple, John and Matilda, who earned their living by making artificial flowers for an Italian dealer. They did this well, it seems; perhaps art and display sat latent within them, too, like a recessive gene awaiting a new generation to make itself apparent. Her father's people had been countryfolk, making bonnets from osiers and willow withes; her mother's parents were bootmakers. No theatrical history in the direct line – but there was a dancer and a comedienne on the mother's side of the family. In the next few years other children followed Tilly into life at Hoxton – Johnnie, Alice, Grace . . . eleven altogether. As the oldest, Tilly soon found herself taking over the mechanical burdens of motherhood. She seems to have been a popular girl; perhaps she was ingratiating; certainly she was always lively. It may have been this that persuaded her Aunt Louisa, the dancer, to display her to a public; perhaps for Louisa it was a kind of gimmick, a draw-card, the child a sort of freak to bring in customers who would stay to applaud her aunt. One knows very little – an unnamed hall, little Tilly not five years old, smiling, her blonde hair shining through the smoke, the din, the half-aggressive laughter, the child turning in a dance, some jig she had been taught, her feet skipping up and down, somewhere to one side a piano playing, two or three of those watching clapping time, perhaps. . . . In any case, the customers were pleased, they threw a shower of coppers; later Tilly would take with her a little basket and when she brought it home, it would be full of coins.

Short of money, John Wood himself took a step nearer the music hall. He became a waiter, working only in the halls; people liked him and called him 'Harry', nobody nowadays knows why. But was it only his popularity that got his name on the bill? Did 'Harry' have the kind of magnetism that would fetch men and women to the halls where he worked, as against the halls which had not taken the precaution to hire him? Or did he actually perform – sing a little, perhaps, tell a few stories? Nobody knows. It must have made the music halls more accessible to little Tilly, whatever her father did there. They were not distant, glamorous, mysterious – they were familiar, places where her father and her aunt worked. All this must have made it easier for her later, not only in choosing what she wanted to do, but in knowing roughly how to go about doing it.

Tilly's next appearance was in evangelical mood. She was asked to perform at the City Temple, that centre of stern, populist Christianity, to sing, or possibly recite, a temperance piece called 'Throw down the bottle and never drink again'. She made this the basis of her next advance – with her sister Alice (later to be very famous, too, particularly in the United States), and two other children whose only brush with immortality this was to be, she founded the Fairy Bell Minstrels. Their act always ended with a sketch based on the song. Tilly would play the drunken husband, Alice the miserable wife; then Tilly would launch into 'Throw down the bottle ...' and bring the house down. The act seems to have been very successful, often asked for at those gatherings which provided free entertainment for the avid public of a pre-electronic age.

Did Tilly put on airs? Did she assume herself grown up? School was little use to her, and indeed in those days for a girl from Hoxton it would not have led anywhere. Her mother found her work in a factory making babies' boots – in a sense, following her own family tradition. Tilly started work on Monday; on Saturday she left. Her mother found her more work, curling the feathers women in those days wore in such dashing profusion. Tilly worked out the week, then left. Again her mother found her work, trimming clothes and objects with beads. On the first day Tilly did a step-dance on a work-table – and left the little factory then and there. One may imagine Mrs Wood's complaints: Tilly was fourteen, she had a lifetime's work in front of her, it was time she settled down, stopped playing her childish games on improvised stages, realised that life was earnest. And one can imagine Tilly's answers, hustled as she may have been by the situation itself into an outspoken determination to make the music hall her career. Was her mother outraged? Did she fear for her daughter's morals, for her security? She must have known about the precariousness of the artistes' lives; did she try to warn Tilly? Or did she too recognise that the girl was already in some sense special, that the way she had with audiences was, if not unique, at least one given to very few performers?

In any case, Tilly won the argument. 'Up and down the City

Road, in and out the Eagle . . .' When the tailors had 'popped' or pawned their 'weasels', their irons, the Eagle was one of the public houses where they would spend their money. It must have been a well-established house to have found its way into the jingle, and The Grecian, its offspring, was one of the earliest music halls to be specially built. Thus it was well known, a little rowdy, free and easy, and not far from Tilly's home. So off she set, wrapped in hopes and that new, glamorous name of Bella Delmore from which she was so soon to be separated. The stage door opens to reveal for a moment the drabness and dirt within, she passes inside; we wait, there is the sound of applause – when she emerges, she will be Marie Lloyd, London's darling.

Marie Lloyd's was not an overnight success. She had to sing for very little, and in some very undistinguished places, for the first few months. But in comparison with the way most performers' careers develop she rose as swiftly and as easily as a skylark. By the end of the following year, she was under contract to one of the big West End houses, the Oxford, and earning up to £100 a week. Her only check, at this stage, came from a threatened court action over the songs she sang. She owned none when she began, singing any that she liked. In those days, however, song-writers would sell exclusive rights to their creations, and performers who bought them expected to be the only ones to sing them. There were a regiment of these writers, most of them very poor, who would advertise their skills in *The Stage* or *The Encore* and, if they wrote something a performer liked, they would be given anything between £1 and £5 for what were in effect world rights for a lifetime. We remember many of these songs – including the one Marie Lloyd herself sang from her earliest days, 'The Boy I Love Sits up in the Gallery' – and we remember the men and women who sang them, but only rarely have we even heard the names of those who first created them. In any case a performer – especially perhaps one who represented a real threat, one who was obviously on the way to the top – was liable to be in serious trouble if known to use songs which were the exclusive property of another. Marie Lloyd learned her lesson, dropped unauthorised material, and before very long was big and successful enough, in any case, to have writers queueing for the honour of having her sing their songs.

The Oxford Music Hall was a showplace for performers. It stood at the corner of Oxford Street and Tottenham Court Road. It had been founded by Charles Morton, who had taken over the Canterbury Arms as an already flourishing sing-song hall in 1849 and

had devised from its slightly rustic and unco-ordinated entertainments the structure upon which music-hall bills were always to be
based: he is often referred to as the Father of the Halls. Marie Lloyd
sang there and did a nimble dance, adding to the happiness of
people who had, under the same roof, just eaten a five-course meal
for half a crown. From now on life became, at least in its externals,
a tolerably comfortable business for her. She was a rising star, later
an established one, and never really faced a time when her public
turned away, chose others newer and brighter, threatened to forget
her. And this was due not only to the person she was on stage, but
also to the person she actually was, the real Marie Lloyd, the true-
life Tilly Wood from Hoxton.

She seemed to give off a radiance during her performance. Again
and again people use that word when they discuss her act, or remember her, fair-haired, her smile bright and inviting, moving forward to the footlights. She was everyone's delight, less like a lover,
more like a favourite relation, the one your heart lifts for when a
visit is announced. She was funny naturally, and her innuendoes,
barbed and flighted with her monstrous, endearing wink, brought
her the reputation of being smutty. Yet she was never 'blue', in the
way that comedians were to be later in night clubs and in the
variety theatres, filling the emptiness between one set of nudes and
the next. She teased her audiences, offered them suggestions they
were only too eager to take up, then laughed at them and with
them. 'I always 'old with 'aving it – if yer fancy it, *if* yer fancy it –
that's understood', she sang in 'A Little of What You Fancy Does
You Good'. And, winking, she would challenge those who watched
her to make what they could of the lines and they, uproariously,
always did.

She belonged in real life, even when she was a star. In a sense
that was the strength of the music halls – the performers spoke the
same dialects as the audience, their experiences in childhood and
through poverty were nearly always similar. Between audience and
artist there were unspoken bonds, a unity of class. Not that the
'toffs' did not find their way to those theatres too, and in their own
way adored the music-hall greats; but rather as in the 1960s there
were pop groups and singers who not only had their roots in the
poorer districts of Liverpool, Newcastle, Manchester and London,
but also never pretended that this was not the case and even went
further by taking from those districts and the people who lived
there the subject-matter of their songs, so in the 1880s music-hall
artists took a pride in their working-class origins. Their acts were

dialogues between equals, dealing with matters familiar to those on both sides of the footlights. Others were – could only be – eavesdroppers. And so Marie, although sweeping on, smartly gowned and glittering with jewels, always remained a Londoner, and all over the world, but especially in London, the people loved her for it.

In her ordinary, off-stage life, Marie Lloyd was warm, impulsive, generous, passionate. She took to people instantly, and often foolishly. She kept up no barriers between the world and herself; she spoke to anyone who would speak to her, exchanged jokes with those who, recognising her, would call her name or offer some of the easy banter of the streets. When, early in her career, it was suggested she should arrange a benefit for herself at the Oxford, she agreed. Those who actually organised it ended rather better off than she – and the money she made she used to buy eighty pairs of boots and shoes for the children of her old school in Hoxton. (An indication of the times – eighty children in one school, in need of footwear.) When she was famous, she would sometimes invite the cabbie who took her home in for a goodnight drink, a chat and a joke. 'Marie? She's a card, our Marie!'

She was generous, was, in fact, 'a soft touch'. But she was more than that. If money is coming in, giving it out again is easy and many people have learned the trick of it. Millions are handed out every year, supporting hospitals, libraries, monasteries, cats' homes; but Marie Lloyd acted, she took time and trouble on behalf of the people who appealed to her, or who asked nothing but seemed to her in need of help. There was the case of a girl, an entertainer also on the halls, who found herself pregnant. She was told she would not be able to work – managements took no moral line, but there was the question of her figure. The girl, who had relied on working for as long as she could to tide her over the months after the baby was born, became desperate. It was Marie who had clothes made which would disguise her condition for as long as possible; and it was Marie who paid for them. It was Marie who went to the managements and begged and bullied them into allowing the girl the engagements and so the money which would give her at least some security. It was Marie who made certain that when the baby was born, both it and the mother were looked after properly. She took the time, she took the trouble, she was generous with herself; and all that was founded on some quality in her which her audiences sensed at once, those strangers who sat about her, echoed her choruses, knew the lines of her face as well as they did those of their own sisters, and the lines of her songs better than they did the Bible.

When she was seventeen, she married. It was, in some ways, a mysterious match. Percy Courtney was older than she and had nothing to do with the music halls. He was a gambler and made a sporadic living as his luck with horses waxed and waned. But perhaps the fact that he came from the world beyond the halls made him attractive; certainly he was attractive in himself, handsome, well-mannered, cool and gentlemanly. He was not like the men she was used to, those who shared the bill with her or those, very much like them, who paid to see her. She fell in love; with her career set fair, marriage may well have seemed an adventure to her, a new territory to conquer.

Mr and Mrs Courtney bought a house in Lewisham. In the gentility of those surroundings, Mr Courtney seems to fade. Nothing can displace Marie Lloyd from the centre of the stage, after all, and when she wanted to be raucous not all the inhibitions of suburbia could restrain her. She was a woman who, making her own way, had thrown off the restraints most other women laboured under. She owned herself: outside the aristocracy few women could claim as much. In Lewisham she entertained and her Sunday-evening parties became famous. But they were meetings for the trade; other people in 'the business' were always the guests, loud men and laughing women, with a slang of their own and experiences from that weird world 'on tour', the maps of which were spattered with the images of landladies and the legend, 'Here be dragons'. Percy Courtney had nothing to contribute to these gatherings, especially when, late into the night, famous artists would try out their new songs and ageing patter on their peers.

Courtney became Marie's business manager, but that meant little. She was in demand, she took the offers she wanted to, she could ask the going rate and rather more – her business manager, husband or no, could never have been much more than a yes-man. Not that she did not look after him. The house was always spotless; Marie treated the maids as she had once done her younger brothers and sisters. She had been stern then, a stickler for cleanliness, and she was still the same. Courtney may have married a music-hall star; he had not been forced to do without a housewife. But it was not really enough; and he fades. Like one of those sad victims of poisoning who litter the margins of Victorian history, he seems to weaken as we look at him. For a while the couple were happy, though the husband seems unconsidered. For a while Marie remained in love; then she was loyal. But Courtney fades, he seems to become slowly invisible; in the end, he disappears. There is no sign that anybody really missed him, nor is his future, post-marital history of much concern. From Marie's point of view, his major effort was fathering a child. It was a daughter whom they called Marie. It may be that it was this that proved too much for Courtney – outnumbered now, about to be overwhelmed, he drifted away. Marie Lloyd's was always a solo act and it was a long time before she realised that life as a whole really demanded a different approach.

Nowadays, stars of variety or pop often make a place for themselves on the legitimate stage, singing in musicals or suddenly appearing in West End plays. The stars of the music hall rarely, if ever, made that transition. They were the kings and queens of their own kingdom, with wealth and a horde of adoring subjects. There was one theatrical area, however, where they were welcome and in which they could face and conquer audiences which normally would never have heard them. That was in pantomime. The Emperor of this domain was Harris, the impresario who had taken over Drury Lane at the age of twenty-seven, with just under £5 in his pocket. He believed in the spectacular and he believed in the talents of music-hall artists. Every winter he would put these beliefs to the test, spending fortunes on productions against which the singers and comedians of the halls could display their qualities.

In 1891 he put Marie Lloyd into her first pantomime: 'Humpty Dumpty', at a salary of £100 a week. Little Tich and Dan Leno were in the cast, together with five hundred other performers. Those who had seen such performers before flocked to the theatre, and so did the thousands to whom they had only been names, strange and exciting figures from a world which to the matrons of Kensington and St John's Wood must have seemed lurid indeed. In 1892 it was 'Little Bo-Peep', and again Marie Lloyd played the Principal Girl. In one scene she had to kneel sentimentally in a nightdress, saying her prayers at her bedside. One night, Little Tich whispered, 'Look under the bed, Marie', and she did, peering under with simulated innocence as she searched for the non-existent chamber-pot. The audience was delighted, Harris less so. It was perhaps his sense of propriety that helped to make him, later, Sir Augustus. He warned her, he nearly dismissed her; but when he cast 'Robinson Crusoe' in 1893 she was back again as Polly Perkins, with Dan Leno as Robinson's mother and Little Tich as Man Friday.

That was the last time she appeared for Harris. She was a solo artist, she liked to feel free to do what she pleased and what directly pleased her audiences. One can imagine her restrained and restive under the demands of an unvarying plot, even one as absurd and flexible as that of a pantomime. She liked to come out on her own, sustained by a welcome and an adoration intended only for her. Perhaps, too, she may have been constrained by the presence of children in the audience, and middle-class children at that. Her nods and winks and dead-pan pauses were intended for people more robust and, though she was always popular, she may have felt a lack of that full understanding which elsewhere supported her. Or perhaps it was the mothers she found difficult, those late-Victorian middle-class ladies, sheltered from the world's realities by the earnings of their husbands and the hard work of their servants, free to believe that poverty and starvation and above all sex were curses brought down on their own heads by the presumptuousness or wickedness of those who laboured under them. When she played in pantomime in 1895, it was in 'Dick Whittington', at the Crown Theatre, Peckham.

The next year she made an overseas tour for the first time. She had travelled the length and breadth of Britain, on the move for months at a time as all the music-hall performers had to be. But now she took her daughter – against the wishes of the increasingly alienated Percy Courtney – and set off for South Africa. Perhaps she needed a new audience to love her; like all 'theatricals', she was always insecure and thus tempted to test herself and her appeal on strangers. She expected to succeed; if she thought she had not, she felt it keenly. When she first played in France and the audience yelled '*Bis! Bis!*', it is said that she stormed away, under the impression that she had been called a beast. It took a great deal of persuasion before she could believe that *encore* was not the French for 'encore'.

So far as South Africa was concerned, she need not have worried. Despite the mixture of nationalities – one speaks of Boer and English; black Africans, so far as most whites were concerned, had not yet stepped forward into evident humanity – audiences took to her with delight. And young Marie, too, made her first stage appearance, billed as Little Maudie Courtney. She was a great success and much admired; there is no record of what Percy thought about this precocious beginning.

The voyage home saw a piece of typical Marie Lloyd behaviour. She travelled first class – she had, after all, both money and status.

Those who travelled with her, however, saw the matter differently; officials and their wives, from the Colonial Office or the great merchant houses, who had strong views on correct behaviour, on breeding, on whom it was proper to rub shoulders with and just how much or how little rubbing there should be on such occasions. But when the moment came to organise a ship's concert in aid of charity – and to ease the long tedium of the journey – they came to her. Would she sing? Would she, perhaps, dance? The great Marie Lloyd, after all – would she? Just six concerts, two in each steerage, second class and first. Would she do that, for charity? She smiled and nodded; her generosity was legendary; she would.

Came the night. The First Class Saloon was packed. Imagine, Marie Lloyd, and just for them! One amateur act after another droned to its conclusion of tepid applause. A final song, perhaps a drum roll, a short announcement – the end. Marie Lloyd had not appeared. They came to her, appalled. Why had she not sung? She smiled – that bright, toothy smile which had lightened the sadness and poverty of a million men and women. She had sung, she told them sweetly, twice in the steerage and twice in the second class. But the first class, what of the first class? 'They wouldn't recognise me – I'm buggered if I'll recognise them!' When it came to war, she owned weapons few others could match.

The century turned. In a sense, much that had been delightful during the Victorian period came to its apogee under Edward VII, and some of what had made the nineteenth century hideous was withering away. If there was something a little overblown in the Edwardian era, it was nevertheless a period which spread its pleasures fairly widely. There was still dreadful poverty and an inequality in society which seemed incurable (and which has not, after all, been cured yet), but there was employment for most, and for many enough money to spend a little now and then on luxuries. The music halls flourished and those artists most in demand whirled about the country, bombarded by applause and sustained by what were, in contemporary terms, enormous salaries.

For a performer like Marie Lloyd, life could be very good. Wherever she went she was treated as a queen. As with film stars later, it was enough for people that they should stand next to her for a short while, unimaginable bliss if they had the honour to help or serve. Marie was hardly the person to respond to the possibilities this opened up by retreating into austerity or asceticism. At Romano's she had her own table near the door, and hardly anyone came in whom she did not know well enough to greet. She went to race meetings, her hair bright beneath the fruit or feathers of enormous hats. She gave parties at her Lewisham house, or later in the house she bought in King Henry's Road, in Hampstead. She was generous to everyone – and 'everyone', she felt, included herself.

What did she give in return? Those many men and women who flocked to see her in Leeds and Birmingham, in Glasgow and Manchester, and above all in London – what did they see, what brought them and captivated them? First, her own magnetism, the brightness, the special verve, made up of the colour of her hair and the flash of her eyes as she winked and the neat, white teeth which protruded over her full lower lip, as though set by nature in preparation for a smile. And then, beyond all this, the person she was, the character she laid out for them to read and which in any case they knew so much about. Then there was her skill in portraying types of all sorts and all ages. She could be an innocent young girl, baffled by the strange unwillingness of her elder sister and her boyfriend to let her stay with them; or she might play an old lady remembering good times in the past; or again she might be herself, sentimental in 'The Boy I Love Sits Up in the Gallery' or offering her full repertoire of double-meanings in a song like 'Twiggy Vous' or 'She'd Never Had Her Ticket Punched Before'. Finally, it was her songs – and the way she sang them. She had an infinity of approaches; a song could become something totally new from one night to another, just as she could become a totally different person from one number to the next. She had an uncanny sense of what her audiences would take and a way of finding the right song to unlock them. She had her moments of difficulty, times when she misjudged the kind of response she would get. Almost always she would manage to put things right by the second or third song, digging into her store of characters and mannerisms to pick out the one which turned indifference or even hostility into acclamation.

There was a time when Mrs Grundy stalked the land, a curious spectre which seems to spend years accumulating righteous indignation like a sort of gas, until the pressure is such that it must rise and float and haunt an astonished world. In the end, someone more inventive or courageous than the rest usually finds the right weight of pin to deflate it for a while, and in the Edwardian period Marie Lloyd was one of those. Her method of doing so illustrates her methods on the stage, for a committee of ravening Grundies, scandalised by what they had been told of the music hall – a place none of them would, naturally, expect to visit for themselves – summoned her to sing for them. They wanted to hear for themselves the filth which was, they were certain, corrupting the otherwise blameless labouring poor. Marie Lloyd placidly agreed. Some of her friends must have been surprised at her docility. Nevertheless, she appeared before the committee of stout Edwardian ladies and gentlemen, and she sang her songs. She sang them straight-faced and clear-voiced, as one sings in a drawing-room. The ladies and gentlemen were surprised. With the best will in the world, or the worst, they could see nothing obscene in this pretty, fair-haired lady in her thirties, or in the songs she sang. Baffled, they said so. Marie smiled. She sang them a song their own daughters were fond of – 'Come Into the Garden, Maud'. She sang it as she sang her own songs, with the winks, the pauses, the exclamations. She added no words of her own – but she added a manner. The ladies and gentlemen blushed. They understood her, as her audiences understood her. Marie laughed at them. The human mind, after all, has its oddities, and one of them is its quirk of being interested in sex and of finding sex very often ridiculous. That was the quirk Marie Lloyd shared and made no secret of, and which she and those who came to hear her enjoyed together. She was never obscene – she had no need to be. As for the committee, it disappeared, as such committees do. The music hall went on for another twenty years, and so did Marie Lloyd.

She sang 'Everything in the Garden's Lovely' and she sang 'Oh, Mr Porter' and she sang 'When You Wink the Other Eye' and the audiences laughed and clapped and stamped their feet and ordered pints of bitter in a haze of adoration. Yet Marie herself seemed not to have learned the trick of love. Percy Courtney was slipping out of her life, and though it was full enough and gay enough, yet there must have been an emptiness at its centre. At the parties she went to and gave, however, and at the theatres where she played, she was meeting a handsome, chipper sort of man and finding herself more and more enjoying his company.

Alec Hurley was a Londoner, a performer, a singer of perky costermonger songs. He was reasonably well known, cheerful, and he was a part of her world. As Percy Courtney slipped into the sidelines with little more than increasingly astringent complaints about how his daughter was being treated and his rights over her, so Alec Hurley moved, noticeably, towards the centre of Marie's affections. A Cockney comedian, he had all the quickness of mind and gaiety of spirit Londoners like to imagine is typically metropolitan. When he sang, he did so in an easy tenor; when he came down to the footlights and leaned over for his moments of patter and back-chat, he had the cheek and high spirits which have always brightened the drabness of the East End's back streets. He never had the genius as a Cockney comedian of Gus Elen, nor were his songs as popular as Albert Chevalier's, but he had his following. He was not handsome, but he was attractive. He had some of the qualities of Marie herself. He made himself moderately famous with a song called 'The Lambeth Walk' – not the one to sweep Britain in the Twenties, but an answer to that American importation, the cake walk. After Courtney, who had been so out of it all, so much the second fiddle, the 'Mr Marie Lloyd', Alec Hurley seemed an ideal choice. Courtney divorced her, and not long before Edward came to the throne, she became Mrs Alec Hurley.

They honeymooned aboard ship; they were troupers, and being on the move was in their blood. They were on their way to Australia, where Marie had been engaged to tour. She was an enormous and instant success. With her working-class background, easy manner, earthiness and plain speaking, she was in herself almost an Australian *manqué*. Never one to bother very much with hotels, she would rent a house and there entertain just as she had in London. The raffish, the Bohemian, the confidence tricksters, the beggars both professional and genuine, the envious and the admiring crowded through her open doors. She had become a queen in Australia, just as she had been one for fifteen years in Britain. She was uproarious with happiness. It is possible, however, that her consort was beginning to be less so. Alec Hurley was a man used to his own high billing and it is unlikely that he took with absolute kindness to his new role, that of Marie Lloyd's husband. Music-hall artists were themselves, totally; what they were was all they owned, in the end. When they stood on a stage, that was what they offered to the public. Anything which diminished them was a danger. Marie's Australian triumph started a struggle in Alec Hurley's breast that time was never to resolve.

In Britain again she started her triumphant circuit of the island once more. She conquered Edinburgh, a city whose rectitude and cold self-righteousness had broken many a performer's heart. All over the country she was plain 'Marie' – even 'our Marie'. She was as much, or more, to Londoners as, three decades later, Gracie Fields was to be to Lancastrians. But she did not lose her pugnacity, nor lose touch with her own origins. When she was slighted, or thought she was, she took care to have her revenge. When furnishing her Hampstead house, she overlooked an upholsterer's bill. She was usually punctilious about paying, as people who have been through hard times often are. Without writing to her, or sending someone to see her, the shop issued a writ. Just before closing time the following Saturday, Marie Lloyd appeared and asked to see the manager. When he saw her, his smile, practised on the wives of a hundred Hampstead merchants, froze and vanished. She did not look like a woman who would take happily to being smiled at. She asked him about the bill, and about the writ, and about his responsibilities in the matter; then, cutting short his limping explanation, she waved her chauffeur forward. She had brought the money, she said, she had brought it in full and in cash – in halfpennies, to be precise. She wanted the money counted and she wanted a receipt for it before she left. Into the afternoon the manager and his discontented staff were forced to work, their Saturday sliding away as they laboured. 'Don't blame me,' she told them as she left, 'blame your bloody guv'nor.' Then she stepped into her car and had herself driven regally away.

In 1906, however, she brought her formidable pugnacity to bear on a cause rather greater than this. For a long time it had seemed to the artists of the music hall, particularly those who were in the middle of the bill or lower, that they were being exploited. In a sense, their position had always been weak. Hundreds of performers were only too anxious to work and except at the very top there was little to choose between them. A juggler was just a juggler, a singer just a singer, one competent acrobat as lithe and limber as any of a dozen others. As a consequence, once hired, a performer was almost completely at the mercy of the managements. It was a question of working according to the terms laid down, or not working at all, and artists were made to perform two, three, sometimes four matinées a week, as well as their nightly spots, without any extra pay; or they were forced to work two theatres, dashing from one to the other, again without any extra money.

Conditions backstage were bad for everyone, even the stars. There was little light, dressing-rooms were bare, poky and insanitary. Often a bucket of water was the only place where people could wash. But the stars had their high wages and their reputations, they had the adulation of the audiences and a reasonable hope of working the year around. Not so the performers who were less well known. They were still in the profession, and so had done better than the thousands who had tried and failed even at that. But often their very success had trapped them – they knew they would never rise higher, yet they were too old, too ignorant of other trades, to start a new career or a different life. And again, wasn't there always a chance, just a chance, that if they found the right song, the right line of patter, the right gesture, smile, or tone of voice, that they too ... that for them also ...? So they struggled on, travelled their thousands of miles a year, to stand up on creaking stages before indifferent audiences in a hundred soot-covered towns – and they took what the managements offered them. Overworked, they drank too much, coughed, spat blood and died.

All through the early years of the Edwardian period, some of the most notable of the music-hall performers attempted to form and make viable their own organisation, the Variety Artistes' Federation. Men like Gus Elen, who were famous enough to demand and get contracts on their own terms, worked for the profession as a whole. Managements tried to discourage them, and there were many minor martyrs among the unknowns of the music-hall stage. But the Federation grew and it began to ask for a new basis upon which the artists could work; it began to make trouble. In January 1907 it brought the music-hall performers out on strike.

In the nature of things, such a strike could not be a hundred per cent. But it was very nearly that, much more so than anyone had predicted – certainly on the management side. Retired performers were desperately rounded up and sent whirling about the theatres. Minor singers found themselves for the first, and often the only, time of their lives near the top of the bill. But the great performers stayed outside the theatres, they remained loyal to their poorer colleagues; they not only gave donations to the strike fund, they went on picket duty themselves. Marie Lloyd went out on picket duty. When audiences in the theatres heard that Marie Lloyd was outside, they came hurrying out to catch a glimpse of her. The blacklegs on the stage were left to their own devices. And Marie would give them a performance – her line of vituperation was personal and earthy, and she had no need for anyone to script her jokes. When the picket she was on tried to stop Belle Elmore from going into the music hall where she was playing in defiance of the strike, Marie restrained them: 'Let her go in – she'll do more for the strike by playing than she will by stopping out!' Belle Elmore certainly did nothing to further her own career by working on – when she finally earned immortality, it was as Dr Crippen's wife and victim. No one the managements could scrape together equalled the drawing power of the stars on the streets outside the theatre. In the end the Federation, loyally supported by the musicians, won its battle; its members were never to be so blatantly exploited again.

Marie Lloyd's career, stellar and glittering, continued. She toured America, where her sister Alice was already a star; when she left, her American colleagues made her a presentation which carried the engraved message, 'To Marie Lloyd, the greatest artiste and the best friend we have ever known.'

She bought two houseboats near Staines and named them 'Sunbeam' and 'Moonbeam'. Here she continued her parties, the voices of her friends raised in patter-song and ballad, their laughter floating out over the quiet river. Legend says that Harry Tate once dived in and came up with water-weeds draped about his upper lip, thus originating the mobile moustache which was to become his trade mark. Once Marie herself fell in the river and nearly drowned. Eventually, 'Moonbeam', where Marie and her husband slept, sank at its moorings. That was the end of the houseboats; Marie stayed for the rest of the summer at a riverside hotel, although the boat had been salvaged. When autumn came, she sold both of them.

Her second marriage was by now beginning to go the way of the first. There was perhaps no room in a life so filled with music hall and friends, with fame and energy, for the quiet in which a stable relationship could be built. Alec Hurley, himself well known and in demand, was not too pleased at taking the back seat. He believed that Marie preferred her public to him; later, that she preferred other men to him. Her humour was earthy, she was frank in her speech and suggestive in her stage performances. He began to drift away, as Courtney had done earlier, to travel his own road, no longer the same as hers.

In 1912 her reputation brought her a public insult – unspoken, implicit, but very hurtful. Edward had died two years earlier, and it may be that there was a sort of heaviness about George V, a new kind of primness. Nevertheless it was for him that the first Royal Command Variety Performance was arranged. Artists of every sort were asked – 150 of them for the garden party which was to be associated with the event. Marie Lloyd was not invited – not as a performer, not even as a guest. It seemed as if the country was on the verge of revolution. The newspapers were full of the story, and nearly all of them were critical of the decision. But it had been made. Marie was both hurt and angry. On the night that the chosen performers stepped one by one out on the stage of the Palace Theatre in Shaftesbury Avenue (and Queen Mary averted her eyes from the disgusting sight of Vesta Tilley in trousers), Marie Lloyd appeared at the London Pavilion. The posters outside proclaimed her 'The Queen of Comediennes' and stated, quite correctly, 'Every Performance Given by Marie Lloyd is a Command Performance by Order of the British Public'. Inside, the crowded house cheered her again and again, demanded one song after another, would not let her go.

She and Hurley were quarrelling now. She was restless, often tired and strained, sometimes ill, but night after night, up and down the country, she performed with all her usual gusto and verve. She was in her forties, but the charm and radiance remained, and with it the love of the people she sang for and about. She fell in love again. She thought it had to be third time lucky. The man she chose was Bernard Dillon, quiet, good-looking, an Irishman with a flair for a song, but a greater one for horses. He was a jockey, and a good one. With him, she felt, there would be none of the professional jealousy which had destroyed her marriage with Hurley. Yet, unlike Courtney, he was a man in the public eye, a man with a life and a following of his own. She was older now, knew what she was about. It would be all right. Alec Hurley divorced her, citing Dillon. She moved to a house in Golders Green and moved Dillon in with her. She might have married him, but she did not. Was she being cautious, nervous after her earlier failures? Did she feel that having been damned by the conventional, she might as well live as they expected her to?

Late in 1913, in any case, she set off on another American tour, travelling on the *Olympic* as Bernard Dillon's wife. In New York a curious reporter wondered why the passenger list nowhere had her name on it. When he, and others, discovered why, Marie found herself again cornered by the fury of the self-righteous. She was taken off the ship and locked up on Ellis Island, that notorious little colony where the United States once kept the criminal and the undesirable. She was finally allowed in – provided she left before the end of March 1914, and, above all, provided she married Dillon within five days of crossing the border from Canada, where she had gone in the meantime. In February 1914, in Portland, Oregon, they were married. In New York she scattered her critics and gathered to her once again the acclamation of friendly thousands. But she had learned a new bitterness, a feeling harsher than anything she had experienced before. When she was leaving, they asked her what she thought of the United States and she pointed at the Statue of Liberty, standing tall at the edge of the Atlantic. 'I think your sense of humour is grand,' she said.

Her third marriage was proving a greater disaster than the other two, even before she left America. Dillon had been warned off the Turf. He drank, he made trouble, sometimes he beat her. In Europe the First World War began, threatening as it rolled on its ruinous and bloody course to make unrecognisable the world Marie had grown famous in. Yet she was still the conqueror, still the one the people flocked to see and hear. It was around this time that she began to sing 'One of the Ruins that Cromwell Knocked about a Bit' and – even better known – 'Don't Dilly-Dally on the Way'. She made these songs into performances, developing for them a complete character – a woman who was good-hearted, happy with a glass of stout, but not perhaps blessed with the brains of some, falling into the slightly bizarre situations with which everyday experience is studded. There was a pathos in the character, a touch of tragedy and a deepening understanding of human nature in the characterisation. If there crept into her work an underlying sadness, it was not to be wondered at.

Dillon joined the army, then deserted. When he was caught, he was prosecuted and punished. When he was with her, he beat her; when he was away, he would get drunk, fight, get himself arrested. Every time this happened, it was news and the papers printed it, with Marie's name prominent. She toured South Africa again, as though in an attempt to escape. She conquered as she had before, but it was not a new world now, nor a new public. She was a wanderer – if there had been new territory for her to colonise, people to dazzle who had never seen her, never even heard of her, she might have leaped at the challenge. Instead, she could only repeat the triumphs she had had already. People told her that she had changed amazingly little, that she seemed as youthful as ever. Perhaps she enjoyed hearing this, and perhaps she felt that her life had stopped, now, at its nadir of misery. Yet she came home, to a public more deeply affectionate than ever.

Off-stage she was frightened and lonely. At night she did not want to go to bed. She organised parties, she invited friends, acquaintances, people she had barely met, people she had not met at all but only heard of from others. The Britain she had known was altering. From her point of view the biggest change was that being wrought by the cinema. At first slowly, then more and more quickly, the music halls up and down the country were closing down, or installing the screen, the pianist or little orchestra, the usherette, by whose light a new kind of patron would find his way to his seat, there to roar with laughter at the permanently caught, endlessly repeated sprawling and dodging and speeded-up running of Buster Keaton, Charlie Chaplin, Ben Turpin and the Keystone Cops. Marie Lloyd herself worked harder than ever, and earned even more than before – £600 a week, at least. She travelled as she had always done, and every night when she stepped on stage the glitter, radiance and exquisite timing were there – and, at the end, the applause, the affection. But off-stage now she was looking haggard. She constantly dreaded messages telling her that Dillon was in trouble once more. Her memory, which had once allowed her to learn a song in a matter of minutes, began to fail her. She felt constant pain, which the doctors said was rheumatism.

So to the final struggle – the Alhambra stage; in the dressing-room the doctor who had warned her not to go on, and in the darkness beyond the footlights the crowded audience whose expectation ordered that she should. And what else could she do, unhappy elsewhere, unfulfilled except when facing that almost palpable adoration? She had no other home, no place but the stage to be herself, had had no lover ever, looking back, but the invisible and multi-headed crowd. They cared as little as she that she was ill, seeing what they had always seen, Marie superb, moving about the stage, singing, 'Outside the Cromwell Arms last Saturday night, I was one of the ruins that Cromwell knocked abaht a bit', staggering now and then as the character demanded . . . and then at the end, to their joy, a new bit of business: she fell! It was superb; they cheered her, standing up, yelling their delight. The curtain came down.

They carried her from the theatre to her house in Golders Green, and there, on 7 October 1922, she died. She was fifty-two years old. Those who had loved her sent flowers. They filled her house, and the garden of her house, and then the house nearby where she had lived before. In the procession, twelve cars filled with flowers preceded the hearse. People came from all over the country to watch her go by. After the service, they filed past her grave – thousands and thousands of them, passing in an uninterrupted flow for hour after hour: an even bigger crowd, people said, than the one which had watched the funeral of Edward VII. 'The Queen is dead, long live the . . .' But there was no one to succeed her.

Lloyd George

IT IS PERHAPS only to be expected that David Lloyd George, so archetypally Welsh, so much the Celtic adventurer, self-proclaimed in many roles yet so difficult to pin down, a man of genuine achievement yet one whose every pronouncement gives off a faint whiff of the meretricious, should have been born not in Wales, but in England. His father came from an old Pembrokeshire family of farmers and yeomen; in 1863, when Lloyd George was born, he was headmaster of a Manchester elementary school and already breaking down in health. Soon afterwards he gave up his career in teaching, took up farming in his ancestral Pembrokeshire, caught pneumonia and died, leaving his wife pregnant with their third child. David was then only a year old; his mother took herself and her children, born and unborn, to Caernarvonshire, where, in a village called Llanystumdwy, her brother Richard Lloyd lived.

Wales at this time, as for many years afterwards, retained about its social institutions the strong taint of colonialism. On the one hand stood a Conservative, English or English-orientated minority, whose hold over the community was sustained by their ownership of land and supported by the Established Anglican Church with its network of schools; these were often the only schools available, and were devoted to training children in their dutiful acceptance of authority and its medium, the English language. On the other hand there was the majority, the Welsh, who spoke their own language, cherished their own culture, worshipped in the chapels of the Non-comformist sects and gave their votes, when they had any, to the Liberal Party.

In 1868 Caernarvonshire returned a Liberal as one of its two Members of Parliament. The consternation of the landlords was expressed by wholesale evictions of those of their tenants whom they knew to have voted for the Liberals. Despite this background, Richard Lloyd never hesitated in expressing his allegiance and at the age of six young David was the only child in his village openly to wear the rosettes of what was then the party of protest. It was thus early in his life that he found himself in the position he was to be in so often over the years that followed – that of openly proclaiming his opposition to entrenched authority.

Because of his uncle's love and concern for the Welsh language and culture, young Lloyd George grew up as widely read in both tongues as his circumstances permitted. In English he had read Carlyle, Ruskin and Macaulay by his middle teens. As for his love of Welsh, that in itself was an affirmation of nationalism and a protest; a Government Commission of Enquiry (composed of Englishmen) had reported on the language in 1846 that it was 'a vast drawback to Wales and a manifold barrier to the moral progress and commercial prosperity of the people ... it distorts the truth, favours fraud and abets perjury', going on to point out that this distressing lingual structure led to various immoralities, of which 'the worst and most common is sexual incontinence, the vice of the Principality'.

Lloyd George's mother never wavered in her ambitions for her two sons; each would become a professional man. David might have become a teacher, had that not meant joining the Church of England; or a preacher, had the Disciples of Christ, the family's particular Noncomformist sect, had a paid ministry. Instead, it was decided that he should become a solicitor and Mrs George and her brother agreed to spend their savings on the heavy fees which the years of training would demand. First, however, David would have to be prepared for the necessary examinations. Polymath and autodidact, Richard Lloyd was his best teacher; they would sit through candlelit evenings, picking their way perhaps through the fables of La Fontaine as both master and pupil struggled with the intricacies of a language neither knew, yet which the qualifying tests demanded.

In November 1877 Richard Lloyd went on a mysterious journey with his nephew. Early in December everyone knew where they had gone, for David had passed the preliminary examinations of the Law Society, and in January he was articled to a solicitor in nearby Portmadoc. He worked hard at both his work and his studies, but his energy allowed him to move into other and wider fields. In 1880 the *North Wales Express* published his first article – an attack on the Tory Government of Lord Salisbury. Two years later, when he was nineteen, he began to give addresses at the chapel at Penymaes where the family worshipped. Richard Lloyd wrote in his diary, 'D.Ll.G. speaking for the first time. O! my dear boy, he did speak so well! Never was anything more striking and profitable.'

In 1884 David Lloyd George finally qualified and opened an office in the back parlour of his home in Criccieth, the small town to which the family had moved. His practice took in neighbouring towns – Portmadoc, Festiniog, Pwllheli – and he had very soon made his mark, notably with the Llanfrothen Burial Case. The Burials Act of 1880 had allowed Nonconformists to hold funerals and be buried in local Church of England graveyards. But at

Llanfrothen the Rector had persuaded one of the donors of land for the enlargement of the graveyard to sign a deed insisting on the use only of Anglican rites. Lloyd George thereupon set himself, somewhat ghoulishly, to discover a potential candidate for interment whose family would be prepared to insist on a burial according to the provisions of the Act. He discovered a Calvinist Methodist named Robert Roberts, indubitably dying and perhaps not unhappy to take part in some posthumous act of religious dissent. Under Lloyd George's advice, the family overcame the protests of the Rector by breaking down the church gate and burying Robert's body beside the grave where his daughter already lay. The Rector sued the Roberts family, Lloyd George defended them and won the case. The publicity this brought both to the Welsh cause and to the young lawyer himself was country-wide and must have been very gratifying for an ambitious young man.

It was just after this that he fell in love – not apparently for the first time and quite certainly not for the last, but with more determination than usual; he wanted not only to win Maggie Owen, the farmer's daughter, he wanted to marry her. She came from a family of Calvinistic Methodists, he was a Baptist. They were faintly Liberal, he was already winging about the county, using and strengthening the ties between Liberalism and Welsh Nationalism. They were wealthy farming folk, he was fatherless and without property. Richard Lloyd, on sectarian grounds, was very much against the marriage. It may be that this barricade of objections made the enterprise more enticing; in any case, after a persistent courtship he married Maggie in 1888, in the Presbyterian chapel at Pen-cae-newydd – which suggests that the families had come to a religious compromise, at least on the subject of the venue.

Meanwhile Lloyd George was building his reputation as a public speaker, as a fighter for Liberalism, above all as a leader in the Welsh cause. As he told a Liberal meeting at Caernarvon, 'I come from the blackest and wickedest Tory parish in the land. It is a parish in which the squire turned the fathers of young children out of their homes because they dared to vote Liberal. But the power of the landlords in Wales will be broken as effectively as the power of the Druids. The great, rugged nationalist sentiments of Wales will rise against the English Ogre, this fiendish she-wolf whose lair is in Westminster. I shall not sleep in my grave until someone knocks and tells me, "*Mae hi wedi mynd*" (she has gone).'

Rhetoric of this sort wooed some and alienated others – for many he was the coming leader, the Moses who would lead them to freedom; for a staider and older minority he was a wild man, not to be trusted. In 1890 he found that most of the Liberals were in fact with him, for he was nominated as a candidate for the Parliamentary by-election in Caernarvon Boroughs caused by the sitting member's death. His opponent was Ellis Nanney, his own village squire, which gave an extra zest to Lloyd George's campaigning. He whirled about the constituency, knocking on doors where no candidate's knuckles had ever sounded before, reaching many of the more remote and inaccessible places on foot. It must have given him an enormous satisfaction that it was against precisely this Tory candidate that he finally won the election – by less than twenty votes, certainly, but those votes enough to send him back to Criccieth a hero, welcomed by a bright flutter of bonfires from all the surrounding hills.

Although most English Members, particularly on the Tory side, regarded the Welsh nationalists with a contemptuous condescension, they had begun to take some notice of them. Much stronger in the House was the group of Irish Nationalists, who, first under Parnell and later, when that gigantic figure had been lopped down by the keen hypocrisies of Victorian England, under Redmond, had for a long time been using the procedures of Parliament as a weapon in their guerrilla tactics against the constitution. These tactics Lloyd George studied and mastered. And, at the General Election of 1892, he held his seat, increasing his majority to nearly two hundred over a new Tory candidate, Sir John Puleston, a Welshman too identified with English causes for his own political good.

Under the great Gladstone, the Liberal Party won that election, but its majority in the Commons depended on the Irish vote; the thirty-one Welsh Liberal Members were almost enough by themselves to erode the difference between the parties, which was only forty. In these circumstances, the Celtic attitude to the Government could afford to become highly conditional; for support, rewards were expected. As Lloyd George said in Conway after his election, 'Why had Wales made sacrifices in the face of unexampled difficulties and intimidation from squires and agents? It was not to install one statesman into power. It was not to deprive one party of power in order to put another party in power. ... No; it was done because Wales had by an overwhelming majority demonstrated its determination to secure its own progress.'

When the Liberal Government took office they passed legislation which must have pleased the radical heart of the young Welshman

– particularly an Employers' Liability Bill and a Bill to establish Home Rule for Ireland. Both these Bills failed in the House of Lords, that curious anachronism which by the nature of its hereditary basis battled throughout most of the last century and a part of this at its own Thermopylae, defending a civilisation it could not help but feel was identical with its own interests. This will have done nothing to lessen Lloyd George's congenital enmity to the Upper House and its over-privileged members. Asquith, then Home Secretary, finally moved a Bill suspending 'for a limited time the creation of new interests in Church of England . . . benefices in Wales and Monmouthshire' – in other words, he made a preparatory move in the disestablishment of the Anglican Church in the Principality. After strong Welsh pressure on Lord Rosebery, Gladstone's successor as Premier, a Bill to complete that task was introduced in 1894 – but before it could pass the Government had been defeated and forced to resign.

Lloyd George, not a man with private means, was faced with the demands of a third election in five years. He told his constituents that unless his expenses were met, he would not be able to stand again. They did so, and he held the seat – as indeed he was to do for well over half a century altogether. He now tried to manufacture a truly Welsh Home Rule party, but for all his influence in North Wales, he was unable to find much leverage in the South. By no means all the Welsh Liberals accepted the policy of Home Rule, and all his efforts to unite them, as well as his much more ambitious plan to unite all the Welsh, Irish and Scottish MPs under the same still-chimerical banner, came to nothing.

In 1896 he came to the first of his close brushes with disaster. Lloyd George was a man who was not only irresistible to women, but one who found most women irresistible. No one's wife or daughter was safe from his advances, and he brought to these adventures the same audacity and charm, the same eloquence and energy, with which he had already dazzled the House of Commons. A friend of his, a Dr David Edwards, sued his wife for divorce on the grounds of adultery with the stationmaster at Cemmaes, a man named Wilson. But in a written confession to her husband, Mrs Edwards admitted that it was not Wilson who was the father of her daughter, but someone unnamed who was then called simply 'A.B.' Soon rumours spread that these initials hid the identity of Lloyd George – and when the confession was produced in court, those rumours appeared to have been proved correct. Counsel on both sides, however, agreed that they were 'satisfied that the imputation ... was without foundation'; it is said that Lloyd George claimed that he had been in Parliament and voting on the night in question, but as Donald McCormick pointed out in *The Mask of Merlin*, Parliament was not in session then. D. A. Thomas, leader of the South Wales Liberal Association, bluntly referred to the parallel case of Parnell's love-affair with Kitty O'Shea, already known to almost everyone in political circles – 'You seem to think the Irish have everything to teach us! It would be better to learn from the lesson of where Mrs O'Shea will lead Parnell – to Home Rule or the Divorce Court!'

Perhaps because of his failure both to get on with Thomas and to capture the whole of the Welsh Nationalist movement, but possibly also because the years in opposition permitted him more latitude, Lloyd George after this period became active in an increasingly wide area of political activity. He made journeys abroad – to South America, to Italy, to Canada. Again and again he rallied his party, again and again harassed the Conservatives, engaged under Lord Salisbury in demonstrating the same complacent stagnation which they were to display under Baldwin forty years later. By 1896 *The Westminster Gazette* could say, 'It is doubtful if a private member has ever done greater service to his Party in Parliament.' And all his work was on the side of reform and against the continuing and strengthened privileges of the landlords, the employers and the Anglican Church – as he told the House in 1899, to its pious consternation, 'The squire and the parson have broken into the poor-box and divided its contents between them. The Tammany ring of landlords and parsons are dividing the last remnants of the money between them.'

That same year, however, brought him his first major political crisis. To the plaudits of an exuberantly jingoist population, the Salisbury Government rejected Kruger's ultimatum and found itself at war with the Boers of the Transvaal: in the Commons, a Member put the case for conflict in a nutshell, 'I believe the war will be brief and that we shall be victorious and that such a result will be to the advantage of the Boers, the blacks and the British alike.' But Lloyd George had already written, 'If I have the courage I shall protest with all the vehemence at my command against the outrage which is perpetrated in the name of human freedom,' and after the war had begun he did not waver in this opinion, nor did he allow his courage to waver. In a sense he saw the Boers as distant Welshmen, farmers of Nonconformist convictions being coerced not merely by an imperial power, but more particularly by such ambivalent builders of personal empires and personal fortunes as Cecil Rhodes and those associated with him. More than that, he had come to detest the supercilious, but very deft, very intelligent Joseph Chamberlain, a man who changed parties when he saw Gladstone clinging to the Liberal leadership, who engineered the downfall of Parnell by persuading O'Shea to sue for divorce, a man who could say, at a dinner at which the Jewish Foreign Minister of Italy, Baron Sonnino, was one of the principal guests, 'I think the Anglo-Saxon race is as fine as any race on earth. ... There is only one race I despise – the Jews, sir. They are physical cowards.' Above all, Chamberlain was suspected – and relatively recent evidence suggests it was not without reason – of complicity in the Jameson Raid and thus in Rhodes's shabby South African manoeuvres.

As a result of his stand against the war, Lloyd George for the first time found himself without the affection of the people. He had always been ambitious and he had, for most of his still-short career, been successful. He had received a great deal of attention and a great deal of praise. Now he was ostracised in his own village of Llanystumdwy, he was stoned in Bangor, his practice declined, his political future looked bleak. Yet he stuck to what he believed and he was among the most vigorous of that minority which steadfastly offered the British people an alternative view to the simple patriotism which had beguiled them, and offered the rest of the world an alternative British view to the one which the government proclaimed.

In 1900 the famous 'Khaki Election' was held at which the Tory slogans suggested that 'every vote for the Liberals is a vote for the Boers'. Lloyd George's support dwindled, slipped and gave under the strain. But he was after all one of the world's natural politicians – again and again he returned to the theme of the Boers' Noncomformity, of their Calvinism. Every word he had to say on that subject must have woken familiar echoes in the minds of his listeners. When polling day came, Caernarvon Boroughs elected him again, his majority increased once more by almost a hundred. This victory was against the national trend, however (the Unionist Government had an overall majority over the Liberals and the Nationalists of 134), and there stretched before Lloyd George another long period in which to exercise his gadfly wings and mobilise his barbs and wounding stings in opposition.

He now became the main target for the Tories – and 'target' in more senses than one. He wrote in his diary, 'Was warned that the Tory rioters threatened to kill me'. He was assaulted on a number of occasions, and so at least once was his wife, who in this, as in so many other assorted crises of his early and middle years, stood unswervingly by him. On one occasion Lloyd George seems almost deliberately to have placed his head in the lion's mouth. Birmingham firms supplied arms for the Boer war. One of these firms was Kynochs, in which the Chamberlain family had interests. Birmingham was a Chamberlain town, sewn up as tight for the Liberal-Unionists Joseph Chamberlain led as is Cook County, Illinois, for the Democrats. Yet it was to Birmingham that Lloyd George decided to go, to address a meeting the mere holding of which he must have known would be an affront to his arch-enemy.

The Chamberlain-controlled Press stirred up expectations of a riot. Labouchere, a rakish Liberal colleague of Lloyd George, asked Chamberlain to use his influence to help get Lloyd George a fair hearing. Chamberlain replied, 'If Ll.G. wants his life, he had better keep away from Birmingham. . . . If he doesn't go, I will see that it is known he is afraid. If he does go, he will deserve all he gets.' The Liberal-Unionists forged tickets in order to smuggle their bully-boys into the meeting. These hooligans had each been primed to recognise Lloyd George by large pictures of him which they had been especially given. Arriving earlier than expected, he missed the first planned wave of violence; on the platform, however, he found time for only one sentence: 'The Union Jack is the pride and property of our common country and no man who really loves it could do anything but dissent from its being converted into Mr Chamberlain's pocket handkerchief.' Then the crowd rushed the platform. Disguised in a police uniform lent him by a constable somewhat bigger than himself, Lloyd George managed to escape. Meanwhile Chamberlain, that respectable Cabinet minister, was in his club, reading a telegram which began, 'Lloyd George the traitor was not allowed to say a word. . . .'

The divisions in the Liberal party over the Boer War were healed as that war receded into history and the Tories became, as ever, their main opponents. Particularly in the struggle against the Conservative desire to support the voluntary – that is, the Church – schools with public money the Liberals found unity. This was especially the case in Wales, where the Anglican schools still forbade the people's language and punished those who spoke it, while hitting at the Nonconformist sects by mixing religious instruction, couched in terms acceptable to the Church of England, with the rest of their curriculum. But it was Joseph Chamberlain, determined on a policy of protection and tariffs in order to make plausible the cause of Empire Preference, who brought Balfour to the point of resignation. Perhaps the latter hoped that the Liberals, split as all radical parties always seem to be, would be unable to form a government. If he did, the diplomatic efforts of a long-headed, unspectacular old Scotsman named Campbell-Bannerman soon disillusioned him; under 'C.-B.' a Cabinet was formed, and in it sat Lloyd George as President of the Board of Trade.

When the Liberal administration came to power in 1905, their first necessary act was to call a general election in order to provide themselves with a power-base in the Commons – or hand responsibility back to the Tories. In the event the country endorsed Campbell-Bannerman's government; they elected 377 Liberal Members and only 157 Unionists. Over on the Left, however, there appeared a clump of men, brilliant or glowering, alarming to those Liberals with the brains to see into the future – fifty-eight Members of Parliament sent to Westminster by that new political breed, the Labour voters. In the dazzle and excitement of victory many may have overlooked their significance; nevertheless, they marked the end of that gentlemanly, paternalistic era in which Liberals and Conservatives, overwhelmingly drawn from the ranks of the educated upper-middle classes, had wrangled over the principles of government. Born out of the desperation of poverty and based on the increasing strength of the trades unions, the Labour Party was to carve away and carry off the very soil on which the Liberals stood. But for the moment Campbell-Bannerman's administration seemed to stand unchallenged. Indeed, its only enemies were inside its own ranks – there was a faction which had wanted Asquith as Prime Minister – and as always that almost sinister array of Tories who sat in coroneted ranks in the House of Lords, a petulant army determined to hurl back or emasculate every effective measure of Liberal reform.

The first problem was solved when in 1908 Campbell-Bannerman's health broke down and he was forced to resign; the second was brought to the point of critical confrontation by Lloyd-George's Budget of 1909. Before then, however, he had proved his worth as well as the pliability of his principles, and had suffered a deep personal tragedy. As President of the Board of Trade he had piloted through the House the Merchant Shipping Act, which permitted heavier loads on ships by raising the Plimsoll Line, but on the other hand guaranteed better conditions for seamen (unscrupulous owners were soon misusing the new provisions and the figures of men and ships lost at sea rose noticeably); the Patents and

Designs Act, which laid down that British patents only covered objects made in Britain; and the Port of London Act, with which he created the Port of London Authority which has run London docks ever since. But in November 1907 Mair Eluned, his eldest daughter, died after an operation for appendicitis. She was seventeen years old, talented and attractive, and for years afterwards Lloyd George could be seen with tears in his eyes when her name was mentioned or when he caught sight again of her portrait. Perhaps his elevation to Asquith's old post of Chancellor of the Exchequer, when Asquith himself became Premier, did something to reconcile him to the circumstances of his life; but he was always a man of intense feelings and it is doubtful if the scar ever disappeared.

As Chancellor Lloyd George could attempt the kind of reforms he had always advocated. In this he had the support of Asquith, who himself initiated many of them – indeed, Beatrice Webb called him 'the greatest radical of them all'. Certainly it was on foundations the Prime Minister had built that Lloyd George constructed his measure introducing old age pensions, against the kind of Tory opposition summed up in Lord Lansdowne's comment that the 'expenditure on the South African War had been a better investment than old age pensions', for war raised 'the moral fibre of the country' while pensions weakened it. Yet throughout the Edwardian decade the standard of living fell for the majority of the population and all the Liberals' reform legislation redistributed not more than one per cent of the gross national income. The decline in the consumption of wheat, sugar and meat, while the population figures rose, indicates how much the poorest sections of society needed and deserved support.

Another point of bitter conflict was the Licensing Bill, which tried to control the sale and consumption of alcoholic drinks. Lloyd George had made his maiden speech on the subject of temperance and, although not a prohibitionist, he would have liked to bring breweries, distilleries and public houses under direct government control. This measure, like other reforming measures, was destroyed in the House of Lords. With the introduction of his Budget, nicknamed 'The People's Budget', in 1909 the battle against the Lords was joined.

In order to provide money for the social services he envisaged, Lloyd George introduced a number of new, or extended a number of old, methods of taxation. A sum of £8 million, he said, would have to be found in order to keep some 700,000 old people out of the workhouse. 'The workhouse may be better than hunger,' he declared, 'but it is a humiliating end for men whose honest toil won for them through life at least freedom, if not plenty.' Another £2 million would go to free those already inside those dreary walls – 'at least 200,000 of these aged toilers who stand at the gates wistfully awaiting the turn of the key with nothing between them now and their redemption but the greed of the Lords'. He increased income tax, clamping a surtax on the highest incomes, and added estate duties; the most unpopular – and, in the event, inefficient – of the new taxes was that levied on the unearned rise in land values. It has been suggested that this measure, which was due to bring in no more than £500,000, was included in order to set their assembled Lordships by the ears. This suspicion is contradicted by Lloyd George's behaviour, some of which was oddly conciliatory, given his overall mood. If, however, it had been intended to rouse the titled and landed members of the Upper House, it succeeded. They did what they had not done in centuries, exercising a right many had thought constitutionally atrophied through lack of use: they rejected a money Bill passed by the House of Commons.

In his demagogic, Celtic way, Lloyd George appealed over their heads, making inflammatory speeches in various parts of the country. 'Who is going to rule the country? The King and the Peers? Or the King and the People?' The most famous of these speeches was made in Limehouse in July 1909. Talking of the manner in which land values had risen, he asked, 'Who created these increments? Who made that golden swamp? Was it the landlord? Was it his energy? His brains? ... It is rather hard that an old workman should have to find his way to the gates of the tomb bleeding and footsore, through the brambles and thorns of poverty. We cut a new path for him, an easier one, a pleasanter one, through fields of waving corn.' It is hardly surprising the Lords vote went against him.

As a result Asquith turned to the country – and came back after the election in a stalemate. He now held his Premiership only with the acquiescence of the Labour and Irish Members. The Liberal Party had begun its slide towards extinction, although paradoxically its policies had never been more radically reformist. In the grip of what must have seemed to him the extremists of proletarian resurgence and Celtic nationalism, Asquith was forced as a preliminary to attempt to curb the power of the Upper Chamber. The Commons, and the (largely absent) Lords, passed a little-amended version of Lloyd George's Budget, permitting the business of government to continue; then Asquith tabled a measure designed to curb the powers of the Lords, notably restricting their veto, which was to be overridden in the event of the Commons voting repeatedly for a piece of controversial legislation. Their lordships should in future be able to delay and modify, but not to stop, laws decided on by the commoners of England, Scotland, Ireland and Wales.

Against this the ancient order of the English aristocracy attempted to make a last stand. Everything could go, they conceded, even the hereditary principle, provided they retained their right to veto. Asquith and Lloyd George were adamant; they declared, to the horror and astonishment of every true, blue-blooded Britisher, that if the Lords refused to pass their Parliament Bill intact, they would create five hundred new Liberal peers who would make sure it became law. The only man who might stand in the way of this policy was, of course, the King, since it was he who at least nominally had the sole right to create new peerages. The Conservatives, however, did not trust the frivolous Edward VII – they suspected him, quite wrongly, of Liberal sympathies and whispered among themselves that he was a traitor. This was an odd view to take, since the King directly represented the Crown to which they owed allegiance, disobedience to which would have made them traitors. When Edward died and George V replaced him, their hopes grew – George V was conventional, George V was dull, George V was a man who believed in the Navy, therefore George V was clearly a Conservative. He would not let them down. Asquith, however, went to see him late in 1910 and asked him whether, should the situation reach such a point, he would agree to create the new peers. After some hesitation the King said he would, and Asquith again went to the country.

It was somewhere around this point that Lloyd George began to negotiate with the Conservative leader, Balfour, about the possibility of a National Government. This would have been based on a compromise which may have offered the Tories many of the measures they were advocating and Lloyd George was condemning, and it would have given Lloyd George, who wanted Asquith shunted up into the House of Lords, the Premiership, since he would then have been leader of the majority party. Nothing came of this – except that it offered any who were uncertain a glimpse of how Lloyd George's mind worked, and that of his quicksilver ally, Winston Churchill.

Asquith, however, won the election again, although no more decisively than before, and once again presented the Parliament

Bill. It went up to the Lords in August 1911 and, despite a move by the backwoods peers to make a last-ditch stand against it (thus bringing about the destruction of the very institution they were supposed to be defending), the House of Lords admitted that power had finally slipped from the landed interest, and passed the measure by 131 votes to 114. Thus, despite his attempts at compromise – which may have been no more than an exercise in keeping his options open – Lloyd George stood on the winning side at last in the battle against what he called, with a comprehensive contempt in his tones, 'the Dukes'. The way was clear for the reforming legislation which he and the Liberals still wanted to pass, determined as they were to prove themselves the party of radicalism and the working man (a doomed determination, as the clamour on their Left grew stronger and more organised).

In 1912, however, there came a new suspicion to darken the glitter of the famous Welshman's career. Sexually he was widely known to be fickle; politically his colleagues knew him to be both indispensable and pliable, a dangerous combination – his principles, while not for sale, were certainly easily detachable. Now, in what was known as the Marconi Scandal, it was his financial probity which came under intense scrutiny. Just at the time when the Postmaster-General was ordering a chain of wireless stations from the British Marconi Company, Lloyd George and, much more expansively, Rufus Isaacs, the Attorney-General, were found to have bought and sold American Marconi shares.

A Select Committee looked into the purchases and, basing their findings on the apparent lack of connection between the Marconi Companies English and American, decided there was 'no ground for any reflection upon the honour of the Ministers concerned'. Lloyd George told the House he had been indiscreet; he said he regretted the purchases. The House possibly thought that the connection of the two companies was closer than the Select Committee imagined, particularly within the sphere of stock-exchange quotations, and that Lloyd George's profit of £743 on five hundred shares, made within two days of their having been bought, was fatter than mere honesty made likely. In any case it divided on a Motion of Censure. Certainly Lloyd George and Isaacs were vindicated and the motion was lost – but only by 346 to 268, a margin too thin to wipe off all the mud.

In the meantime Lloyd George had been one of the main pilots of the new National Insurance Bill, to some extent based on Belgium's and Germany's contributory schemes. For the first time employee, employer and State were joined in a compulsory alliance to underwrite an insurance scheme which protected the health of the lower-paid workers and gave some shelter from the effects of unemployment for those in certain selected, but basic, industries – shipbuilding and engineering were two. The scheme was not nationwide, no one had yet coined the term Welfare State, the Beveridge Report was still decades in the future, but for Britain this Act, passed into law during 1911, became an essential part of the measures devised by the Asquith Government in the first dozen years of the century which were to be the pattern and foundation for much of the social legislation which has followed them. What was important about it was not so much its provisions as the mood it set and the responsibilities it accepted. By implication, it told the country that the time had come when the benefits of industrialisation ought to be shared out more equally, and that from its profits its casualties could be cared for or appeased. Much of the detailed work on this Bill was done by Bottomley's *bête noir*, C. F. G. Masterman (see p. 58), but it was Lloyd George who was the prime mover behind it. Although he was often insincere, often wavered in his allegiance to his principles and never acted as tough as he talked, it is true that throughout his life he honestly felt that 'all down history nine-tenths of mankind have been grinding corn for the remaining tenth and been paid with the husks and bidden to thank God they had the husk'.

Between 1912 and 1914 Lloyd George, like the rest of the Liberal Government, found himself faced – and, indeed, outfaced – by the challenge of Sir Edward Carson and his implacable Protestants in Northern Ireland. Supported by the Tory Party, Carson challenged not only Asquith and his Cabinet, but the whole notion of Parliamentary supremacy. Seeing the clear possibility of Home Rule, with Dublin the capital of a united Ireland, he refused both to accept the imminent decision of the House of Commons nor any responsibility for the constitutional crisis this refusal would have provoked. Bull-headed, he stood for independence, and in the name of loyalty to the Crown offered to drag the country into civil war. Firmness at this point would have changed Anglo-Irish relations for ever. The arguments which have raged up and down Ulster since 1966 (couched in precisely the same terms and uttered by what seem precisely the same people as in 1912), punctuated as they have been by the heavy thunder of explosions, would not have had sixty years of bitterness in which to root. But neither Asquith, nor Lloyd George, nor Winston Churchill could find the necessary firmness or support to stand up to Carson and his Ulster Volunteer Force. Indeed, so far as Lloyd George is concerned, it is plausible to suppose he had more personal sympathy with the Calvinistic Protestants of the North than with Nonconformity's traditional enemies, the Papists, in the South. It was Lloyd George who went to see Redmond, the Nationalist leader, in order to put to him the proposal that Ulster should be excluded for the first five years from any Home Rule provisions. It was thus from Lloyd George that Redmond first learned that the Liberals, whose legislation he had supported and whose majority had rested on his acquiescence, were not after all going to pay their political debts in full. For him it was doom – Irish nationalists were not prepared to settle for half a loaf. But into the middle of this tense situation there intruded in 1914 the wider calamity of the First World War.

Here Lloyd George had not been among those astute enough to predict the near approach of the conflict. It was, of course, a situation in which the intransigence of the Austrians towards the Serbians (whether inspired by Berlin or not) caught many observers unprepared. Not all of them, however, were saying, as Lloyd George was eleven days after the Sarajevo assassination, 'In the matter of external affairs, the sky has never been more perfectly blue', nor imagining that Anglo-German 'relations are very much better than they were a few years ago', as he did on the day Austria delivered her ultimatum to the Serbs. Nor, when the crisis became more clearly discernible, was he among those prepared to leap patriotically to the barricades. As late as 2 August he seems to have wanted to remain aloof from the whole business; only the crossing of the Belgian frontier by strong German forces finally made him realise that Britain had now been given no real alternative to war.

Another suggestion for his change of mind has been made – that if he had not accepted the Cabinet decision to send Germany an ultimatum at this point, a Coalition would have been formed there and then, from which he was told he would be excluded. Whatever the reason, once he had changed his attitude he took up the new direction this indicated with the same all-consuming vigour that he did any of his projects, whatever shift or mixture of principles lay behind them. First, he had to calm the City, whose financiers, caught by the advent of war without either the experience or the foresight to cope with the changed situation, panicked – Asquith said of them, 'They are the greatest ninnies I ever had to tackle. I found them all in a state of funk like old women chattering over their teacups in a cathedral town.' By a number of measures Lloyd George managed to prop up the banking structure and the unsteady currency; he then turned to the problems of meeting the enormous and increasing costs of the fighting. Part of the necessary money was raised by War Loans, short-term borrowings from a people now earning higher wages and encouraged to lend their money to the government for the best of patriotic motives. On the whole Lloyd George preferred to raise the funds he needed through taxation – as he said in November 1914, 'Every twenty millions raised annually by taxation ... means four or five millions taken off the permanent burdens thereafter imposed on the country.' Those who had to cope with the post-war economy ten and fifteen years later may well have wished that this was a policy that could have been adhered to.

At the same time he plunged with all his originality, imagination and intelligence into those responsibilities of strategic planning which fell upon the wartime Cabinet. John Buchan wrote of him, 'Of all the civilians I have known, Lloyd George seems to have possessed in the highest degree the capacity for becoming a great soldier. But he might have lost several armies while he was learning his trade.' Certainly he realised that the stalemate on the Western Front, already established by the end of 1914 and not thereafter to be much modified in the three years that followed, should and could be broken. He wanted to fight in the Balkans, where Austrian and not German troops would have to be met, and he wanted to fight in Turkey. Entrenched military opinion was against such a widespread and daring series of ventures – neither Kitchener in London nor Joffre in Paris thought much of what was coming to be known as the 'Easterner policy'. There was in 1915 the attack on the Dardanelles, inspired by Churchill and for various reasons a complete fiasco, which confirmed the experts in their orthodox convictions. Indeed, they needed little more for this than the sight of Lloyd George and Winston Churchill standing shoulder to shoulder on the other side – such a coalition of mavericks could not, they must have felt, be right. Yet, at the end of 1915, the only changes in the situation had been those for the worse; substantially, nothing had altered in the West at all.

By this time, Lloyd George was head of the Ministry of Munitions in the new Coalition Government (brought about partly by unofficial contacts between Lloyd George and the Tory leader, Bonar Law), where he was responsible for supplying the various war fronts. Here he operated somewhat like Lord Beaverbrook at the Ministry of Aircraft Production during the Second World War. He overrode procedures, scandalised civil servants, arrived early and left late, and expected others to do the same. At the same time, he conducted a personal vendetta against the War Minister, Kitchener. The War Office's Ordnance Department had been in charge of munitions – according to Lloyd George, inefficiently. It is hard to substantiate this claim – the Allies were short of shells, certainly, but so was every one of the armies caught up on the Western Front. Kitchener had expanded the production of shells twenty-seven-fold, which involved an extraordinary mobilisation of resources. Another point of conflict was the question of voluntary recruitment, which Kitchener continued to favour, as against Lloyd George's demand that conscription be introduced. It had always, of course, been one of the basic tenets of the Liberal Party that conscription had no place in a free society, whatever the circumstances; on the other hand, no one had envisaged circumstances like those in Europe in 1916 and 1917.

Lloyd George was a practised and unscrupulous intriguer; his manipulation of information, both secret and public, was masterly, though rarely ethical. There seems no question that he wanted more power and that he was prepared to stop at almost nothing to get it. He was in secret communication with Sir John French, his ally among the Generals – in this attachment a lonely figure. He leaked Cabinet secrets, when it suited him to do so and when it would advance his cause. He was not alone in this, of course. As Kitchener told Asquith, 'You I can trust, but all these damned politicians talk to their wives – except for Ll.G., who talks to other people's wives.' Certainly part of his animosity against Kitchener was caused by the fact that he had thought Asquith would give him the War Office, and that he seemed to feel thwarted at his not having been given it. So marked and well-known was this feeling that when in June 1916 the cruiser *Hampshire* sank, with Kitchener aboard, there were those who whispered that somewhere in the story of this disaster there would be found the secret guiding hand of Lloyd George. He certainly made a great fuss about the possibility of his going with Kitchener, who was on his way to Russia, although there seems never to have been any question of his going. He certainly talked about Kitchener's journey to other people though, and mentioned both the name of the ship and the date of her departure – a slightly thoughtless revelation given the pervasive nature of German espionage. For the country Kitchener's death was a tremendous blow to its morale. For Lloyd George it provided the opportunity he had expected thirteen months earlier – he came at last to the War Office.

While helping to prosecute the war against Germany, and doing so with endless energy as always, he also continued his battle with the Generals, this time reaching a stalemate reminiscent of the Western Front with Sir William Robertson. His long-term objective, however, was the Premiership, not only because he was ambitious, but also because by this time – with Winston Churchill discredited by the Dardanelles failure – he thought himself alone among politicians for speed of thought and quickness of apprehension. There seems no doubt that, with the exception of Asquith, his colleagues were intellectually his inferiors, and Asquith had neither his energy nor his self-confidence. His most immediately helpful effort at the War Office was to insist on a reorganisation of the transport systems in the West and in Mesopotamia. But he felt himself hampered by the reluctance of the Generals to take much notice of his strategic ideas, and by the unwieldy nature of a Cabinet whose more than twenty members, of conflicting parties, were expected to arrive at immediate and crucial decisions. There was a move to create a War Council, with Asquith retaining some overall, presidential control, but Lloyd George being charged with the actual day-to-day running of the war. This was suggested by Hankey, the Secretary to the Cabinet, but it is clear that such a division of command would have made matters worse rather than better. On the Tory side, Bonar Law havered and veered, enticed by the delicate bait which Lloyd George spread for him – if Asquith would stand down for anyone, it should be for Bonar Law. The 'if' was sizeable, but the prize beyond was dazzling enough for Bonar Law not quite to be able to see the snag. On the Liberal side there was division, some Ministers rallying round Asquith, some trying to keep the Cabinet undivided, some considering Lloyd George the necessary man to lead the war effort.

An oddity appears here, for this opinion persisted despite Lloyd George's declared pessimism. Those who were close to him knew that he thought the war as good as lost. One reason for his opinion was the decision of Robertson and his colleagues of the Imperial General Staff to attack on the Western Front – or, as Lloyd George put it, to repeat 'the bloody stupidities of 1915 and 1916!' Those who take his view of the military's decisions will see his actions in provoking the fall of the Asquith Government as one which may have saved the thousands of lives which would otherwise have been wasted in yet one more futile effort. Those who feel the Generals were right and that an attack early in 1917 would have proved more victorious than the one which actually took place (which I would have thought the harder case to prove) consider his efforts at that time little short of treason, prolonging the war and thus causing the deaths of the thousands who fell in its last year.

What seems beyond dispute is that his manoeuvres at this period were often squalid. He leaked his opinions to *Reynolds News* and possibly, by way of Dawson, to *The Times*. He spread his idea of Asquith's flabbiness among a wider and wider circle of acquaintances, emphasising his own impatience to pick the war effort up by the scruff of its neck and thrust it in the right direction. He flirted with, but never accepted, the terms of some accommodation with the Prime Minister. The crisis continued. With more firmness Asquith might indeed have ended it – in a way, the final proof of the truth of Lloyd George's indictment lies in the fact that he was allowed to make it at all, even if only by implication. The Tories were undecided – Lord Lansdowne had presented a memorandum to the Cabinet suggesting the possibility of a negotiated peace, and Asquith had not condemned it as the rest had done. This was in the style of the man, which tended to avoid the denunciatory. In that wartime mood of chauvinism, however, so skilfully milked in another context by Bottomley, the idea gained strength that without Lloyd George at his side, Asquith might waver. Henderson, the Labour leader, declared that he and his would be willing to serve under Lloyd George. Gauging his moment with a guerrilla's instinct, Lloyd George made the final move – he resigned. The pressures having grown too great, knowing he could not now carry on, Asquith almost disdainfully handed back his Premiership. Bonar Law leaped for the bait which had been so tantalisingly before his nose so long. He saw the King, then he saw Asquith. But Asquith, as Lloyd George had always known he would, refused to serve under anyone. Bonar Law's claim lapsed. On 7 December 1916 Lloyd George became the Prime Minister. He was fifty-three, popular, admired, at times adored, by a population sometimes as much dazed as dazzled by his charismatic oratory, his changes of pace, his sleight of hand, his deft leaps and somersaults on the high trapeze of politics.

As to how Lloyd George ran the war there has been much debate. The war was won, therefore he ran it well. The war was long, therefore he ran it badly. He was let down by the Generals. He let the Generals down. His ideas were right, but implemented too late. His ideas were wrong, and their implementation led to avoidable disasters. What is true, and remains true across the political desert of the Twenties and Thirties, the smoke and dust of World War Two and beyond the booming voice and jowly determination of Churchill (a giant whose shape has distorted history for many of his contemporaries and obscured great men who came before him), is that in Lloyd George the British people found the leader they could respond to, the voice they were prepared to hear. As Churchill was to be nearly three decades later, Lloyd George was a focal point for national morale. It was not in the end what he did or organised or planned that mattered so much as the mere fact of him, his presence. In this, ironically, he took the place of his arch-enemy Kitchener, that heavily moustached Field Marshal who had been seen by the people as a bulwark against invasion or defeat. It was now Lloyd George who, as Clemenceau did in France, personified the defiance and determination of the whole country.

Yet he made mistakes. Almost at once he cancelled the plans of Robertson, considered variants of the 'Eastern' policy, then abruptly authorised the French General Nivelle to mount an offensive in the West after all. It is hard to tell now what Nivelle's failure proved – Lloyd George's defenders might say it meant that he had been right to consider a Western offensive a mistake, his critics that Robertson's well-planned attack would have worked, where Nivelle's hastily-prepared one never had the slightest chance. On the other hand, he favoured Pétain's strategy over that of Haig – solid defence as a basis for sudden, unexpected attacks, rather than massive, sustained and grinding assault – and if that had been agreed on, the waste and horror of Passchendaele might have been avoided. Yet even here his position was not clear-cut, for in May 1917 Lloyd George had said in Paris, 'We must go on hitting and hitting with all our strength until the German ended as he always did, by cracking,' thus putting in a nutshell the case for a war of attrition. Moreover, his own insistence on allowing the glamorous Nivelle his campaign lost Haig the early months of the summer; had he been able to move then, the sticky hell in which his armies perished might never have been reached.

Lloyd George's dislike for Haig was tempered by a fear of the political consequences of removing him – not least the slightly paranoid thought that the pig-headed Field Marshal would lead a *putsch* against him – and this left him in a position of neither supporting Haig's plans nor countermanding them. Much later, he was to attack Haig and the rest, particularly in his *Memoirs*, and history has for the moment accepted his general view of their deficiencies, but there seems no doubt that Lloyd George managed with hindsight to slide away from that burden of blame which may yet be rightfully assigned him.

Where he was right, however, was in his advocacy of the convoy system, which was adopted by the Navy only just in time to avert the threatening victory of the German submarine fleets. Where he was even more crucially right was in demanding and finally helping to create a unified Supreme War Council, and a single command for all the Allied armies on the Western Front under the imperturbable Maréchal Foch. And at home he organised food rationing, he saw to the control of wages and prices, he extended the capacity of the shipbuilding industry and – in the long term one of his most significant reforms – he recognised the contribution women had been making to the national effort by offering to them for the first time a franchise, limited though it was.

For a while, in 1918, it seemed as if after all the war was to be lost; the Germans smashed their way closer and closer to Paris and the four years of desperation looked as though they might in spite of everything end in bitterness. But that tide turned – in August he could tell the House of Commons, 'The enemy have done their worst, they can do no more, and if we only hold together we will have the greatest triumph for liberty the world has ever seen.' On 11 November he announced from Downing Street, 'The Armistice was signed at 5 am this morning, and hostilities are to cease on all fronts at 11 am today.' And then, with President Wilson and with Clemenceau, he had to struggle to create the peace.

To secure his base, he needed to be endorsed by the country and thus, on 18 December, there was held the first post-war General Election – the 'Coupon Election' at which the Coalition put itself up for the nation's approval. Lloyd George used this to pay off one score. Earlier in 1918 Major-General Sir Frederick Maurice had charged him with trying to whip up support for his policies by quoting inaccurate figures, purporting to come from the Front. There was a censure motion, a debate, and a vote. Lloyd George won – but Maurice had been right. Perhaps it was this knowledge nagging him which made the Prime Minister so bitter. In any case, he refused to give his 'coupon', his endorsement, to any candidate who had voted against him at that division. In the event, the candidates he had endorsed came back in overwhelming numbers to Westminster – they had won 526 seats out of 707. But most of these were Unionists; his own Liberal supporters numbered only 133, while a splinter group of less than forty glowered at them from the Opposition benches, virtuous in their continued support for Asquith and purity. Lloyd George had saved himself, but he had destroyed the Liberal Party.

He had done more than that. Campaigning on a platform which demanded the prosecution of the Kaiser and other German leaders, payment of vast indemnities by the Central Powers, and the expulsion from Britain of all 'enemy' aliens, he raised up for himself a sort of monster which, like Frankenstein's, was later to prove beyond his control. The public opinion he had aroused played a large part in forcing through the excessively harsh terms of the Versailles Treaty and so helped prepare the way for what we consider the Second World War, but which was really World War One, Part Two.

Lloyd George, however, once installed as Prime Minister, with his heterogeneous army of MPs behind him, was enough of a politician to realise that he no longer had a true political base. His party had vanished and he was, in effect, a prisoner of the Tories. That he did not seem to be so, and was able to pursue his own policies to some extent – softening the implacable peace terms Clemenceau proposed, for instance – was the result entirely of his own ability in calming or swaying the House. He needed a centre Party of his own, and for that he had to have money. To get it he began the Lloyd George Fund. The temptations inherent in the situation are immediately apparent and there is nothing in Lloyd George's personal history to suggest that he had the austerity of mind even to desire to resist them. Soon rich men were handing to his Fund large sums in the expectation of favours – and the favour they most frequently expected was an Honour. For Lloyd George, a man who had once helped coerce the monarch into at least threatening to create five hundred peers and who had spent a lifetime of increasingly ritualised hatred for squires, landlords and members of the Upper Chamber, this must have seemed an amusing human weakness it would be absurd not to put to practical use. He ought to have remembered Palmerston's comment when similarly approached: 'The throne is the fount of honour. It is not a pump nor am I the pump handle.' For those who did think in these terms, Lloyd George's actions were perturbing.

That the Fund benefited seems clear. The highest price for a peerage is said to have been more than £150,000 and a barony was handed across the counter for £80,000; a knighthood went for some £12,000. Between 1916 and 1923 Lloyd George nominated nearly a hundred new peers, double the normal average, and seemed to care hardly at all who received them. Sir William Vestey, for example, had moved his business to Argentina to avoid the war and its taxes, thus throwing 5000 men out of work, yet Lloyd George gave him a peerage. 'Why is it that only the very rich men seem to get the honours?' asked a Labour Member of Parliament, and a great part of the country muttered, 'Why indeed?' This criticism became so vociferous that eventually the Prime Minister was forced to agree that a Royal Commission should inquire into the whole question of honours. Fortunately for him he was out of office when it brought in its report; it may have been for that reason that its conclusions were surprisingly gentle, only Arthur Henderson, the Labour leader, who was a member, dissenting from its verdict, saying, 'I am of the opinion that the Commission might with advantage have made a more searching inquiry than they have done.'

In this scandal, as in the Balkan machinations which brought Lloyd George down in the end, there appeared briefly the sinister figure of Sir Basil Zaharoff, the international arms dealer. He had crossed Lloyd George's path, one cannot but doubt profitably, while Lloyd George was Minister of Munitions and he himself an agent for Vickers. Now he seems to have been involved in Lloyd George's stand over the Treaty of Sèvres, which was to do to Turkey what Versailles had been designed to do to Germany and Austria. It handed Smyrna and a large part of Asia Minor to Greece, to the enthusiastic applause of the Greek leader, Venizelos. Unfortunately a dictator had arisen in Turkey, Kemal Ataturk, a man much more astute and determined than anyone in London then seems to have realised. He insisted that he had not been a signatory to the treaty and thus felt justified in firmly and even forcibly resisting Greek encroachments – a firmness which may also have owed something to secret support he was receiving from France and Italy on the one hand, and Russia on the other.

For a short while it looked as though Lloyd George's efforts here would lead to another war. This was, if not more than the Tory Party could tolerate, enough at least to allow them the appearance of a justified impatience. They withdrew their support from Lloyd George and, when the dust and the electioneering had finally settled late in 1922, it was found that Bonar Law had become Prime Minister at last, at the head of a Conservative administration, while Lloyd George sat, finally powerless, the leader of fifty-five National Liberals.

In 1923 he took what was becoming the British way to lick his wounds, and went on a speech-making and lecturing tour of the

United States and Canada. Everywhere he went he was received with wonder and applause. He made many friends, although it is doubtful if he influenced many people. His days of making a real impact in the world were over. He had ended his own career and had also brought to an end – with help of one sort from the Tories, and of another from the Labour Party – the long story of the Liberals. It is questionable if they could have survived in any case in a political system dragged Leftwards by the advent of a Socialist party, but his methods of achieving and holding power certainly helped in his party's destruction.

His wife died in 1941; she had stayed loyal to him through disasters and humiliations, although by the end he had long exhausted her tolerance. In 1943 he married again, this time his secretary, Frances Louise Stevenson, who had been his wife in all reality for many years before. He remained a Member of Parliament until 1944; then he took an earldom, perhaps with some reflections upon the long journey he had made from the candlelit cottage room, poring over La Fontaine, to this new curiosity tamed by the honours and traditions of the Establishment: Earl Lloyd-George of Dwyfor. Early the next year he began visibly to weaken; on 26 March 1945 he died.

Lloyd George was a charmer, a buccaneer, a man who understood poverty and never forgot that understanding, who despised the system which had created it, yet who used that system, was used by it, and in the end succumbed to its pleasantly-baited temptations. He was a man of appetites, a quicksilver character never to be pinned down by anything as clumsy as a principle. He ran his feuds as he did his endless *amours*, only just out of sight. He was a foreigner, who seemed to see the English-dominated social system as something which, until it could be changed or overturned, was there to be plundered of its riches and its women. Yet he was more, more than a great orator, than the self-seeking confidence trickster using the democratic system and its Parliament to help himself to power, prestige and gold. He was among the first to take the social conscience of the English middle classes and use its energy to create the detailed legislation which, in its extensions and developments, led in the end to the social system we have today – a system geared, however inefficiently and partially, to such ideals as concern, equity, security and fairness. If he was one of the last great voices of the Whig ascendancy (however atypical of them he himself was), he was also one of the first great voices of Social Democracy in Britain.

E Nesbit

THE STAIRCASE dark, winding down into a deeper darkness. All about, the smell of mould and damp, of a graveyard, subterranean eternity. The small girl grips the hand of her older sister hard, hard; the steps are slippery and the child is frightened. An iron barred door at last, the key grating in an ancient lock, the hinges moaning and the prowling echoes thrumming a reply. Within, lamp-lit, charnel-house horror: 'skeletons with their flesh hardened on their bones', she was to write years later, 'with their long dry hair hanging on each side of their brown faces, where the skin in drying had drawn itself back from their gleaming teeth and empty eye-sockets. Skeletons draped in mouldering shreds of shrouds and grave clothes, their lean figures still clothed with dry skin, seemed to reach out towards me . . .' The child still, silenced by terror, the scene biting into her memory with an incisiveness nothing was ever to erase.

E. Nesbit was eight or nine then. She was in Bordeaux, with her mother and her dying elder sister, Mary, the latter caught by consumption, which killed so many of the Victorian age's young. The scene, the situation, the witnessed horror, the bereavement to come – all are part of the continuing paradox of Edith Nesbit's life. For not only in the children's books which made her famous – *The Treasure Seekers*, *The Would Be Goods*, *Five Children and It* and so on – but also in nearly all her fiction for adults and in her poetry, there is a serenity, even, despite the humour, a naïveté, which makes a strange contrast with the drama, the tragedies, the long poverty, the enduring unconventionality and the passion which dominated so much of her private existence.

Would it be claiming too much to see in this paradox something typical of her times? The surface serenity of her work, acceptably disturbed only by the horror stories she sometimes wrote, hid the turmoil beneath. It was as if her books, despite her own left-wing political convictions, were part of that tacit late-Victorian and Edwardian conspiracy which pretended, publicly at least, that all was for the best in the best of all possible worlds. Yet Edith Nesbit was far from being a hypocrite; it was simply that, like most of the world she lived in, she seems to have had no problem in reconciling the starkness and indiscipline of her private experience with the detached sentimentality of her public voice. Only in her books for children, perhaps, where the sentimentality was overtaken by genuine feeling, was there no need for such a reconciliation. It is this which makes them successful to this day; it is the dichotomy between work and self which has sent the poetry she set such store by into a deserved oblivion.

She was born in 1858, in London. Her father, something of a scientific prodigy in his youth, a student under Dalton, the famous chemist, and director of the school his own father had founded, died when Edith was only four years old. Her mother, now twice-widowed, had capabilities of her own, however, and took over the running of the academy, keeping it going for several years. From these early years there comes one story which might have figured in Edith Nesbit's books: she and her two elder brothers having decided to run away – more for adventure than unhappiness – they collected everything they thought they would need, and everything they could not bear to part with, in a tablecloth. They tied this up and prepared to set off – only to find their bundle too heavy to lift, and departure as a result impossible.

When Mary first became ill, Edith was sent to the first of the boarding schools in which she was to languish for periods of varying length but undifferentiated misery. This was Mrs Arthur's, a small, perhaps pleasant enough but inefficient establishment in which she was bullied. In her next school she had the bad luck to come up against a teacher who disliked her – not always without reason, given young Edith's delight in playing jokes on others. In her own recollections, at least as they are written down, the terrors and miseries of her early childhood, or those parts of it spent away from home, loom perhaps exaggeratedly. Reading between the lines, it sometimes seems that what she could not quite bear was the lack of special attention, the getting her own way, which she had been used to. Certainly when her mother decided for the sake of Mary's health to take the older girls abroad, Edith pleaded so effectively to be taken along that her mother took her out of school and did as she asked.

It was while on the way to the warmth of Biarritz that the party stopped at Bordeaux and little Edith – or Daisy, as everyone called her – found herself face-to-face with those staring, petrified faces in the underground vault. As a result she would for years start up in the night, to face insomniac hours crowded with luminous skulls, appalling shapes huddled under white sheets, or curtains, light fittings and shadows transmogrified into the beckoning arms of the dead.

As Mrs Nesbit and her daughters were to spend a considerable time in France, Edith was sent to stay with a French family at Pau. Here she made friends with a girl, Marguerite Lourdes, who – one sees her gravity and concern across the decades – made Edith both a friend and an object of concern. They quarrelled only once, Edith was to recall later; Marguerite had asked her not to wear her best dress to a party, for it made her own look so shabby, but Edith, always headstrong and even selfish until second thoughts corrected her, decided nevertheless to 'put on my blue silk'. Delighted with her appearance, she went to the kitchen to show off, curtseyed to the cook and fell backwards into a tub of washing. Marguerite laughed and made fun of her, whereupon – harbinger of furies to come – she grabbed her friend and ducked her. Madame Lourdes refused to let Edith go to the party – but Marguerite brought her back a sugar coffee mill and assurances that she had not enjoyed a moment of it, and in a welter of promises and apologies the two girls made up.

Ill health, now in one of her sons, sent Mrs Nesbit back to England. Edith left Pau, never to see Marguerite again, and was sent to a school run by a Mrs McBean. She ought, she wrote later, to have been happy at this school, had she been capable of finding any school congenial; she expected week by week to be sent for by her mother, who after looking for somewhere to live had finally decided to set up house in Dinan, in Brittany. A date was arranged – but on its eve Edith was rather insensitively told at dinner that she would have to wait another two days before setting off. She burst into tears hysterical in their intensity; her misery became so entangled in her mind with the flavour of the blackcurrant pudding she was eating that she could never stand the taste of such pudding again.

Mrs Nesbit's house, at La Haye, near Dinan, stood between a farm and a walled garden – 'There never was such another garden, there never will be!' – where, amid the haylofts, the yew trees, the bushes of berries and trees of fruit, with the spinneys and pathways of the countryside beyond, Edith and her brothers played at pirates or explorers, adventures which may well have been rehearsals for the stories she was later to write.

In the name of that great god, Education, Mrs Nesbit sent Edith away to a boarding school in Dinan, presided over by a Mademoiselle Fauchet. But Edith, arriving five days early, never discovered how she might have enjoyed life there, absconding before the rest of the children arrived. In the spring of 1869, however, she was sent away again, to an Ursuline convent-school, and she stayed there for most of that year. She seems almost to have enjoyed it; in any case, she exercised her mind on such theological niceties as the doctrine of transubstantiation. All the same, when the time came for her to return to her mother late that same year, the letter the good sisters sent to announce her arrival seems to convey a certain sense of strain. One of the things which disturbed them was the discovery, among the bric-à-brac she was leaving behind, of two empty wine-bottles. Such precocity might well seem worrying in a convent, even a French one.

Edith's brothers were by now in Germany, and so she was next sent there to continue her schooling near them. There seems no doubt she hated it. One can imagine a child of her determination and singularity, with a cast of mind which was to remain all her life unconventional and Bohemian, faced with the exigencies and narrow-mindedness of German pedagogic discipline. She tried three times to run away: once only hunger drove her back, when all she had found to eat during a whole day as a fugitive had been a single raw turnip. A result of this whole period was a detestation of the Germans; in a couplet she produced at the time, she wrote,

> God! Let the Germans be suppressed
> So that Europe at last may have a rest!

With the outbreak of the Franco–Prussian War, it became necessary for her to return to her mother. Since Mrs Nesbit still lived in Brittany, the journey had to be made by way of Southampton. Shipped from there to St Malo, Edith found herself stuck on board a ship which for nearly four days hung about in mid-Channel, waiting for fog to clear; all she had to read was a set of nautical tables and she afterwards considered this the most boring period of the whole of her childhood.

Back in England again, the Dinan paradise closed now for ever, Edith found herself part of a new household, that of a doctor, a friend of her mother's. This seems to have been dreary in that brooding, self-righteous, mid-Victorian manner novelists of the time have made familiar. There were few books, and those that were about were either religious or soggy with moralising, and although there was a piano, it was kept locked. As always, Edith fought back, exercising on the doctor's medicines her curious faculty for playing pranks. She found the medicines, made up ready for his various patients, waiting on a surgery shelf to be collected. She emptied all the separate bottles into a large jug, mixed it well, then refilled the bottles. She then spent several days of excited dread, wondering what the consequences might be and fancying herself coming forward at the doctor's murder trial with a dramatic court-room confession, saving his life and reputation at the last moment and, incidentally, leaving not a dry eye in the house. It says something about the advances in medicine in the century since that, as far as she ever knew, no one actually came to harm, despite the impartiality of her dispensing hand. She finally wrote a letter of complaint and lamentation to her mother which the doctor's wife, in the high-handed manner of the day, opened and read. The result of this interception was that Edith was sent home and the doctor's friendship with the Nesbits nearly came to an end.

At about this time the consumptive Mary became engaged to a young, blind poet, a friend of Swinburne and of the pre-Raphaelites. Edith always remembered meeting Rosetti, and was delighted at the talk and the vivacity of this circle of people with whom she now and then mixed. One wonders how much this early, if passing, acquaintance contributed not only to her own already half-formed desire to write poetry, but also to the life-style she was later to follow.

Late in 1871, however, Mary finally died in France, where her mother had taken her for one last attempt to rescue her health. Grief-stricken, Mrs Nesbit returned to England to make her home there. Edith was sent once more to school, this time at Brighton, while her mother searched for a suitable house. Once again, Edith found conformity too difficult and the struggle against it brought too much misery. She was delighted when her mother asked her to come and live in what was for the next few years to be her home, Halstead Hall, in Kent.

It is hard to judge what effect this itinerant, multi-national, intermittently unhappy childhood had on a girl now nearly fourteen. Judged by today's standards, it seems an upbringing that must have led to emotional deprivation. On the other hand, many of the middle-class young of the period expected to be sent away to school, to be sent away early and to stay away for a long time, and even when at home to see their parents comparatively rarely and often in rather formal circumstances. Edith, however, was a child who doted on her mother and on the company of her brothers and sisters. She must have felt often that she had been sent away almost as a punishment, particularly when she knew that the older daughters remained with their mother. Perhaps it was a need for stability which later led her to stay with, and unremittingly to love, a husband who caused her much suffering for many years.

Halstead Hall, however, she loved, writing years later of 'the roses and the ivy which clung to the front of it, and the rich, heavy jasmine that covered the side. There was a smooth lawn with chestnut trees round it, and a big garden, where flowers and fruit and vegetables grew together, as they should, without jealousy or class-distinction ... From a laburnum tree in a corner of the lawn we children slung an improvised hammock, and there I used to read and dream, and watch the swaying gold of leaf and blossom.' Nearby, the railway had recently driven a cutting, and there she and the other children often used to play together. One fancies that this cutting reappeared, years later, in *The Railway Children*, as did, perhaps, some of the games she played and the adventures she had.

She was at this time a mixture – a sort of tomboy, always running or swimming or climbing, but also reading omnivorously and writing, rather secretively, more and more verse. She had always written poetry, almost from the moment she had learned to write, but now she was becoming increasingly serious about it. Yet she and her brothers added Sphairistike to their accomplishments at about this time – a game which, when more widely popular, became more prosaically known as lawn tennis. This had been set up on a nearby vicarage lawn and, when the game was over, Edith made herself popular with the young children of the vicar by inventing stories for them. Very shortly, however, she was to find herself, even though on a modest scale as yet, addressing a far wider, though only slightly more sophisticated, audience.

Her half-sister, Saretta, had already pseudonymously published a number of small pieces; now, at the age of fifteen, Edith was herself in print. The *Sunday Magazine*, a periodical uplifting in intention, accepted a poem of hers, 'and I got a cheque for a guinea – a whole guinea, think of it!', she wrote later. From this time on Edith found that her poems, written with an almost dangerous facility, were in some demand. They were moralising, impersonal and rather bad, and such magazines as *Argosy* and *Good Words* were very pleased to publish the decorous messages they contained.

Late in the 1870s, Mrs Nesbit found herself in that staple situation of widows in Victorian melodrama: she was running short of money. Halstead Hall had to be left behind, and with it the idyllic life its surroundings had offered a dreamy, yet active, adolescent. By now, however, Edith was coming to the end of childhood. Back in London there was some talk of a Stuart Smith, mention of an engagement, a future talked of when she would be married, although she herself seems to have had no very strong feelings for the man involved. He remains faceless and all but anonymous, being no more than a passing name in her story. Yet he played a decisive part in her life. He worked in a bank, and Edith went there to change a note. While she was there, he introduced her to a colleague: Hubert Bland. (Edith herself later suggested they had met over picnic strawberries, and so indeed they may have, realising each other then for the first time, becoming instantly aware in a manner that for Edith at least was to remain life-long and unique.)

Hubert Bland was an impressive man. He looked it; those who knew him testified to it. He was vain, but both men and women would take an instant liking to him for his charm, and for the swift working of his keen and agile mind. He was an adroit debater, an upholder of thought-out positions, yet never solemn or portentous. He was a man who listened well, as good debaters must, and always offered others the tribute of respect and attention he expected from them. Even children were treated with the same gravity of attention.

Here, then, was Edith, young, unconventional, used to a freedom of thought and action unusual in a young lady of her class at that period. To be listened to, to have her ideas seriously considered, to have her sense of humour appreciated, to have someone, as she felt, with whom to share her unique world – these must have made the months that followed her meeting with Hubert Bland a heady time for her. This man, with his slightly Roman nose, his firm yet well-proportioned mouth and chin, his fierce, monocled glance, might have been made for her to fall in love with – a conclusion which his private income and good North Country stock did nothing to falsify. That he was also a practised seducer of women was something Edith would not have heard about, nor probably would have known how to cope with if she had.

For three years she and Hubert were engaged. She showed him the walks and meadows about Halstead Hall, before she had to move, spent hours talking and walking with him, writing letters to her closer friends about him when he was not there. In 1880 she married him – in the registry office in the City of London, with none of her family or friends apparently present. She was just under twenty-two years old, some three years younger than he; and she was seven months pregnant.

Hubert Bland and his wife took a small house in Lewisham. He had left the bank, to start up in business with a partner. On his marriage certificate he is described as a 'brush manufacturer'. But shortly after they had taken their new house, he fell ill with small-pox. He almost died, but struggled through, recovering after weeks of fevers and weakness. His partner took the opportunity Bland's absence gave him, and absconded. When Hubert had recovered his health, he found himself the father of a small son, and penniless.

For Edith Nesbit, had she remained the wife of a brush manufacturer in a modestly successful way of business, life might have been more comfortable; but it might have been very much less satisfying. She always wrote at least partly for money; certainly this was true of her books for children. Had she not learned need, she might never have hit on a way of satisfying it. She would have written her sugary poems, brought out a slim, overdecorated volume, and subsided into a middle age made silly by good causes. Instead, she had to become a professional, although her route to achievement remained arduous and roundabout. She began, with a friend, on the stages at smoking concerts and private functions, reciting monologues and duologues, some of which she had written herself. She then turned to stories and articles for the newspapers and magazines of the day. Hubert Bland, now recovered, his mind active and his pocket empty, was persuaded to attempt journalism too, and it at once became clear that he had considerable talent for the craft. A little money began to come, in fits and starts, into the Bland household.

It was at this time that Edith first met Alice Hoatson. She had brought a story she and Hubert had written to *Sylvia's Home Journal*, a magazine for women. Alice Hoatson, the reader for the magazine, fed her with sandwiches and cocoa, promised to read the story that day, liked it and had it accepted. But Edith arrived next morning again in a state of apologetic distress. Hubert had sold the story already; would the magazine take a story she herself had written in its place? Again Alice Hoatson read and recommended; from then on Edith became a regular contributor to the magazine – and to the *Weekly Dispatch*, the periodical which had taken the original story.

Another way by which Edith made money at this time, and for some years to come, was by painting, and writing the verses for, Christmas cards. On one occasion she was late with a batch of these and, when the manager of the firm which had commissioned them, a man named Aaronson, refused to accept them, she burst into tears. Thus softened, Aaronson paid her rather more than he had promised, and from then on took her as one of his regular suppliers. She had the force and energy not only to work for her living, but to go out into a commercial world with which she must then have been totally unfamiliar, and cope with it successfully – on its own terms, if sometimes by her own methods.

Her private life, too, was about to display to her a section of the world's darkness which must have been as unfamiliar and far more distressing. After three years of marriage she discovered that Hubert was still nominally engaged to a girl called Maggie, whom he had known before he became her husband. When she went to see this girl, she found that not only did Maggie genuinely believe herself still Hubert's fiancée, but also that she was the mother of Hubert's son. Her strength of mind in making the visit was matched by her subsequent generosity: she befriended Maggie, she helped her as she could, and the two women remained close until Maggie died eighteen years later. There is an odd quality in the manner in which Edith accepted this situation and those which were to follow. It is as if she were constrained to love where Hubert loved. She had, of course, never judged by the ordinary standards of the world – it was precisely this nonconformity which had made her schooldays so difficult. Yet the generosity seems almost excessive, her affection for the women her husband made love to a little extravagant. Certainly she was swayed by him, leaned on him a great deal, allowed him to lead and shape her opinions. Yet she was strong-minded, intelligent, passionate, with a warm temper which she never really learned to control. It makes her behaviour in these cases – despite the warmth and generosity of her nature – a little difficult to understand fully. Acceptance and a sort of resignation, a belief in Hubert's freedom and her own, would have been enough and consonant with her temperament and her opinions. But she often went further, a quirk which stands further examination.

Certainly Hubert's behaviour forced her to take some sort of attitude to the other women in his life, if only because he found, used and discarded so many of them. With him one gets a sense of that Victorian and Edwardian underworld, the unspoken, almost unrecorded history of those times which such as Frank Harris and the energetic 'Walter' write about. Hubert was an attractive man, vigorous and vain, and it was almost impossible for him, so it seems, to hold back from any possibility of a sexual encounter. The unknown 'Walter' kept his adventures largely confined to the working classes, always glad of an extra half-crown, or the ladies of the town; from Hubert no one was safe, not even the wives and daughters of his friends. Edith's response was not only to accept this, but almost actively to encourage him by her attitude; on the other hand, of course, she also – later and possibly with some reluctance – took lovers of her own.

Edith, with her quick mind, her tall figure and dark, penetrating eyes, her strong nose and wide, well-formed mouth always made an attractive and intelligent hostess. It was at this time, however, that she began more widely to entertain, an art at which she always excelled and which she took perhaps as seriously as any other she practised. Not that she permitted any formality in her house; she loved to fill it with congenial, lively people, unconventional in opinion, behaviour and dress, and if possible young – certainly in heart. As a result, and because of Hubert's socialist convictions, now on record in the articles which were beginning to make him well-known, the Blands became sought-after, people whose acceptance established one in certain of the artistic and political circles of London.

It is not to be wondered at, therefore, that they should have been founder members of the Fabian Society, that intellectual power-house of the democratic Left, which despite its small membership exerted for eighty years an enormous influence on the burgeoning and finally victorious Labour Movement, and which even today is by no means a spent force. Hubert Bland was the chairman at the society's first meeting and for the following twenty-six years was its Treasurer and a member of its Executive. Many people – Bernard Shaw, Havelock Ellis, Sidney and Beatrice Webb among others – were involved in this new venture, and with some of these, particularly Shaw, the Blands were to become lifelong friends. Indeed, there seems no question that around 1880 Edith fell in love with him, a possible attachment with which Shaw dealt in his usual manner – an odd mixture of embarrassment, wit and kindliness.

All the time, both Blands kept on writing. Hubert perhaps had rather the better of this, for at least he had convictions to sustain him. Edith, on the other hand, hammered out a series of unmemorable potboilers, while at the same time trying to run a household, look after her children – to Paul, the first, had now been added her daughter Iris and a second son, named after her interests of the time, Fabian – and educate herself. She read Buchner and Mill to sustain her socialist convictions, and kept herself spiritually alive through occasional trips to the country and by writing the poetry she always felt she was destined for. She remained Bohemian, unconventional, attractive; she was, for instance, one of the first women to smoke in public, carrying tobacco and papers wherever she went. There is at times about her something of the air of a *poseuse*. She struck attitudes, she demanded attention, she sought admiration and, had she not been both intelligent, humorous and generous, she might well have been one of those tiresome women whose secondhand opinions and attention-getting mannerisms make tedious so much of artistic and political life.

In 1886 Hubert Bland became the editor of a periodical called *Today*, and what that meant in terms of at least local prestige can be gauged by the machinations and intrigue which surround the getting of such an editorship in George Gissing's novel, *New Grub Street*, written less than ten years later. (Indeed, some idea of the whole ambience of the Blands' life at this time may be gained from this book.) He was now established among the radical intelligentsia of London. *Today* published the early novels of Shaw in serial form, the first English translation of Ibsen's *Ghosts*, articles by William Morris, Havelock Ellis, the critic William Archer and the American poet Walt Whitman. The Blands' household, now established in Blackheath, remained a centre where the advanced of the day liked to meet, discussing and dissecting the world over dinner and far into the night.

By this time Alice Hoatson had joined them. After several years as a journalist, she appeared one day on their doorstep, answering an advertisement for a companion-help. Edith was probably pregnant with Fabian and needed assistance. It must have been a surprise for Edith to see this slim, self-effacing woman, whom she had known only among the chatter and expertise of magazine offices, offering her services in this domestic post. She was dressed with a perhaps exaggerated quietness, in a shade of grey which brought them spontaneously to the nickname she always had thereafter: 'The Mouse'. 'In that case,' she is supposed to have replied, 'I'll call you The Cats!' and 'cat' each was thereafter. No one is quite sure why Alice should have applied for this position, but since the Blands were by then well known and also the friends of those already famous, it might have seemed a glamorous opportunity for someone who until then had been separated from such a world by a narrow but clearly defined distance.

In the same year, 1885, Edith and Hubert jointly – under the name Fabian Bland – published a novel, *The Prophet's Mantle*, the title of which was more resounding than its fate. The following year, however, Longmans brought out a collection of Edith's poems, entitled *Lays and Legends*, and this had considerable success. It was very much in the manner of the times: Swinburne, Rider Haggard and Oscar Wilde were among those who, in letters at least, praised all or some of her verse. Of one of them, indeed, Swinburne wrote that it 'struck me as singularly powerful and original, the sort of poem Charlotte Brontë might have written, if she had had more mastery of the instrument of verse'.

With more money coming in, the Blands now began to take expansive holidays, renting houses in the country and inviting to them parties of their friends. The tomboyish elements in Edith's character still remained – she enjoyed riding, swimming, boating, could do fancy skipping or a high-kick and would explore the local byways and lanes perched high on a solid-tyred tricycle. Her life was on the whole pleasant, although there was still a considerable amount of drudgery attached to the ways by which she helped to earn the family's living. Yet there had been a progression, a gradual winning of some sort of position; her poems were spoken of and widely read, her stories were in demand, she had her children, with whom, despite her sometimes uncertain temper, she spent a considerable and happy time. She was hostess to the young and the intelligent, she was healthy, reasonably successful and widely admired.

It was at this time that Alice Hoatson became pregnant. Unmarried, her future seemed uncertain in the moral labyrinth which made up these aspects of late-Victorian society. She kept the father's identity a secret; he was not, she said, in a position to help her. With her customary generosity Edith decided not only that Alice, 'Mouse', should remain with them, but that, since she could not bring up the child as hers, the Blands would take it as one of their own. Six months after the girl, Rosamund, was born, Edith discovered how appallingly she had been deceived: Hubert was himself the child's father, her own children were this newcomer's half-siblings. Furious, she asserted her own rights. Hubert told her that if she did as she threatened and threw Alice and her daughter out of the house, he would leave with them. This was a quixotic decision, since there seems no question that he always preferred Edith, not only to Alice Hoatson, but to the innumerable others whom he pursued. But Edith, after all, had her position and her talents; perhaps he thought it was Alice who really needed him. It may, of course, have been no more than a bluff. In any case, faced with the prospect of the collapse of a relationship as vital to her as that with her mother had been during her childhood, Edith capitulated.

Thus there was set up what must have been rather a strained *ménage-à-trois*, and it is hard to see quite who had the worst of it – Edith, faced with the constant reminder of her husband's infidelity, or Alice, seeing her own daughter brought up by a woman the child thought of as her mother, while she herself remained in the background, a housekeeper, a sort of superior servant. Edith was certainly, during this and many other periods, very unhappy. At such moments she would feel Bland's influence over her to be baleful and malevolent, and she would long for someone equally strong, but good, to come and break that influence down and bear her away to a happier existence. Yet she could not leave Bland. Partly, perhaps, this was a matter of law – a woman in those days had to prove not merely adultery to obtain a divorce, as a man did, but also physical cruelty of the most extreme and direct kind. There was also her clinging nature, curious in a woman otherwise so free, but partly, too, one suspects the reason must be sexual and one thinks of Stekel's 'the tragedy of the physical', the plight of a woman held by unbreakable chains to the man who first gave her full sexual satisfaction. In any case, whatever combination of weakness or generosity or pure love there was in Edith, she always did forgive her husband and she always continued in her affection to him – even when she fell in love with others.

And she did, of course, fall in love with others. She was full of vitality, very attractive and becoming well known. After Shaw, around 1890 she was on the verge of eloping with Richard le Gallienna, the writer, who was several years younger than she; in the mid-1890s there was a young man named Noel Griffiths; as late as 1905 she was asking the Egyptologist, Dr Wallis Budge, to run away with her, a thing he might have done had his position at the British Museum not seemed to him too satisfying to be put in jeopardy. How many of her men-friends were actually her lovers is not known, although there is no question that some were – just as there is little question Shaw was not. Hubert Bland's view of these affairs is also unknown; one supposes that his own adventures kept him too occupied at the relevant times really to notice. His advanced principles might have allowed him to accept matters as they were, although he was never pro-suffragette, for example, and thus probably subscribed to the double standards of contemporary morality. It is the case, of course, that many men who feel the need to pursue women other than their wives are hurt and discomfited to discover that their wives sometimes pursue men other than themselves.

Through the 1880s E. Nesbit continued to appear in newspapers and magazines, and in 1886 her second collection of poems, *Leaves of Life*, appeared. It was not the success that the first had been, nor was the second collection of *Lays and Legends*, brought out early in the 1890s. As well as her journalism and her poetry, she organised a Christmas charity for the poor children of Deptford. At one time the parties she gave there had over a thousand children at them, but even for her this proved too strenuous and the parties, at least, she gave up. This, and the dinners and gatherings over which she presided, as well as those leisurely holidays, meant that what she and Hubert earned – he was by now a regular contributor to the London *Daily Chronicle* and a number of other papers – was very quickly spent (the Blands were always scrupulous about their bills).

It was in 1890 that she wrote the first of her books for children, *The Voyage of Columbus*, a verse narrative. She continued working in many other genres, however, as she was always to do; her poems appeared in, among other magazines and collections, *The Yellow Book*, proof that she remained in touch with what was then the most modern of contemporary movements. Some of this and other verse was collected in a new volume, *A Pomander of Verse*, but despite her own opinion of herself as a writer, more significant for the development of her talent may have been *Pussy Tales* and *Doggy Tales*, stories for children she published at this time. After more work for children, the first of the stories relating the adventures of the famous Bastaple children began to appear in the *Strand Magazine* during 1898. E. Nesbit had begun the work which was to make her famous and, for a long period, wealthy, and which has brought her to at least the fringes of immortality.

Yet, even as she explored her own constant and uncanny awareness of what it meant to be a child, she also responded to the world she inhabited. Despite her socialist convictions, the late-Victorian passion for self-glorification which had struck the English did not leave her immune. Trouble in South Africa, the reputation of Kipling, the sense of expanding frontiers in distant places, religion and justice being brought to the savage, the ignorant and the uncivilised, Victoria's enthusiastically celebrated jubilee, all seem to have combined into the inspiration which caused her to write her *Songs of Love and Empire*.

In 1899, however, *The Treasure Seekers* was published, and with it came the public acclaim and financial success which had always until then eluded her. The *Strand Magazine* instantly commissioned a new series of stories, at a princely £30 each, the first of a succession of such commissions, and each set of stories was later published in book form, to sell world-wide and for year after year. As a result of this success, the Blands moved to Well Hall, in Kent,

David Lloyd George 1863–1945
Below, with his wife and daughters Olwen (right) and Megan

Edith Nesbit 1858–1924

Charles Stewart Rolls
1877–1910

Sir Frederick Henry Royce
1863–1933

Daisy, Countess of Warwick (*1861–1938*). Below, with her son Maynard

the house where Edith was to live for many years thereafter, which she always loved, and which was to see her at the highest points of her career and the lowest points of her life. She described it in several of her books: 'There has been a house there since Saxon times. It is a manor, and a manor goes on having a house on it whatever happens. ... It is a very odd house: the front door opens straight into the dining-room ... and there is a secret staircase, only it is not secret now – only rather rickety. It is not very big, but there is a watery moat all around it with a brick bridge that leads to the front door. Then on the other side of the moat there is a farm, with barns and oast houses and stables, or things like that. And the other way the garden lawn goes on till it comes to the churchyard.' That is from The Would Be Goods, but through all her descriptions of the place her delight and fascination with it always shine through. As was almost usual with the places where she lived, the house was seriously thought to be haunted; both her mother's house in Dinan, years before, and Halstead Hall had had similar reputations. This, however, never worried her – indeed, she probably welcomed it as an additional attraction.

Yet her happiness in finding Well Hall, and in making it fit to live in – a long and arduous task, the completion of which she celebrated with a generous house-warming in her best style – had in the balance of fate perhaps to be compensated for. In 1899, she give birth to a child which was either stillborn or died immediately afterwards. She had been almost inconsolable years earlier when she had had a similar disaster; now her grief took on some of the heaviness of tragedy as she realised that at her age this had probably been her last opportunity of again becoming a mother. And it was at this time that she discovered that Alice Hoatson was pregnant a second time – once more, as thirteen years earlier, by Hubert. Edith again made the self-sacrificing decision to take the new baby as her own. Thus she gained, after all, a final son, and though it might have been at some emotional cost and the gesture itself was, perhaps, partly self-dramatising, she always stuck loyally to the decision she had made. Also in that same mixed and desperate year of 1899 her half-sister, Saretta, died.

For a while Edith herself was threatened – a local doctor told her she had cancer and that, although she would of course be operated on, she had little chance of ever recovering. She behaved with courage and even gaiety, facing with valiant vivacity the party of house-guests who were as usual there for the Well Hall weekend – and if here again there was an element of self-dramatisation in what she did, it is also true that the part she chose might well have been a gloomier one, much more demanding of the sympathy of her family and friends. The weekend over, she saw the relevant specialist, who told her the original diagnosis was nonsense. 'Well, anyway,' as she told one of her guests, the poet Laurence Housman, 'I found out I wasn't afraid of death!'

Not her own, perhaps; that of others proved harder to bear. Her son Fabian was by now fifteen. In him, more than in her other children, she seemed to see herself as she had been in childhood. He was, it seems, both lovable and adventurous, mischievous in ways that were attractive rather than hurtful, helpful and generous, though with a will and character of his own. Throughout early 1900 he had suffered from a series of colds and in the autumn it was decided that he should have his tonsils out. The doctor and the anaesthetist travelled out to Well Hall. Everyone was pleased that the slight operation was at last to take place, freeing Fabian from the recurrent nuisance of a sore throat. It was mid-morning; in the kitchen, lunch was being prepared, a maid was laying the dining-room table. Upstairs, his instruments ready, the doctor waited as the anaesthetist prepared the boy for the operation.

Why did Fabian never recover? Was it the fault of the anaesthetist? Or had he some unsuspected physical condition, which made the anaesthetic dangerous? No one seems to know. For hours Edith, Alice Hoatson and Hubert tried somehow to revive the boy. The doctors left; then Hubert, to give his sister the news. Still Edith ran about the house, fetching and filling hot-water bottles, laying them about Fabian's body, as though somehow to keep the warmth of life in him. She took the sixteen candles which had been bought to celebrate his approaching birthday, and she stood them about the bed where he lay and lit them, as though the love they symbolised would somehow revive him.

When finally she had to admit herself defeated and Fabian gone, she despaired. She turned on Alice Hoatson – why had *her* children lived, to stay under that roof, to prosper and grow, while her own lay dead? Never one to restrain what she felt, whether love or fury, she now offered this strange sharer of her life the full weight of her bitterness. No doubt Alice herself understood her, understanding tragedy; but Rosamund, passing, overheard. She was old enough now to make sense of the words, to realise not only that the brilliant, the delightful Edith, upon whom she had doted, was not her mother, and that 'Mouse', unconsidered, almost despised, was; but also to feel that revelation as a most fundamental betrayal. She had been robbed, as it were, of her sense of who she was, of her place in a household where she had imagined she belonged by right. Not only that, she had discovered that the people whom she most loved and trusted had lied to her throughout the whole of her life. It was many years before Rosamund really recovered any of the early affection she had felt for Edith, or got over even some of the bitterness she felt as a result of that day's revelation.

It was with these tragedies and disasters that Edith's years at Well Hall began – but also with the triumphs and successes of *The Treasure Seekers* and *The Would Be Goods*. In 1902 she brought out *Five Children and It*, another of her immensely popular books for children, and *The Red House*, which many think the most deft of her adult novels. Not that these ever attained any great distinction; it was as though she could get a uniqueness of voice only into those works which drew on her memory and knowledge of childhood. Nevertheless *The Red House* went into several reprints and certainly did nothing to diminish her reputation. Meanwhile she played the hostess with an undimmed energy and all the power her now much greater financial resources gave her. Everyone called her 'Duchess', or sometimes merely 'Madame', and she must have made a curiously imposing figure. She always wore long, flowing robes, in various colours and variously decorated, Turkish slippers, and silver bangles to the elbow. These last were presents Hubert used to give her – one every time she published another book. As one guest who knew these gatherings has written, 'The party never flagged once the Blands had appeared. A friendly atmosphere hung about them, an atmosphere of festivity. They were intensely *lovable*. . . . After dinner we danced in the cleared drawing-room, and there were games and more talk. . . . The dinner and the dancing and the talk lasted so long that most of us missed last trains and slept where we could, the men usually finding accommodation in the garden cottages. Next morning it was considered in the best taste to depart by an early train without seeing our hosts.' H. G. Wells used to go to these parties, and Laurence Housman, and Berta Ruck, the novelist, whom Edith helped greatly in her early days, and G. K. Chesterton and many others – and so did that egocentric and intensely difficult man, Frederick Rolfe, the author of *Hadrian VII*. It is perhaps the greatest tribute to the 'lovable' nature of the Blands that Rolfe, who managed to quarrel with everyone, including his most generous benefactors, remained on friendly terms with them.

In 1905 Edith brought out a new book of poems, *The Rainbow and the Rose*, dedicated to her daughter Iris and to Rosamund (their names symbolised in the book's title), which suggests that, despite what she had said to Alice Hoatson at the moment of her anguish five years before, she made little distinction between the affection she felt for the two girls. These poems, like so many of her others, were destined more as masks for her real nature than revelations of it. 'Right or wrong,' she wrote, 'I could never bring myself to lay my soul naked before the public.' This is the kind of self-guarding attitude out of which great poetry is unlikely to be written.

It was as a poet, nevertheless, that she principally regarded herself, and as a novelist and short-story writer; despite the delight she took in the delight of her juvenile public, it was only *force majeure* that she became a writer for children. It is no surprise, therefore, that she appeared in 1907 as one of the co-founders of a literary magazine with very serious intentions indeed. Called *Neolith*, the first issue drew contributions from, among many others, Shaw, Chesterton, Gerald Gould and, of course, E. Nesbit herself, while such artists as Brangwyn and Charles Sims provided the illustrations. Edith, given to drama, tended to have fits of weeping during editorial meetings, which did nothing to aid the committee's rather dubious efficiency. Nevertheless, the magazine continued to appear, later issues printing contributions by Laurence Housman, Andrew Lang, Lord Dunsany and many others. By the end of 1908, however, *Neolith* had become rather more trouble than its founders had anticipated, and, as is the way with such projects, it came to an end with one last, resounding number. It had, nevertheless, been a brave venture – as magazines of this kind must always be – and one which had perhaps drawn work of a higher quality than is usual. It may have been its weakness to have no real *raison d'être*, although in this country the literary scene has never had much time for manifestoes or professions of artistic or even political faith.

It was during this period that she conceived her last and perhaps fatal passion. She came to the conclusion that the works attributed to Shakespeare had actually been written by Francis Bacon. She is not alone, of course, in holding to this theory – the English intellectual classes have always taken badly the possibility that their major poet should have had neither the birth, breeding nor education for the post – but she was rare in the single-mindedness with which she attempted to find the proof. She was of the school which imagined that hidden cyphers in the text would reveal the truth of the plays' authorship. She tried desperately to match her knowledge of mathematics, always sketchy and unreliable, to the strains of deciphering the codes she was sure were there. When this failed her, she would call on the skill of her more scientific friends, notably the brilliant young scientist later to become the world-famous Professor Andrade. He wrote of these efforts of hers, 'She was by nature quite incapable of mastering the meaning of mathematical symbols and arguments. ... As the figures were frequently copied down wrongly, this did not make as much difference as might be supposed.' What did make a difference, however, over the years to come, was the amount of money she spent in her attempt to unravel the secrets she was sure lay interwoven with the lines of the plays. Bernard Shaw for one was convinced that this was the main cause of her comparative poverty later.

She continued to write, as before, for children and adults, in prose and in poetry. But from the last years of the Edwardian decade onwards her abilities began to decline, although she remained popular for some time thereafter. Superficially, at least, she remained as energetic as ever. She entertained and, an imposing lady, now, her figure thickening, its breadth and height made commanding by the same long gowns she still affected, she worked hard, yet retained both her high spirits and her childlike qualities, breaking off even in her late fifties for a game of hide-and-seek and spending time on the construction of the splendid models she named her 'magic cities'. Chessmen, candlesticks, dominoes, ashtrays, wooden boxes or blocks – anything she could think of would be added to these cities; and in 1912 she actually exhibited such a one, with its arches, domes, minarets, strange statuary and spreading trees at the Children's Welfare Exhibition, at Olympia. She wrote a new book for children, entitled *The Magic City*, and a book on children's pastimes which included instructions for building one of these elaborate models.

In 1911 she published *A Wonderful Garden* and two years later *Wet Magic*, the last full-length books she was to write for children. Childhood, the feel and physical sense of it, still shines through these pages, but when she wrote them she was once more unhappy. Hubert, who had always suffered from a disease of the eyes – his monocle had not been affectation – seemed now finally to be losing his sight. The Blands spent a great deal of money on treatments, but these did little good and in 1914 Hubert at last went blind. He was only fifty-eight, still apparently vigorous, still intellectually active.

Thus the parties and the entertainments dwindled; there was neither the spirit nor the money to keep them going. But in that summer of 1914 Edith went on holiday with John Bland and two of his friends. Hubert remained at Well Hall, with Alice Hoatson and another lady who was then living there. He dictated his usual article for the *Sunday Chronicle*, stood up, complained that he felt giddy and fell, despite Alice's efforts to support him. 'I am not hurt,' he said; then died.

Thus it was he who, after all, left Edith. There had been no way for her to break her dependence on him while he lived; now that he was dead it was a year before life began to stir in her again. It is hard to say what exactly his loss meant to her, just as one does not know precisely the shape of her love for him, the ambivalence of feeling she must have had. But that she needed him in some fundamental way is clear; his loss altered the whole geography of her existence.

Later that same year she herself became ill with a duodenal ulcer. Operated on, she hardly survived; when released from hospital, she had a relapse. When she finally recovered, the First World War was taking from her the world she had known and in which she had been successful – was perhaps taking too the young men who, now old enough to die, had as children been her first wide and loyal public. Edith's own attitude to the war was that of a simple-minded patriotism – perhaps not untinged by that detestation of the Germans she had learned forty-five years earlier as a schoolgirl. But despite her own attitudes, the War was largely a disaster for her. It and her ill-health prevented her from working. The friends she loved to have around her were widely scattered and she would not have had the money to entertain them as she liked even if they had remained nearby. Her son Paul was in the Army, her daughter working at the Woolwich Arsenal, Rosamund abroad. John Bland was at school, to go on from there to a medical training at Cambridge made possible by the generosity of Shaw. Edith herself was awarded a small Civil List pension, £60 a year, and was also given help by the Royal Literary Fund. In addition, she began to take in paying guests at Well Hall.

In 1917 she married again, a marine engineer named Thomas Terry Tucker, but always called 'Skipper', who seems, like Edith herself, to have discovered how to retain within himself a childlike capacity for make-believe, without in the least impairing his capacity to cope with the realities of life. He had begun as a rivet-boy in the shipyards, had spent many years at sea and now ran the Woolwich Ferry. In many ways self-taught, he had seen her from a distance in the early days of the Fabian Society, when he would be among the audiences at the open lectures given by such luminaries of the socialist firmament as Bernard Shaw. For a long time before they married Edith had relied on his good sense, his practicality, his cheerfulness. 'After the cold misery of the last three years,' she wrote to her brother, 'I feel as though someone had come and put a fur cloak around me. . . . I feel as though I had opened another volume of the book of life (the last volume) and it is full of beautiful stories and poetry.'

'Skipper' became, in time, her collaborator in a number of tales with a new and nautical flavour. Indeed, her conversation became peppered with the technical terms of the sea, and when, late at night, she would sometimes go to cook for him on his ferry, it was as though they played at being sailors together, like children, and if he was 'Skipper', she was 'Cook' or, occasionally, 'Mate'.

Despite her new happiness, the practical advice of 'Skipper', the writing she was still doing, and the paying guests, it was clear by the end of 1921 that Well Hall had become too expensive to keep. Early in 1922 Edith made the last move of her life, to Jesson St Mary, a mile or so from Dymchurch. There she and 'Skipper' had found two single-storey buildings left behind by the war – one had been an Air Force photographic laboratory. They made everything shipshape, doing as much of the necessary work themselves as they could: the bedrooms were 'cabins', the kitchen 'the galley', the drawing-room 'the saloon', while the two bungalows themselves were named the Longboat and the Jollyboat. Here, in this make-believe craft, Edith gradually became weaker over the following two years. She had brought out her last novel, *The Lark*, in 1922, and a volume of short stories a year later. She also brought out *Many Voices*, a last collection of those poems, often sentimental and even turgid for the taste of today, overwritten and fundamentally insincere, to which she nevertheless always wished she had devoted the whole of her writing life.

After four days of pain and struggle, she died early in May 1924. She was buried in the churchyard of St Mary's in the Marsh. There is no tombstone – she asked that there should not be. Instead, 'Skipper' carved a plain wooden panel to stand above her grave: 'Resting – E. Nesbit, Mrs Bland-Tucker – Poet and Author'.

Rolls & Royce

THE MATCHMAKER was Henry Edmunds, a friend of Rolls, a shareholder in Royce's company. It was his patience and diplomacy that persuaded Rolls to make the journey to Manchester, where Royce had his works and the three assembled prototypes of his first car. Rolls and Edmunds travelled down early in May 1904 – uncharacteristically, perhaps, by train – to test the car and meet its maker. Both Charles Rolls and Henry Royce must have known or guessed that each of them needed someone like the other: Rolls wanted a new and preferably British car to sell through his Fulham garage and West End showrooms, Royce a way into the labyrinthine but expanding motor market. They met for lunch at Manchester's Midland Hotel; no echo comes to us from that meeting, no phrase or prophecy to catch our imaginations and drag us back to that intersecting point of two extraordinary lives. A door is opened, a servant bows, a curtain is whisked aside, there is a glimpse of a heavy, mercantile dignity, jowly men in tight collars sitting red-faced over white tablecloths, then the curtain drops back: silence.

Yet the meeting has a significance which extends beyond the fact that its outcome was to be an incomparable motor-car, one of the defining artefacts of the century. At one level it was a coming together of the genius and the visionary, the maker and the dreamer; at another, that of the designer of a machine and the man of action who will use it; at yet a third, there was the way they had qualified to speak together, and the fact that they could do so on level terms, which exemplified both the continuing inequalities and the startling changes which were the paradox of the English social system during the Edwardian decade. Mr Royce, after all, had come from nothing, while the Hon. Charles Rolls was the son of a peer; what linked them was their fascination for and mastery of the burgeoning technology of the age.

The barriers they had to overcome were sizeable in a country where at one extreme children still ran barefoot through the streets while at the other an aristocrat like the Earl of Derby might pay £50,000 a year in household expenses. There were over a million domestic servants at the turn of the century. Many of these had come from the increasingly depopulated countryside. The towns were magnets which drew with all the power of an expanding industrialised economy; by the Edwardian age, more people lived in cities than outside them. Domestic service was one compromise between the field and the factory; yet paradoxically again, the very technology which forced so many millions to live in squalor, gave a few among them totally new possibilities of escape.

This was still the period of inventions, one new application of the discoveries of science leading to half a dozen others. The cinema, the telephone, wireless telegraphy, electric light – marvels seemed to appear almost daily in the thirty years before 1910. Above all, of course, there was the motor-car, that upright, clattering, foul-smelling and unreliable machine called, at first perhaps with some disdain, the horseless carriage. Jean-Joseph-Etienne Lenoir had invented a vehicle which, using petroleum vapour and with electrical ignition, ran successfully in the 1860s. It was, however, from the work of Karl Benz and Gottfried Daimler in Germany that the modern car was to derive. Benz was on the road in 1885, and Daimler a year later, both with petrol-engined vehicles. The French were not far behind – the Marquis de Dion and Emile Levassor, of Panhard-Levassor, were designing, redesigning and producing cars by the beginning of the next decade.

These new forms of transport transcended not only distance and the muscle power of horses, but also many of the barriers of class. On the one hand, there were the landed and the moneyed who accepted these machines as new and fascinating toys, surrogates for, or even complements to, exploring, big-game hunting and the new athleticism; on the other, there were the inventors and technicians, many from the lower-middle class, who took to the machine-age with an energy which suggested that a century of industrialisation had finally thrown up a new religion. For the rich young men the development, and even more the racing, of motorised tricycles, motor-cars and, a little later, aeroplanes, became an arena of daring and adventure more accessible and less hackneyed than the jungles of Africa or the dun plains of India. But for their poorer and often much more dedicated colleagues these new forms of transport offered their only opportunity for self-assertion; at last they too could make their mark on a world in which both the factory and the sprawling city seemed instruments of a conspiracy to keep most men not only impoverished but anonymous.

Neither Rolls nor Royce fits absolutely into these categories, for both of them were too involved in what they were doing to be much concerned about what was extraneous. For Royce a machine seemed to issue a compelling challenge to improve it; he was one of technology's platonists, harassed all his life by the ideal of mechanical perfection. Rolls, on the other hand, was a man seduced by novelty, who understood that the petrol engine had made a formidable alteration to the way people would henceforward live. The story of the development of motoring in Britain is his story and he transferred his allegiance from it only when the petrol engine made an ancient dream come true, and man – in the long, lean, Yankee shape of the Wright brothers – began with greater skill and confidence to take to the air.

The world Charles Stewart Rolls was born into, on 28 August 1877, was ordered, traditional, comfortable and walled about with certainties. Britain was the most powerful trading and manu-facturing nation the world had ever seen, fed by – and to some extent feeding – an empire which took in a quarter of the world's population. Despite the political and educational reforms of the previous fifty years, it was a country still in the hands of the landed aristocracy and the more or less new upper-middle-class which tried to live like them. Although Rolls was born in the family's London house in Kensington, his home was a clumsy neo-Gothic pile called the Hendre, near enough to Monmouth for Charles's father to serve two terms there as mayor. Typical of rich men of the day, Henry Allen Rolls took his duties to the local community seriously. Apart from serving as Mayor, he spent five years in the 1880s as MP for the constituency and all his life regarded those on and around the six thousand acres he owned with an autocratic but sincere High-Tory paternalism. His grandfather had been an earl, his wife's father a baronet, and he was indirectly related to that bluff and victorious sailor, Lord St Vincent. When Charles was three, he was himself raised to the peerage, his new title of Lord Llangattock suggesting a Welsh nationality which in fact none of the family could claim by blood.

Charles, having sullied the Monmouthshire Sunday by an un-authorised excursion on a steam-roller – probably his first recorded drive – and shown his technical aptitude by rigging up an electric bell connecting his bedroom to the stables, was sent to a Vicarage School in Berkshire, where at the age of thirteen he was seventh in a class of eight at mathematics, bottom in Latin, 'bad' in geography, and in Bible history 'remarkably poor'. Thus prepared, he set off for Eton where, after a poor beginning ('. . . forgetful and irregular, sometimes even to vanishing point!') he began by 1893 to improve academically to the stage where at least the Army was being con-sidered as a career (certainly he joined the College Volunteers that year, suggesting he took the idea seriously). On the other hand, his technological interests had surfaced the year before in letters which had persuaded his father to install electricity at the Hendre, and improvements for this still exercised his mind. By 1894 his house-master was assuming that Charles's 'chosen career', in which he had 'very considerable ability', would be in the field of electrical engineering.

With a little coaching Charles Rolls achieved the necessary standard and found himself at Cambridge University, reading for a degree in mechanical engineering and applied sciences. This he enjoyed, particularly the visits three times a week to the workshops. What he was doing now had more relevance to the life he intended to live than Latin or geography. He also took up cycling, a sport then almost at the end of its vogue with the upper classes, winning a half-Blue, although not, as legend insists, becoming the University team's captain. In May 1895 he certainly did appear before the public as a cyclist – charged with riding without lights and fined half a crown, with two shillings costs.

By the following year, however, the bicycle had begun to be superseded in Rolls's mind by a new and much more compelling interest. In February 1896 he spent a weekend at the home of Sir David Salomons, President of the Self-Propelled Traffic Association, the first motoring club in Britain. There he had a ride in his host's Peugeot, 'which was delightful, and we attained a speed of 20 at one time', as he wrote enthusiastically to his father. Pointing out that he intended 'going in for one of these some time', Charles added a phrase which suggests that his intention was not new, since he had been 'saving up for a considerable time for this purpose'.

It was in fact towards the end of that year that Charles Rolls bought his car, also a Peugeot, despite the strong interest – later to be revived – which he had earlier shown in Panhards. In November 1886 the Locomotives on Highways Act raised the speed limit from 4 mph to 12 mph, also abolishing the need for one of the obligatory crew of three to walk twenty yards ahead of every mechanically propelled vehicle and warn of the monster's approach. When Charles took possession of his car at Victoria Station, however, the new regulations had not yet come into force. In the station yard he was stopped by a policeman and summoned for not having sent before him the necessary messenger with his red flag. Charles, one of whose most conspicuous traits was a dislike of parting with money, talked the constable out of severity and set off for Cambridge. He averaged 5 mph, which suggests that on country roads and in the middle of the night he took rather a lofty view of the existing legislation; certainly he records with some delight night-shirted figures leaping to lonely cottage windows as he passed, awakened by the rush and racket of his pioneering progress. As water boiled away, he renewed it from ponds in nearby gardens; despite the din and the excitement, he went to sleep at one point, awakening to find himself still on course.

From now on the name of C. S. Rolls was to appear with prominence in the motoring and general Press of Britain. As a driver and as a member of committees, delegations and clubs domestic and foreign, he became identified with the new pastime of motoring. The fact that he was the son of a peer, with all the background and connections this implied, would have brought him the interest of the new reading public, even if he had not pursued his role of one of motoring's ambassadors. At this age he was, despite a tendency to jowliness, sufficiently good-looking to act the part, having a firm chin and short nose reminiscent of the young Churchill. After the turn of the century he tended to sport a small, rather military moustache which, with his bursts of loud laughter and penetrating glare, must have given him at times a rather overbearing appearance.

In 1897 Rolls bought a four-cylinder Panhard, the car which a year earlier had won the Paris-Marseille-Paris race at an average speed of 14.5 mph. He must have valued speed highly to have bought it, for he spent £1200 on the car, no negligible sum before the First World War. It is true, though, that he never seems to have made speed the only consideration, and never went in for the stripped-down, over-engined lightweights in which some young men were increasingly threatening life and limb – both their own and that of bystanders.

The moment at which Britain entered the motor age in the fullest sense occurred, with a nice sense of precision, in the first year of the new century. The date was 23 April, the time 7 am. That was when the first of over sixty cars left Hyde Park Corner for the Thousand Mile Trial, an excursion designed both as a test and a shop-window for this new form of transport. Rolls was among those who wanted, and got, a two-hour lunch break every day, not because of any aristocratic notion of leisure, but in order to allow the people of the places where they stopped to have a good look at the cars. He was a crusader in a cause and thus a more than useful publicist.

Rolls himself drove his Panhard, but at the beginning seemed, a little uncharacteristically perhaps, perfectly prepared to keep within the legal speed limit of 12 mph. As the Trial progressed, however, and he found himself losing contact with the others taking part, he began to accelerate. Once he had taken this decision, there was little else in the Trial which could compete with him; as the *Yorkshire Gazette* wrote edgily, 'Those who motor with the Hon. Charles have merely to say their prayers and hold tight.' In the speed trial at Welbeck, he was timed at over 37 mph, by 10 mph the fastest of the day, and eventually won the Trial's Gold Medal for the best performance irrespective of class.

The Trial brought into prominence another man who was to play a great part in the Rolls-Royce saga, Claude Johnson. He was the man who organised the whole event, no easy matter in days when few motorists had travelled further than a hundred miles in a day, when there were hardly any garages, and petrol, if available at all, had to be bought at the nearest chemist's shop. The success of the Trial, therefore, was in large measure due to its organisation. Later Johnson was to show the same skill in putting and keeping together the disparate and sometimes antagonistic parts of Rolls-Royce Ltd.

By 1901 there were over 10,000 motor-cars in Britain; the task of merely pointing out that such vehicles existed, were viable, safe, and not damagingly liable to breakdown, was largely over. It was necessary now to consolidate the position and, perhaps, to play some part in the commerce which was beginning to thrive on the foundations the pioneers had laid. In January 1902 Rolls opened a garage at Lillie Hall, Fulham. Motoring had become an expensive pastime for him – not only that, he had become a devotee of ballooning, which also seemed to demand an endless expenditure on items large and small. Thus, for the Panhard, he might have an annual tyre bill of around £200, while a balloon envelope could cost anything up to £70 or £80. The Hon. Charles was fortunate in having a father who, although a little bemused by his son's activities, was generous enough to continue lending him money. The garage in Fulham was begun with a capital of £6500; later, the West End show rooms were to take over £20,000 more, in direct loans or bank guarantees, saddling Rolls's company with debts which, although partly covered by legacies due to him, might have put it in jeopardy. A certain rearrangement of last wills and testaments by Lord Llangattock helped to make matters more secure.

At the beginning, C. S. Rolls & Co. was largely a one-man operation, based on Rolls's experience and reputation. It was his contacts in the world of High Society which brought in customers for the cars he sold – mainly Panhards, whose concessionaire he was –

and for those he serviced. In his garage there was space for 200 cars; the place had, after all, once been a skating rink. Charles himself spent much of his time demonstrating models to prospective customers and even teaching those who bought cars from him to drive – such an arrangement was a common part of the contract in those days. In 1904 Charles took Claude Johnson in as a fellow-director, and with his organising ability seemed fairly set for a continuing prosperity.

At this point, however, things began to look unexpectedly shaky. The Panhard, to which Rolls had remained loyal, had not moved with the times. In a period of swift technological change this was disastrous; those who bought motors were often knowledgeable, or knew someone who was, and what they wanted were the latest refinements of which news constantly came to them by way of the specialist newspapers and magazines. The choice before a prospective buyer was vast, too. By 1906 there were over 800 car manufacturers in existence and although many duplicated each other's efforts, either by accident or unconcerned theft, the discriminating man in not too much of a hurry could almost always find the precise vehicle which best suited him. The last thing he wanted was an outmoded Panhard, even if it was offered him with all the weight of the Hon. Charles's recommendation behind it. Among the customers who remained loyal to Panhard and Charles Rolls, however, were a number of illustrious personages, one of them Lord Llangattock himself, who bought his own first car in 1903.

Throughout 1903, therefore, Rolls was trying to work out some way of climbing out from under the full weight of his Panhard concession. At one point it seemed he was contemplating the idea of marketing a light and relatively cheap car; at another, he and Johnson began negotiations for the right to retail an electric brougham – a comedown indeed for a man who had always ferociously insisted that the future lay with the petrol engine alone. It was therefore at something near a crisis in the affairs of C. S. Rolls & Co. that Edmunds, in March 1904, spoke to Charles about the Royce, a two-cylinder motor-car designed and put together by a relatively obscure Manchester firm specialising in the manufacture of dynamos and electrically operated cranes.

In March 1904 Henry Royce was celebrating his forty-first birthday. To him Charles Rolls may well have seemed a semi-mythological figure, alien, incomprehensible and untrustworthy in the secure fastnesses of his aristocratic birth, university education and newspaper-fostered glamour. On the other hand, Royce, who had had no thought of motor-cars until he bought his first and disappointing model in 1902, may never even have heard of Rolls. It seems unlikely that he had much time to read the papers.

Henry Royce's father had been a miller in the small, Lincolnshire town of Alwalton, not far from Peterborough. Nobody knows where Henry went to school, or even if he went at all, although it seems likely that he did, long enough at least to learn to read, write and do simple sums. In any case, he was still very young when his father's business foundered and the whole family moved to London. There the ex-miller, once a man with friends and a place in the scheme of things, became ill. The children, Henry among them, had to go out to work. Like others before him, he worked selling newspapers and brought his shilling or so a week home to his mother. When he was nine, his father finally died and it is certain that in the days before education was compulsory he is unlikely to have gone to school again. The conditions under which the Royce family now lived were desperate and cruel, and Henry's main meal of the day was sometimes no more than two slices of bread soaked in milk. But details of this period are scanty, for the hardness of it stayed with Royce all his life and he hardly ever spoke about it. For a time he worked for the Post Office, delivering telegrams, and there seemed no way out of the trap of poverty into which he, with so many million others, had fallen. The great cities swallowed them and ground them and digested them, to excrete them finally into their cramped, untended graves.

When deliverance came, the microscopic chance from which genius and application would build a career, it was through the intervention of an aunt: the incident has the air of having been contrived by Dickens in benevolent mood. Henry would sometimes spend short holidays with this aunt, who still lived not far from Peterborough. She therefore understood his frustration and realised the possibility that he might despair. Without telling him, she went to the works of the Great Northern Railway and asked about the possibility of an apprenticeship. There was one available, at £20 a year. One has to realise the changed value of money and what the average income of the lower-middle and working classes was to understand what a burden this good lady took on when she agreed to pay such a sum. Henry was now fourteen; it was the year that, elsewhere, the future Lady Llangattock was giving birth to her son Charles Stewart.

Henry's landlord was a Mr Yarrow, a skilled mechanic whose

skill was also his hobby. In a shed in his small garden he had put together a workshop, and there Henry would go after his working day was over, to learn from the tasks he and the older man would take on between them. But after only three years this meagre period of what must have seemed happiness came to an end. His aunt fell ill and gave up her work; the annual £20 dried up and with it went the apprenticeship. At seventeen Henry Royce found himself semi-trained and unemployed. But he knew that the great industries were centred on the North of England and that Peterborough could offer him little more. He said his farewells, packed his bag and set off northward, on foot, trudging across an England dotted with figures like his own, stubborn men refusing to admit that the chances of an unregulated economic system had left them without opportunity or hope.

It was finally in Leeds that he found work – eleven shillings for a 54-hour week, in the factory of a small tool-making firm. He had come full circle – the squirrel-in-a-cage activities of a Post Office messenger had been translated into his present drudgery, the opportunity to do anything useful or rewarding with his life was as far away as ever. Working from six in the morning to eleven at night, unable to afford enough food, decent lodgings or new clothes, he may well have felt that the trap had finally closed on him.

By chance, however, he saw an advertisement in a newspaper: the Electric Light & Power Co. in London were looking for a tester. Henry Royce sat down and wrote an application – it is unlikely that he spent long over the fact that he knew very little about electricity. In any case, at this stage of its development, very few people did and none of this minority appears to have applied, because within a few weeks he was back in London, settling into lodgings in Kentish Town and learning his new trade.

The more Henry studied, the more convinced he became that electricity had a marvellous future – and he studied very hard. He went to night-school, to lectures, read everything relevant that he could find. Already his gift for applying himself totally to the task in hand was becoming not only apparent but one of his greatest assets. Thus his opinions on the matter hardened, despite the many criticisms to which the new system of lighting was being subjected. Not that these were unearned – the supply of current was unreliable, sometimes fluctuating badly, at others being cut off entirely. Yet Royce knew, as many people did not, that these were problems of design and construction and had nothing to do with the inherent qualities of these systems. For some electricity remained too mysterious a power source; it worried them, arousing their prejudices and superstitions. Their enmity was an article of faith rather than a rational attitude taken after examination of facts – they felt threatened in ways which now seem more extraordinary to us than electricity did to them.

For an engineer like Henry Royce, with a brilliant grasp of the principles of whatever he worked on, this opposition must have been infuriating. And in 1883 he was to meet it head on, not in London but in Liverpool. The Electric Light & Power Company was instigating a pioneer scheme for lighting the Merseyside streets. At the same time they were trying to persuade the owners of theatres, music halls and so on to install electricity. Henry Royce travelled north-west as chief electrical engineer on the project. He was twenty years old.

Almost at once the new scheme began to lose money. The opposition was too solid, the generators perhaps a little too unreliable. Hard-headed Merseyside businessmen were not easily to be inveigled into investing in the hare-brained and the newfangled Every year people came up with some new idea and expected it to be taken up and financed. Things were perfectly all right without the new lighting; why put down hard cash for alterations no one really needed? The Electric Light & Power Company withdrew – but was forced to leave Henry behind, a kind of casualty of this unsuccessful industrial sortie. His old post in London had been filled and his new one in Liverpool no longer existed – there was no room for him in the company.

By thrift and good fortune, Henry Royce had by now become a capitalist – he had saved at the rate of almost a pound a year, and now, at the age of twenty-one, had £20 in the bank. He could afford to sit and think for a week or so, to look around a little. What he saw when he did look round was, first of all, a young man named Claremont who shared his own enthusiasm for the artefacts of this modern age, particularly his belief in the future of electrical power. Claremont had done a little better than Royce – he owned some £50. So between them they had a capital sum they would be mad to fritter away; both were young, both were experts, both saw the opportunities in the new technology. Their money ought to be used to give themselves a toehold in the dawning age, and the toehold they chose was a small workshop in Cook Street, Manchester. It was there that F. H. Royce & Co. opened its doors in 1884; it suggests something of the force of Royce's character that Claremont, who put up the major share of the pitiful sum they began with, had no place in the company's name.

Beginning in business with precisely £2,530 less than Rolls was to have some fifteen years later, Royce and Claremont decided to specialise; their first product was a lamp-holder. They lived above their workshop, worked long hours, struggled to make a living. Royce, dissatisfied with their progress, then came up with a new idea: an electric door-bell which would ring wherever you wanted it to in the house, and which, selling at one shilling and sixpence, was cheaper than anything comparable on the market. Orders began to mount; they took on a mechanic, a man named Ellis. The work-load increased on each of them, and their hours rose to meet it. They ate where they stood, at the bench; or, in Royce's case, not at all if someone did not bring food to his attention. When the ordinary, necessary work was done and Claremont had gone to bed, Royce would tinker on into the night with some invention or improvement which he saw as possible. Often Claremont would come down in the morning to find Henry still in the workshop, upright over some piece or drawing of electrical machinery, fully clothed, fast asleep.

What Henry Royce eventually came up with was a new and improved dynamo. This was a class or two up from lamp-holders and door-bells. Capital and unit costs would be higher, but profits correspondingly great. It would provide them with the financial platform from the stability of which they might be able to move on into the field of larger electrical machines. The nights now became endless periods of concentration in the silent workshop. Royce always had the ability to concentrate on the problem he had chosen, to the exclusion of all the rest of the world – his own needs included. With this vigour of investigation and thought, it was only a matter of time before he was demonstrating his new dynamo to a succession of Manchester and North Country firms. All were impressed – the back-street, hand-to-mouth days were over.

In 1893 (while the Hon. Charles Rolls was in his last year at Eton) both Claremont and Henry Royce married. Brothers in effort as they had been, it seems fitting, in a sentimental, late-Victorian way, that they should have married sisters. Royce bought a house in Cheshire, at Knutsford; he was travelling the road of the successful industrialist. His firm took on a young man to look after the money – an accountant called John de Looze, who soon became an indispensable member of the team. Not only did he keep their books straight, he also did his best to make sure that Royce now and then took a little nourishment. He would send a boy out, carrying a glass of milk and a sandwich, with instructions to keep pestering Royce until he had taken them.

The success of the dynamo freed Royce from the ordinary drudgery of factory work. He was employing a staff now; he could sit and dream and struggle over the new ideas which crowded his brain. He gave up his office to de Looze, who now took control of all the firm's paperwork. His own workplace was a small table and chair in the corner of the workshop, beset by the noise of the machines about him. He seemed to hear nothing but, intent on his drawings, would settle in to steady hours of work as the little factory hummed and clattered, then sank into its evening silence.

In 1894 the company went public: Royce Ltd, 'electrical and mechanical engineers, and manufacturers of dynamos, motors and kindred articles'. Henry Royce had his platform and it is clear from the description that he was thinking big. He and Claremont, with a friend who had put up some money, were the directors, and de Looze was the secretary. No one would question Royce's decisions in the new set-up, any more than they had in the old.

Royce was less an inventor than an improver. He detested the shoddy and the unreliable. His standards were always higher than almost anyone else's, his specifications – to himself as to others – more exacting. Now he devised a new and better electrical crane, a machine which gave so little trouble and was so well made that in a short time its reputation was widespread. By 1899 there were orders worth more than £20,000 on the books. It was time to expand: the company issued a prospectus and borrowed the £30,000 or so it needed.

But now, in an odd way, the destinies of Henry Royce and the Hon. Charles Rolls began to converge. Just as Rolls was to experience a decline in business during these years before the two men met, so Royce found that the sales of his dynamos were being threatened by new imports from Germany and the United States, while the market for heavier machinery, like cranes, had contracted during the uncertainties of the Boer War. At the same time Henry Royce too had caught the enthusiasm of the age – nearly a decade after Rolls, he had bought his first car and been converted to this new form of transport, with all the obvious and exciting developments in the future that it implied. His car, a second-hand French 10-hp Decauville, certainly carried him about the lanes and roads near his Cheshire home, but it carried him noisily and stopped both unpredictably and too often. Royce, not a man to feel easy in mind when near a faulty machine, began to tinker with it. He redesigned parts over the weekend and during the week, when they should have been busy with other work, apprentices at the works of Royce, Ltd, would make them for him. He climbed over and under the cars of his friends, and in 1903 he decided to build a motor-car of his own. In some ways, even commercially the idea was not a bad one, since one way of countering a declining market is to launch into something absolutely new. And in the first decade of the century dozens of firms, often with only a local reputation, were involving themselves in the construction of motor-cars: where today is the Ryknield from Burton-on-Trent or the Rothwell from Oldham?

Royce's first decision was one which almost prevented Rolls from ever co-operating with him: he decided that since the main cause of breakdown in an engine was overheating, his first priority was to make space for a sizeable water-cooling unit. This involved a contraction of the space available for the genuine working parts and so formed the basis of his decision to build a two-cylinder motor. It was this which Rolls, whose experience was that two cylinders gave you a noisy and uneven run, found difficult to accept, right up to the moment when he actually heard that engine start.

No one knew very much about motor-engines; there were few components available and those that were often failed to meet Royce's demanding standards. Most of what he wanted he had to design, or redesign, from scratch. At the beginning, he designed and made his own carburettor, he designed the ignition system, he made his own distributor, he simplified the ignition control, he devised his own drip-feed system for lubrication, he perfected one of the best braking systems then on the road and springs giving one of the most comfortable rides. His gear-box, although stiffer than some, made it almost impossible to engage the wrong gear by mistake. In other words, he went piece by piece and item by item through everything that was known in motor-engineering, and whatever he examined he found faulty, and whatever he found faulty he improved. Noise was the basis of some of the most vociferous anti-motoring criticism, and he designed a new exhaust system and silencer to cope with the problem. He wanted reliability; he ran his new engines for thousands of hours on the bench. He wanted superlative engineering; there is a record of his losing his temper with a mechanic who told him that something was 'good enough'. For Royce things had to be absolutely right, they had to be perfect.

Henry let the rest of his life slide away. His car obsessed him. Night after night he would work through until the small hours; his wife, waking alone, would find him downstairs with drawings spread before him, absorbed, possessed. At one point he spent three days and nights at the work-bench, resting occasionally in a chair. And he made those about him work as hard; it was as if no mere person had any independent existence. The machine was god and everyone owed it their total allegiance – what it demanded, they had to give. Hully, the works manager, would fight to keep staff working on the cranes upon which the firm's income still depended. Royce would demand their help with his car. Claremont, trying to keep the peace, sometimes felt a little of Royce's enthusiasm; perhaps more often he would share the doubts of the others about the motor-car and the time and money it was eating up.

The moment of revelation and decision arrived early in the spring of 1904. The official reports gave the date as 31 March, but this was to avoid unseemly jokes by irreverent reporters. It was on 1 April that the Royce had its first test run. It looked very like the Decauville which had brought on the whole enterprise, for Royce was a man obsessed by machinery, not styling. The car had, however, been almost entirely built in his own workshop and to his own exacting standards – a mechanic who had found the front axle half an inch out and bent it level had been forced to scrap it and make a new one, although it meant delaying the car's completion. The possibility of perfection haunted Royce and no one was ever permitted to hamper his efforts to achieve it. The Royce – registration number M 612 – was wheeled out of the workshop and one can imagine the excitement as its engine was started. It travelled for fifteen smooth, trouble-free miles, its engine quiet, its passage comfortable. Royce had crossed the threshold into his new business – and, as it turned out, into a kind of immortality.

Two more Royces were built. The first Henry took for himself, the second he gave to Claremont. (Not a gift without drawbacks; Royce used it so extensively as a travelling test-bench for his new ideas that it became extremely unreliable – so much so that Claremont placed a plaque in front of the passenger seat: 'If the car breaks down, please do not ask a lot of silly questions.') The third Royce, which the factory thought the best, was taken fatefully by Henry Edmunds, a man widely known among motorists, who had quite recently become a member of the board of Royce Ltd: Edmunds the matchmaker, the link between Royce and the in every sense distant Rolls.

For some time Rolls resisted Edmunds' suggestion that he should travel to Manchester to test the new car and meet its maker. He felt that Royce and his motor should come to him. But Panhard sales continued to decline and he was driven on by his own dream that C. S. Rolls & Co. should introduce and market a successful and profitable British car which would take on the Peugeots of France, the Minervas of Belgium, the Mercedes of Germany and beat them for style, reliability and speed. Perhaps the Royce would be that car and for that possibility he would even travel as far as Manchester!

His final objection, that two-cylinder cars were noisy and unreliable, did not survive his first drive in the Royce. When the car was brought back to London he called his partner, Claude Johnson, although it was the middle of the night, and insisted he tried the new motor. So, in the deserted streets of the West End, a more and more jubilant Rolls and a Johnson of increasing enthusiasm savoured the smooth running and muted engine-noise of the prototype Royce. It must have been almost then and there that they decided to become Royce's sole agent, if the older man would agree. For Royce, who was unknown, an outlet into the attention and the pockets of the motoring public by way of the prestigious Charles Rolls must have been better than anything else he could have hoped for, and it was not long before all the arrangments had been made and the contracts were signed. With de Looze acting for Royce and Johnson for Rolls, it is no wonder that everything on the administrative side went so smoothly from the first.

The first public allowed a long look at the new car was that which crowded into the Paris Motor Show of December 1904. Rolls had a stand there; he had hastily rearranged it to show the Royce chassis and engines which was all that the Manchester factory could make available at the time. Outside the exhibition hall, however, he also provided the one Royce free to be brought over, a 10-hp model which incorporated some of the improvements to bodywork and seating which Rolls had asked for. This impressed most of those who were given a run in it – as the man from *The Times* wrote, 'When the engine is running one can neither hear nor feel it', proof that this quality has been drawing the respectful testimony of critics during the whole seven decades of its existence.

After the Paris Show Rolls and Johnson decided that it was time to be a little more detailed in the agreement they had with Royce. Negotiation decided that the Manchester firm should supply the London salesrooms with four models – a 10-hp two-cylinder which would sell at £395, a 15-hp three-cylinder at £500, a 20-hp four-cylinder at £650, and a six-cylindered, 30-hp monster which would cost £890. All these cars would come on the market under a new name – the Rolls-Royce. The agreement was signed on 23 December 1904; Britain had founded her own prestige marque.

At Manchester twenty of the two-cylinder cars were begun almost before the turn of the year – and on these there first appeared the Greek-temple radiator which was from then on to mean Rolls-Royce to an increasing number of people. Probably the idea for this came from Rolls, the salesman, who always had one eye steadily on style. One of the three prototypes became the factory's workhorse, making deliveries and collections for the next thirty years. So confident was Rolls of his own car's reliability that when he had to meet the Duke of Connaught at Folkestone, still at the end of 1904, he drove the seventy-five miles from London on the morning of the appointed day, an act of courage at a time when breakdowns could often still be counted at so many per dozen miles. Although his firm were still agents for Panhard and, more recently, the Minerva, it was clear from more than the fact that his name was on it that the Rolls-Royce was now Charles's main motoring interest.

He had, however, another passion – since 1901, he had become a balloonist of repute. This was a sport still gaining in popularity among those rich enough to pursue it, and by 1905 house-parties, where ladies and gentlemen sipped champagne and consumed their carefully prepared cold chicken while floating in convivial serenity three thousand feet above the common herd, had become quite frequent. The Aero Club had been formed and Charles worked for it in a semi-official way; when a full-time Secretary was found necessary, it was he who interviewed applicants in his office at the Conduit Street showrooms.

Henry Royce, meanwhile, thrust on in his almost inhuman way at Manchester. A chassis, once built, would be test-run by him and an apprentice on the way home after work; if Henry thought he heard an untoward noise or noticed an unexpected and unwanted eccentricity in the machine, he would stop at once and begin to tinker with it. In this way the journeys were made unpredictable and the fifteen miles could sometimes take hours. Another of his quirks was to come into the workshop as it was closing for the weekend at midday on Saturday to look for a finished car to take him home. If none was ready, he would point to a partially assembled motor – that would be the one for the journey. Everyone then had to take their jackets off again and help finish the machine so that Royce could drive it home to Knutsford. Whether this devotion to duty by the workers was based on loyalty or fear is not now easy to understand, but one suspects their feelings for him must have been ambivalent. Certainly he asked no one to work harder than himself; it was perhaps his staff's misfortune that his notion of a working day seemed inexhaustibly elastic.

In 1905 the first of the Isle of Man Tourist Trophies was held – the speed limit still imposed in England made racing there impossible. Johnson, with an eye to publicity, offered the judges the use of one of the new 30-hp Rolls-Royces. Rolls and a friend of his, Percy Northey, were each to drive a 20-hp model. Rolls, as was his custom when his interest was fully aroused, went about his preparations with the meticulousness of a Montgomery preparing for battle. He made special runs to ensure the cars would be within the limits of petrol consumption laid down. He took the cars to the Isle of Man early and as a result could recommend the gear ratios necessary for the race in good time for Royce to make the modifications. In a practice lap he drove his own entry round the course at an average speed of 33 mph. It was in a state of elated optimism that he came to the starting line in his long-bodied, open motor. The air must have vibrated with the raucous yelling of each of the forty or so models as one at a time they first coasted away, then started up and thrummed off at the carefully regulated intervals. The Spyker, the Simms-Welbeck, the Arrol-Johnston, the Star, the Argyll, the Clement, the Darracq, the White, the Minerva, the James and Browne, the Thornycroft – their names call like the keening of ghosts; and with them were others still with us: the Vauxhall, the Cadillac, the Peugeot, the Daimler, the Wolseley. Off they all went on their time trial – leaving ignominiously behind them Rolls cursing in his car.

First away, he had tried to engage one gear, then another, had struggled for a little way, then, hearing a sudden loud crack from beneath him, had realised that his race was over before it had properly begun. The strength of his fury was only matched by the ferocity of his excuses; not even the fact that Northey came in second, 0.2 mph behind the winning Arrol-Johnston, could damp down his accusations of sabotage. The chances are, in fact, that the disaster was Rolls's own fault for trying to engage a gear while still coasting downhill, his engine dead. Later he would insist that some 'loose pieces' had somehow made their way into the gear-box, an unlikely possibility, given Royce's perfectionism and his own meticulous preparation for the race.

In May 1906 Rolls took Northey and the two TT cars to Monte Carlo for what he said would be a general appraisal of the way they went. In fact Charles was going to break the Monte Carlo–London record, made over the roads of France, so pleasantly free of the speed restrictions which still irritated and confined the British motorist. For the journey, Rolls took champagne and tea – the former for his own consumption, the latter for his (one hopes mutinous) companions. They made good progress to Lyons, despite heavy rain; later, overshooting a fork in the road, they lost two hours through Charles's impatient refusal to turn back. Nevertheless, they reached Boulogne having averaged 27.3 mph, over three miles an hour faster than the average speed of the record they were trying to beat. Now, however, they had to wait three hours for a ferry and later lost themselves in the wilds of South London, with the result that although they beat the previous record, it was only by one and a half minutes.

For that year's Tourist Trophy Charles again began to prepare early. He brought in wire wheels, although Royce refused to venture £40 out of the company's meagre kitty for the improvement; Johnson paid for the wheels himself. One gets the feeling that Henry, bent over the Manchester workbench in all his old absorption, hardly understood the difficulties or the value of what his partner was attempting in the wider, public world. For him a machine was an end in itself, its perfect design and assembly the only sensible ambitions open to a man of reason. Nevertheless, de Looze arranged that the intermediate lap times should be sent from the Isle of Man to the Cook Street works by telegram.

Thirty-one cars started in 1906; the Arrol-Johnston was there, to defend its title, and so were more of the marques which showed for a moment or so on the tides of the new industry, only to sink almost without trace – cars like the Vici and the Hardman and the Climax. This time it was Northey who ran into ill luck; his front spring broke during the first lap. On the second lap Charles, a minute ahead of everyone on time, overtook the Arrol-Johnston, which had started ahead of him and had been timed at nearly 40 mph on its first circuit. By this time, however, it was having problems with its tyres, while the Minervas were failing through clutch trouble, the SCAR was running out of petrol and the Argyll had been brought to a halt when its floorboards fell out. As the Rolls-Royce lapped a Bianchi, a stone smashed Charles's goggles, cutting his face. His mechanic, Eric Platford, passed over his own pair and they went on without stopping. By the fourth and final lap, Rolls was a good ten minutes ahead of the second car, a French Berliet. He eased a little over that last lap and in the end the gap was not as wide as it perhaps might have been, but he won at an average speed of 39.3 mph, nearly 4 mph faster than the French car and 5.4 mph faster than the speed the Arrol-Johnston had reached the year before. Charles took the time to point out to reporters, with some modesty, that most of the credit must go to Royce in Manchester – 'Mr Royce, the designer and builder' – before setting off for Paris to take part in the first of the Gordon Bennett International Balloon Cup races. This was won by a Lieutenant Frank P. Lahm of the US Army, who flew 402 miles in just over twenty-two hours, landing at Fylingdales in Yorkshire – a feat which, if repeated today, would probably set in motion the early-warning system guarding the approaches to the Western World.

Charles himself, fresh from his hectic circling of the Isle of Man, may have felt a sense of release as the unpredictable breezes sent him floating out over the French coast. For thirteen hours he had wavered over France; now his trailing rope narrowly missed three steamers before he was able to throw down a note as he came in over Hastings, not waiting, however, to see his message retrieved by a well-trained dog named 'Little Nell'. He then disappeared for several hours, pleasant for him but anxious for his friends and family. Turning up in Norfolk, he explained that he had landed nowhere near a telegraph office. He had been airborne for over twenty-six hours, and won awards for the flight of the longest duration and for the best flight by a British entrant, coming third in the race overall.

In all these excitements, one commercial reorganisation was also significant. The Rolls-Royce car was to be backed by a company, Rolls-Royce, Ltd, thus cutting out the complications of having two separate firms handling manufacture and distribution. C. S. Rolls & Co. disappeared, while Royce Ltd became strictly manufacturers of electrical equipment. Claremont was made Chairman of the new company, with Royce himself, Rolls and Claude Johnson as directors, and with them a new name, that of Arthur Briggs. In a sense he was the prime mover behind this new marshalling of resources, since it was he who at a key moment had agreed to raise an essential sum of money.

All this had come about once it was plain that the works at Cook Street had become too small for the amount of business Royce was being asked to do. He began to look around for another site, travelling all over the industrial Midlands. His choice narrowed to two possibilities, Leicester or Derby. What decided him was an offer of cheap power by the electricity company in Derby. Royce and Johnson agreed that enough land should be bought to allow for expansion later; given the continuing increase in their sales, this was hardly over-optimistic. Henry Royce, although no architect, set to as usual and designed buildings which could be used at once while at the same time forming the basis for future extensions. Thus the moment arrived at which the necessary finance had to be sought.

Rolls-Royce issued a prospectus – Royce, it told the world, would be chief engineer, Rolls technical managing director, Johnson commercial managing director, Claremont chairman and commercial adviser. The firm's cars were already acknowledged as among the best to be found anywhere, and had indeed proved it; yet, perhaps because the whole industry was so new, the public was oddly reluctant to produce the £100,000 loan asked for. The Rolls-Royce bankers had insisted that £50,000 had to be subscribed by a certain date, otherwise the plans for the new factory would have to be shelved. As the date drew near, the directors, their mathematics doubtless made precise by crisis, reckoned up that they had the promise of £41,000. Then de Looze remembered Arthur Briggs, a Yorkshireman who had been enthusiastic about the Rolls-Royce car during the first year of its manufacture. He took the train for Harrogate, where Briggs lived, put to him the company's dilemma and received on the spot an offer of £10,000 – on condition that Briggs was given a seat on the board. He became a director.

Now Royce, the future location of the works settled, bent over his drawings again; it was time for a new car. This was to be of six cylinders, the biggest to date. Not only that, it was to have the radiator mounted on a flexible base, to prevent the breakages which sometimes occurred on the rough roads of that time. Each cylinder was built with its own expansion chamber which led directly into the exhaust system, allowing the engine, despite its greater size, to run as quietly as ever. Royce, able as always to focus almost exclusively on the problem before him, settled into his familiar routine of working each day until he dropped, waking too soon to work again. Running endlessly second to the machines he adored, his wife began almost unnoticed to droop and pine. His own health made those about him anxious, but hardly slowed him at all.

At the 1906 London Motor Show Rolls was able to display the chassis and engine of one of the new cars, and one completed model. Described as the 40–50-hp model, it became the hit of the exhibition. Claude Johnson, with his usual flair for publicity, applied silver plating here, aluminium paint there, until the car gleamed like something magical. Thus the 'Silver Ghost' was born; for twenty years the name was to be synomymous with that of Rolls-Royce itself.

In May the following year the car was given a long-distance test, travelling from London to Glasgow at an average speed of over 20 mph. But Johnson was not satisfied; this was the time of long-distance endurance trials. A 40-hp Wolseley-Siddeley had been driven for 10,000 miles only a short while before and Johnson wanted to do better. It was decided to drive the car 15,000 miles and then have it examined piece by piece by experts from the newly formed Royal Automobile Club. The same car, the original 'Silver Ghost' – or, more prosaically, AX 201 – was driven by a team which included Johnson himself, Rolls and Eric Platford. The car stopped once, when a petrol tap worked itself shut and cut off the fuel flow. At the end, the cost of replacing all the worn parts the examiners could discover came to a princely £2 2s. 7d. As a result, when two slightly more powerful cars, named the White Knave and the Silver Rogue, were entered for the 2000-mile RAC Reliability Trial of that same year, Johnson put down a £1000 stake: any car could win it by beating the Rolls-Royce over a special 15,000-mile trial, to begin immediately after the RAC event. No one accepted the challenge – his cars had been accepted as pre-eminent. In a sense the Silver Rogue's win in the Reliability Trial was almost a formality. From this time on, the honours followed thick and fast; it seemed as if no one could match the steady, near-silent running of these lean, long-bonnetted machines.

Eight years after the first Royce car had travelled its fifteen trial miles, the new works in Derby opened. The transfer had taken place without suspending production, a task which exercised all Henry Royce's energy and technical ability. For almost a year he had hardly had time to come home and have a decent night's rest. In a sense he no longer had a marriage; since his apprenticeship his first passion had been for what he could create from metal and wiring out of the ingenuity of his brains and the patient skill of his hands. He and his wife had adopted a daughter, but his real children travelled in the quiet and comfort of their near-perfection about the roads of Britain and, increasingly, the world.

Charles, in the meantime, although his enthusiasm for the motor-car had helped to build up not only his own business, but motoring itself as both an industry and a pastime, was now on the threshold of a new phase in his life. He was a man who belonged to that first decade of the century in a way few others did. He understood that new forces were moving in the world, that the new technology and the way it extended the scope of individuals was not simply exciting, but on the way to changing the lives of millions, the structure of whole societies. He understood this not analytically, but through action, through taking part, as pioneers and colonisers must always have dimly understood their historical roles. He was a man who by instinct lived on the frontier and when that frontier was marked by the clouds of dust rising behind the clattering racket of the automobile, that was where he was to be found. But the frontier was shifting. The internal combustion engine, having annexed to itself the two dimensions of horizontal space, was taking man into a third.

On a promotional visit with Rolls-Royce cars in 1906, Charles had visited the Wright brothers. In 1908 Wilbur Wright was in France and when motoring affairs took Rolls to Paris, he used the opportunity to renew his acquaintance with the aviator. By this time men like Farman and Delagrange and, briefly, Blériot, had already taken to the air. Charles had flown in over a hundred balloon ascents and once in an airship, a craft he viewed with some reservations. Now he went up for the first time in a heavier-than-air machine, travelling as Wilbur Wright's passenger. 'Once clear of the ground,' he wrote in *The Times*, 'the feeling of security was perfect ... We tore along at a speed of 40 mph. ...' After this he could hardly wait for the Wright aircraft he had ordered from Shorts' to be delivered. He decided to follow Wilbur Wright's example, and learned to fly initially in a glider. By 1909 he was among the first Britishers to fly, although his friend and rival, Moore-Brabazon, later Lord Brabazon, that year became the first man to fly an all-British plane for over 250 yards. (A sense of the attitude these young men took to their new sport may be gained from Moore-Brabazon's ascent with a pig as passenger – as he pointed out, it proved that under some circumstances pigs could fly.)

By 1910 Charles had decided to attempt a two-way crossing of the Channel – Blériot had flown from France two years earlier, and that flight had been emulated by others, but not beaten. Henry Royce, concentrating on producing the Silver Ghosts at Derby, although he was kept informed, thought very little of his partner's venture. For him the air was something one breathed. Indeed, within the firm of Rolls-Royce, and particularly on the board, the feeling was gathering that Rolls would have to make a choice about where his first allegiance lay. For Rolls such choices were instinctive; he followed his love of the moment. In 1908 he found time for balloon races, motor-car trials, a conference on roads in Paris, his flight with Wilbur Wright. He was a man of great energy, after all, fanatical about his fitness and about the food he ate, given to appearing in his office at odd and unexpected hours, tearing with his habitual vehemence into the problems that faced him, then driving off for his business routine of demonstrating the Rolls-Royce, before charging away on another of his own adventures. From 1909, however, he seems to have begun to disengage himself from his official involvement with the motoring world, and to some extent this jeopardised the positions he held in the Rolls-Royce hierarchy. A factor in this was not only Royce's non-comprehension of what Charles was now doing, but the active if still friendly opposition of Claude Johnson.

Rolls arrived at Dover early in May 1910. For a month he waited for the right conditions, both in his aircraft and in the weather. He made trial flights; once he nearly hit an old lady during a landing, breaking a strut while taking avoiding action. A little later a water pump broke. Then, on 2 June, the weather cleared and he took off at 6.30 pm. In forty minutes he was over his destination in France, the airfield at Sangatte, had dropped a message for the Aero Club de France, then turned and, after flying a little distance over French soil, had turned for the Kent coast again. For a while mist troubled him, but some ninety minutes after take-off, having circled Dover Castle in a slightly bravado gesture, he landed once more. The crowds had to be held back by soldiers from the nearby military school. The only comment he seems publicly to have allowed himself was in a speech at a dinner given in his honour, when he said that it had been the first time he had succeeded 'in taking ten gallons of petrol in and out of France without paying duty'. It was after this flight that he finally asked the board of Rolls-Royce to relieve him of such routine tasks as demonstrating the new models. He had found a way forward, he did not have the intention of remaining earth-bound.

Charles Rolls was now one of the small group of aviators more and more in demand at meetings up and down the country. These were hazardous affairs, the tiny box-kite planes circling small airfields in rain or gusty winds, their pilots risking life and limb for what seemed little more than a sideshow thrill for the audiences.

The largest of these meetings in 1910, however, was a rather grand affair arranged at Bournemouth, with royalty among the patrons and a motorised battle of flowers among the attractions. Flyers like Cody, the French aviator Audemars, Grahame-White and Moore-Brabazon were there; the Hon. Charles could hardly have kept away.

One of the competitions, scheduled for the second day, was a quick-starting and landing contest, in which the fliers had to aim at a white circle marked on the ground. This was a competition Rolls badly wanted to win; it was a proof of human skill, rather than mere mechanical endurance. (Royce's attitude might have been different.) In a gusty wind, he took off – Audemars, who had crashed already, had tried unsuccessfully to dissuade him. As he passed over the spectators' enclosure and aimed for his target near the judges' box, he seemed a little high to some observers – about seventy feet up. He would, they thought, have to make a dangerously steep descent if he was not to over-shoot. As he came out over the open space of the airfield, he dropped the nose of the French-Wright, and as he did so, everyone there heard a loud snap. A part of the tail-plane had given way. The aircraft came down, abruptly and with a heavy, ominous sound. Rolls was thrown well clear and for a moment the spectators thought he had survived without injury. Instead, he had been killed instantly.

Rolls died at the end of what would in any case always have been his decade. Edward VII had been buried a month or so earlier, in May. In another four years his Britain, his Europe, would disintegrate to the growl and hammer of guns on the Western Front. Flying was becoming institutionalised, as motoring already had been. It was becoming more and more commercial, a business run by professionals. The First World War only accelerated a process which would have cramped and confined him anyway, as it did his friend, Moore-Brabazon, the holder of the first pilot's certificate, as Rolls was the holder of the second. Unlike Royce, whose technical brain continued to keep him at the forefront of his battle, Charles Rolls would, one feels, have become more and more an anachronism in the Twenties and Thirties when the possibilities he had already envisaged became reality, with all the limitations and disillusionment this involves. Alternatively, if he had survived that coming war – one cannot imagine him not forcing his way into the Royal Flying Corps – he might well have died in some lonely battle with distance, a rival for the Alcocks, Browns and Lindberghs who followed the early pioneers. But flying was to remain a matter of courage and endurance, a game for young men; perhaps Charles Rolls's was the more graceful end.

Henry Royce mourned his partner – and the following year almost joined him. He had a severe breakdown in health, and it was the care and solicitude of Claude Johnson which, perhaps, saved his life. Again, in 1912, only a timely operation saved him – Johnson had to fetch him back for it from his Mediterranean villa, in a Rolls-Royce especially equipped as an ambulance.

Royce, however, recovered. In the war, armour slapped about his famous engines brought them into almost every front line; even the sand-powdered columns of Lawrence of Arabia used them. His engines, in a development which would have pleased Rolls, powered the warplanes which fought in the new battles of the air. This, like his first motor-car, involved his facing entirely new problems, since what was demanded was an engine producing 200 hp, power almost undreamed of until then. Six months of work incredible in one who had been ill so recently brought him the solutions that were needed. And by 1918 Rolls-Royce engines were producing almost double this amount of power. The Vickers Vimy in which Alcock and Brown flew the Atlantic during the first full year of peace was powered by Rolls-Royce.

So the triumphs piled up – and the personal disasters. That his wife had died may have seemed an event which made little practical difference to a life long geared to the demands of the workbench and the drawing board. In 1926, however, Claude Johnson died; aged only 63, he had been not only the organising genius who had moulded the famous firm into an efficient selling and manufacturing unit, but had also become a friend in a way which Rolls, perhaps by his nature, could never have done. One gets a sense, looking at Claude Johnson through the print of those who write about him, of a gentle man, a peacemaker. Rolls was very different, infinitely restless, endlessly active, not given to affection – hardly, judging from his childhood at the Hendre, used to it. There, each member of the family had had his own quarters, a separate coming in and going out. There had been loyalty, but little warmth. The sons had not married. An inner coldness, perhaps inherited or certainly learned early, persisted in him. The place in Royce's life which Charles Rolls, had he been a warmer, easier man, might have filled was in fact taken by Johnson, and his loss must have been deeply felt.

A last challenge: the Schneider Trophy air races. Between February 1929, when the Air Ministry suggested a British entry, and

September, when the race was held, Rolls-Royce developed a power-unit which propelled the special Supermarine at a speed nearly 50 mph faster than the Italian entry. That was the first of the three wins which were to see the Trophy come to Britain, its outright winners. And the Supermarine was the technical base upon which the Spitfire, that round-winged hunter of the Battle of Britain, was to be developed.

Henry Royce was nearly seventy now, as always not very strong. Yet his brain still worked in the old way – when he saw anything which seemed badly designed or badly made, he would whip out pencil and paper and design it anew, or demand from the Derby works a better article. He took up farming (he had always looked a countryman, after all), read everything he could on the subject – on soils, on fertilisers, on irrigation – and it was not long before the local farmers, until then scornful as always of the newcomer, were making journeys to learn from his methods and the condition of his fields and orchards.

His seventieth birthday, in March 1933, brought him letters and cables from all over the world. He had been knighted, he had become a great man. One wonders what he made of the long journey he had taken, of the hardships and the endless effort which had carried him through the years. What did he regret? His lack of children? His wife, pining, then dying, overshadowed by the intensity of his ambition, his perfectionism? He seemed content. A month after his birthday, he died. In a sense he was more a Victorian than an Edwardian. He was the archetypal self-made man; his rags had been appalling and the riches they turned to were enviable. He was in fact that epitome of Victorianism, the great engineer. It was his passion for the motor-car, when it seized him, which made him an Edwardian. He stubbornly remained a motor-car man, until war forced him to move on. Even Rolls could not shift him from his era.

For me he will be forever associated, not only with the cramped Manchester workshop, illuminated by his energy and clear, meticulous vision, but with those long dusty roads of the century's first decade, the goggled, leather-clad drivers wafted high above the hedgerows as chickens and small children scattered in fear before their stately progress; then, later, with those long, powerful bonnets, paradoxically both thrusting and temple-like, and the longer bodies, comfortable, many-seated, those cars which brought new standards to the chaos of motor-engineering; and always, of course, with Charles Rolls, eternally young, eternally obsessed, concentrated behind the high steering wheel as he whirls the car that carried both their names up the long hills and round the swooping curves of the Isle of Man.

After Henry Royce died, the red of the initials which decorated the Rolls-Royce radiator was changed to black, as a signal of perpetual mourning. Yet while the car exists, perhaps we should suspend such grief. Like all creators, Royce lives on in what he made.

Daisy Warwick

ENRY MAYNARD was secretary to Lord Burleigh, the sagacious minister of Elizabeth I, and for his services was in 1590 granted Easton Lodge, near Dunmow in Essex – a reward which suggests a level of restraint and diplomacy not all his descendants could boast, and especially the last of the direct line, Frances Evelyn, who was born in 1861. She seems, however, to have inherited some of her father's temperament: Charles Maynard was a man who set London by the ears on more than one occasion with his violent tempers, his escapades and his drinking, dying at the age of fifty and leaving only two daughters as the last of the Maynards, thus proving himself a delinquent even in the matter of progeny. It was, therefore, to the three-year-old Frances, the older girl, that the bulk of the Maynard estate went when her grandfather Viscount Maynard died. Most of the family, who had been so eager to hear the will read that they prevented the servants from clearing the breakfast table, responded to this information by hurling pieces of cheese at his lordship's portrait. One can see their point when one realises that while his daughter Charlotte found herself with an annuity worth £1000 a year, the rents alone from these estates would bring Frances £20,000 a year; it is no wonder that she grew up believing that money was a commodity as natural to her use as air or water.

Frances's mother, who had herself been Charles Maynard's second wife, married once more and Frances, by now known as 'Daisy', found herself in the care of a stepfather, Lord Rosslyn, a Scottish peer who brought to the 14,000 acres of the Maynard estates which his new wife administered 3000 acres of his own, under some of which lay most lucrative deposits of coal. Lord Rosslyn seems to have cared for Daisy, but to have brought her up – or more accurately had her brought up – in the rather severe manner common at that period. For example, the girl wore her mother's cast-off clothing, and by no means the most colourful articles of that either. On the other hand, he fostered in her a love of birds and animals which never left her and which later in life became one of her great interests. Daisy's upbringing was typical, again, in the patchy nature of her education, left to the unpredictable abilities of governesses (who were largely without either formal education or training themselves) and the whims of her parents. Her life was rather solitary; children of her class were kept to themselves in those days, ostensibly to protect their innocence, more practically, one supposes, to keep them from interrupting the serious business of adult conversation. Lord Rosslyn, a man of wide contacts in the sporting and political world, must have provided a sharp-witted girl many glimpses of a high life from which she was nevertheless strictly excluded; one visitor whom she did get to meet, however, was the beautiful Lily Langtry, the 'Jersey Lily', not then launched on the career which would culminate in her becoming the first of that great triumvirate of royal mistresses of whom Daisy herself was to be the second.

In 1878 Daisy and her sister, Blanche, travelled with their parents to Edinburgh – their father, to a muttering of criticism, had been made Lord High Commissioner of the Church of Scotland, a position which involved a ceremonial procession through the city. Seated in the second carriage, the two girls must have found their situation an extraordinary contrast to the serene seclusion of their Essex home. Daisy, fair-haired, with eyes of an extraordinary blue, caught the attention of many people during the days that followed, despite the fact that she was only sixteen; certainly this seems to have been the occasion on which Francis Greville, Lord Brooke, heir to the Earl of Warwick, saw her and fell in love with her. At twenty-three, presentable if a trifle jowly, and with his father's estates to come, he must have seemed to himself an eligible suitor. In Lord and Lady Rosslyn's opinion, however, Daisy was still far too young to marry, and Lord Brooke promised not to tell her what he felt about her for another two years.

While keeping Lord Brooke at arm's length, the Rosslyns looked around for a more eligible husband – one, that is, who would be worth every penny of the £30,000 a year Daisy's estates were now bringing in. It is one of the root causes of the survival of the British aristocracy – most of whom are in any case *parvenus* by the standards of Europe's *Almanac de Gotha* – that they have always thought cash of greater importance than lineage when arranging their marriages, although naturally preferring when they could get it a combination of the two. Since Daisy represented in herself such a combination, it is not to be wondered at that those who saw themselves as guiding her destiny felt that a mere Earl need not be the limit of her ambitions. Indeed, for a while it seemed as though they would be able to barter her fortune for a position as high as they could have hoped for – in the Royal Family itself. Leopold, the fourth son of Queen Victoria, a rather sickly young man whose inherited haemophilia had more than once brought him to the edges of crisis, was the only one still unmarried. The Queen was not absolute on the question of her children's marrying royal cousins – as she pointed out when her daughter Louise married the Marquis of Lorne, the family could not all afford to marry foreigners who, however heavy in title, tended to be rather light in the purse. That Disraeli, the Queen's old friend, now Lord Beaconsfield, was in favour of the match also helped a great deal. Beaconsfield, therefore, was deputed to estimate the young lady's worth by taking her out to the theatre, where she seems, despite her insistence that it was *Romeo and Juliet*, to have seen *Hamlet*, an experience which she had the sensibility to find deeply stirring. Beaconsfield, too, enjoyed the evening for his report was favourable and Lord and Lady Rosslyn were summoned to bring Daisy to Windsor for closer inspection. Daisy was to write much later, 'I was agonisingly shy in the presence of this mysterious Queen who lived alone and secluded. . . . But self-consciousness was my usual state of mind in those days' – not to be wondered at in a girl not yet eighteen. Despite her own agonies, however, she seems again to have passed the test, which her income in any case weighted heavily in her favour, and it was with this match already half-arranged that she was launched on Society with a coming-out ball on her eighteenth birthday. For this, a special suite of rooms was built at Easton Lodge and – it was December – decorated with flowers rushed for the purpose from the South of France.

In the world which Daisy now entered what was required of a woman, apart from breeding or (if possible, and) a fortune, was that she be beautiful – and to her delight Daisy, who had been plain as a child, discovered that she was. In the space of a few months, it seems, her shyness vanished, her diffidence was consigned to the nursery and the schoolroom. She acquired poise, self-confidence; even, very soon, audacity.

She might have made a serene, even perhaps a popular, daughter-in-law of the Queen. Unfortunately for Victoria's plans, neither Leopold nor Daisy actually welcomed the proposed marriage. Indeed Leopold, according to Daisy herself (she was not, however, the most reliable of witnesses), asked her to make a stand against it, pointing out that 'it would be easy to engage the Queen's sentiment in favour of my first love'. As for the Prince, 'he cared for someone else, whom he took great care not to name'. Despite a certain amount of pressure, Daisy adopted this course and stuck to it. Victoria was reported to be displeased; later, no doubt, she took a rather different view of what by then she might well have thought of as a lucky escape. Leopold left for an arranged visit to Canada, and a month later Lord Brooke became engaged to his future Lady.

The *World* commented, a little sourly, that 'it is a satisfaction to know that that grand old historical monument, Warwick Castle, can now be restored by its noble owner, without continuing the appeal to the general public for the necessary funds'.

After some acrimony over the marriage settlement, the wedding took place in 1881, rather splendidly in Westminster Abbey – although the horses, startled by loyal cheers, broke free of the ancient and decrepit Warwick State Coach and departed for the reception alone, leaving the happy couple in a state of dignified if slightly embarrassed immobility at the Abbey doors. They honeymooned at Ditton Park, lent them by the Duke of Buccleuch, their idyll interrupted only by a royal summons to Windsor, where Victoria insisted that Daisy wore her wedding gown and asked her to sign a birthday book, which she did – to everyone's consternation – in her maiden name.

A year later she did her dynastic duty and produced a son; whereupon she entered with some energy into the life her social position almost demanded. She and her husband moved to Easton Lodge, where she entertained a wide variety of guests, many of whom were aristocratic but all of whom were rich. It soon became apparent, however, that Lord Brooke's passion for hunting, shooting and fishing, the principal excitements of the English gentleman, were not entirely shared by his wife, fearless and capable horsewoman though she was. The great outdoors was not, she felt, her proper arena, despite Lord Brooke's assertion that 'a good day's shooting or fishing is second in point of pleasure to nothing on earth'. Thus began a new phase of her life. There was – there has always been – among the aristocracy and the rich an alternative set to that which was preoccupied with field sports. For them the delights of the chase were more rarefied, perhaps, the quarry both more elusive and more delightful, though possibly no less delicious when caught. In one sense it may be said that the excesses of the Regency continued among these people without a break, despite the Victorian gloom which arose from the still-mourning Palace on the one hand and the new, ultra-careful middle classes on the other. It is, of course, not to be wondered at if a company of young, excessively rich and excessively arrogant people, unburdened by the necessary disciplines which a shortage of money forces on the rest of the world, should have devoted most of their time and energy to the pursuit of pleasure and that, for many of them, such pleasure should have been found in a complexity of liaisons, affaires, flirtations and adulterous passions. The centre of this world was a group of people called, collectively, the Marlborough House set; and their centre was the Prince of Wales.

All through his youth Edward, the heir to the throne, had been treated to the full weight of the upbringing we now think of as typically Victorian – repressive, authoritarian and prudish. Throughout his adult life, partly because of the way he had reacted to this education and as a protest against what she saw as his profligate habits, his mother had kept him as far as was feasible from becoming involved in any genuine responsibility for the affairs of state. Unable therefore to grow and develop, prevented from fulfilling the duties he had been trained for, the Prince of Wales threw himself more and more into a life of pleasure. Marlborough House (which had been modernised at a cost of £60,000 of tax-payers' money in the year of his marriage to Alexandra) and Sandringham, a 7000-acre property bought out of his own capital for £22,000, were the principal centres of his existence. To these in 1869 was added the Marlborough Club. The Prince himself had founded and installed it, in the premises opposite Marlborough House in Pall Mall, after he had had a quarrel with the committee of White's over his desire to smoke in that club's morning room.

From these three inter-connected nuclei Edward ruled over his own dissipated, promiscuous and occasionally riotous kingdom. In that kingdom marriage was a liberation for young women, released as they were from the bondage of virginity and the need to make a good marriage – and the more beautiful they were, the more complete was their liberation. Lady Brooke was a very beautiful woman indeed. As for Lord Brooke, he, according to her own account, 'from the beginning of our life together . . . seemed to accept the inevitability of my having a train of admirers'.

Thus, when during the third and the fourth year of her marriage, Lady Brooke twice more became a mother, there may have been some doubt, at least in her own mind, as to these children's true paternity. And it is during this period that a name is found among that 'train of admirers' whose appearance there was to have important consequences: Lord Charles de la Poer Beresford. He was a naval commander, a man of great dash and courage, popular with his men and destined to become an admiral. He was almost notorious for his ease of manner when with the Prince of Wales, once replying to a royal invitation, theoretically never to be refused, with the telegram, 'Can't possibly. Lie follows by post.' He was handsome and audacious, and he made the strongest possible appeal to Daisy. He and his wife were often at Easton Lodge; and on occasion, of course, he visited the house unaccompanied.

By 1886 relations between these two passionate people had reached a pitch when the normal discretion which surrounded such private arrangements was beginning to wear thin. It seems as if the game of love had suddenly turned serious and that the conventions which bound the couple had become too cramping. Lady Charles Beresford later wrote to Lord Salisbury about the time when 'the Lady came into my room and volunteered of her own accord to inform *me* of the ... "liaison" between herself and my Husband – and of her intention to elope with him! and how I determined not to sacrifice Lord Charles's career to such an insane project by taking him home with me on the spot!' And Lord Charles once publicly renounced his wife during a dramatic confrontation at Newmarket, to the horror of his somewhat steadier brother, Lord Marcus.

Two years later, passion spent, at least on one side, the love affair came to an end – Lord Charles broke it off, with very little fuss to start with, partly because he found that he was not after all Daisy's only lover. Daisy appears to have taken this abandonment with some self-control, at least until she learned that Lady Charles had become pregnant. To be usurped in her lover's affections by anyone as banal as his own wife, a woman who had even tried for a while to be her social rival, seems to have enraged her – perhaps by now she had accepted a rather high-romantic view of the kind of life she was leading and expected Lord Charles to retire into a monastic and celibate austerity. In any case she wrote him a letter, which everyone who read it thought outrageous, demanding in peremptory and outspoken terms his immediate return. Lord Charles was away on a visit to Bismarck, a fact which Lady Brooke might have forgotten in her fury, or might perhaps have deliberately overlooked. In any case it was Lady Charles who opened the letter and was not over-pleased to read it, particularly a passage which seemed to imply that she had no right to bear a child by her own husband. It is perhaps enough to say that when the Prince of Wales read it, he thought it the most shocking letter he had ever seen, and Daisy mad to have written it.

Both ladies spent the spring in the South of France, continuing a barrage of enraged missives there; when they returned, Lady Charles took to the law. Predictably she went to George Lewis, the solicitor called in to help unravel almost every scandal in high places for nearly four decades, who, although skilful at shepherding his society clients through the mud and ambuscades of a court action, was perhaps even better at making sure matters never reached a court at all: in 1902, the year after Edward's accession, he was created a baronet. Lewis now warned Daisy she had better leave Lady Charles alone, or she would face legal sanctions. Enraged and seeking some outflanking manoeuvre, Daisy took a somewhat extreme step – she appealed to the Prince of Wales for help.

What was it she wanted exactly? Support, certainly, in a war fought from fortified positions upon the slopes and among the peaks of the social system. She had also, by this time, become rather nervous of what she had done and wanted the letter back. An open scandal would involve her own husband, who after all had his own political career, however desultorily he pursued it; there were even signs that Lord Brooke was growing a little restive – his complaisance as a husband did not extend to opening the doors of Easton Lodge for the world to goggle at the hectic peregrinations of her ladyship within. So Daisy went to Marlborough House and, as it were, threw herself on Edward's mercy; she needed, she said, his assistance, his protection, above all his intercession with Lady Charles, with Lewis, with anyone who needed to be persuaded that she should have her letter again. For a man like Edward there was only one possible response to such an appeal – as she wrote later, '... suddenly I saw him looking at me in a way all women understand. I knew I had won, so I asked him to tea.'

At two the next morning Edward called on Lewis and saw the letter; the next day he tried to persuade Lady Charles to give it up. She refused, unless Daisy agreed to keep away from London for the whole season. Thereupon Daisy applied her new leverage with the Prince, and when he saw Lady Charles a second time he hinted that perhaps, if she did not give up the letter, it would be she who would spend the season in exile. Lady Charles, although shaken, still refused to hand the letter over, but her position of what had seemed strength was sapped. Lewis, avid for royal invitations, became cooler in her cause; she found herself excluded from house parties and gatherings where Lady Brooke appeared as a welcome guest; worst of all, she realised not only that Daisy had become Edward's mistress – perhaps the most coveted social role of all, at least for women of the Marlborough set – but that she herself, by bringing their feud into the open, had been the cause of this love affair's beginning.

Lord Charles, always hot-tempered and never afraid of the Prince, went to see Edward, to protest at the way his wife was being treated; he called Edward a blackguard and a coward and even offered to strike him, before leaving the country to take command of his ship, perhaps appropriately named *Undaunted*. Beresford, like many who reform, took his new status as dutiful husband more seriously than might some who had never succumbed to the temptation to stray. In any case, with his departure Lady Charles lost her last undeviating champion and was left to survive the social Arctic she had created as best she could; from this spiritual wasteland she could only watch with fury and frustration as Daisy became queen in that curious society of which Edward was king.

The affair of the Beresford letter, however, was not over; in the meantime, later the same year, the Prince became involved, though only as a witness, in the Tranby Croft scandal. Lord Rosslyn was ill and dying, otherwise Lord Brooke and of course Daisy would have been among the guests at Tranby Croft who saw Sir William Gordon-Cumming apparently unmasked as he cheated at baccarat. (He is supposed to have pushed his counters with his sleeve, a surreptitious gesture which increased his stake, and thus his winnings, once the outcome of a hand was known.) The baronet signed a confession and a guarantee that he would never play cards again, but when he found the promise of secrecy he had been given had been broken and that all fashionable London knew the story, he sued his accusers for libel. According to rumour it was Daisy who had whispered the story to her friends, having heard it from Edward, although she always denied that this was so; nevertheless, pictures of her appeared in American newspapers captioned 'The Babbling Brook'.

Edward was among those who had to give evidence in the case, which Gordon-Cumming lost, and he was rather heavily attacked, both in the court and outside it, especially in the Press. He himself always resented being called a gambler, since he took gambling to be the staking of money one could not afford to lose; it is the case, however, that at the house parties he attended such games as baccarat were always and necessarily arranged and that he took with him wherever he travelled his own set of counters, marked with the feathers of the Prince of Wales. He was taken severely to task for what seemed his profligate habits – as *The Times* wrote, 'What does concern and indeed distress the public is the discovery that ... his "set" are a gambling, a baccarat-playing set'.

It was at this rather shaky point in his fortunes, when he was perhaps sustained only by the love felt for him by his new mistress – in his letters he was already addressing her as 'My darling little Daisy wife' – that Lord and Lady Beresford re-emerged. She had all this time been addressing to her naval husband, irritable under Mediterranean suns, a stream of complaints about the way she was being treated; he now responded by writing a letter of violent tone to Edward: 'I consider that from the beginning by your unasked interference and subsequent action you have deliberately used your high position to insult a humbler by doing all you can to elevate the person with whom she had a quarrel', it ran in part. It is an odd letter for a career officer to write to the heir to the throne and one wonders whether Lord Charles was too enraged to care or Edward too negligible to be feared. In any case he warned the Prince that at 'the first opportunity that occurs to me I shall give my opinion publicly of YRH and state that you have behaved to me like a blackguard and a coward'.

It was time for the intervention of a wiser and older head – and it was to Lord Salisbury, the Prime Minister, that Lady Charles sent her husband's letter, with a full if biased account of what had taken place so far: an attempt, it may be, to force the hand of the Establishment by threatening in this oblique manner the Prince of Wales. Lord Salisbury wrote to Beresford, reminding him, curiously, of his duty to Daisy – 'It must not be your face or hand that brings her into any disgrace because she yielded to you' – and the angry husband agreed to moderate the terms of his communication to the Prince, permitting Edward graciously to explain his own intentions in the business, thus perhaps settling it to everyone's satisfaction.

At this point, however, there appeared a pamphlet, written by Mrs Gerald Paget, Lady Charles's sister, and entitled *Lady River*, a thin enough disguise for Lady Brooke, given the scurrilous nature of its contents. 'Any lady who can get a copy,' wrote the periodical *Truth*, 'and who announces "a reading", finds her drawing-room more crowded than if a dozen prima donnas ... were on the bill of fare.' But *Truth* was unable to quote from the pamphlet for fear of prosecution. Thus the crisis broke out afresh – Lady Charles insisting Daisy should be barred from the court, Lord Charles writing further vitriolic letters to the Prince, Lord Salisbury meanwhile trying to keep everyone in negotiation, the Queen quiescent, and, above all, the whole matter secret. As for Daisy herself, she is said to have been quite willing to be barred the court, a place whose privileges she had never really enjoyed although they had been open to her all her life; Edward, however, refused to let anyone directly raise the subject with her. At last sanity and Salisbury had their way: formal letters were exchanged between Lord Charles and Edward, Daisy was barred the court, but only for a while, the damaging letter was returned and, perhaps to everyone's relief, finally burnt. It says something for the tolerance of the Establishment that Lord Charles, despite all this, did finally become an admiral.

Edward seems to have been quite genuinely in love with Daisy; if he had not been, her involvement of him in the business of the Beresford letter might have cost her the relationship. It is hard to know what Daisy really thought about him. He was twenty years older, being then around fifty, stout, his beard greying, with the Hanoverians' German accent and imperious expression and the habit of wearing a rather ridiculous curly-brimmed hat. He seems to have been a simple man, little given to thought or much concerned with the abstract or the intellectual. She was a noted beauty, slender, with a wonderful complexion and eyes of a penetrating blue; more than that, she had a mind and a will of her own, which were later to bring her to conclusions, particularly political conclusions, very far removed from those common among her class. It seems almost impossible to believe that Edward, heavy in both body and mind, although gentle in many ways and with a deep capacity for loyal friendship, could fully satisfy either her senses or her still thrusting, expanding intelligence. She herself, as always, is inconsistent in her own accounts – sometimes saying that, in time, she actually came to love him, at others that he bored her. It is likely that if the man had not been the Prince she would hardly have looked at him twice; since he was, she took the trouble to learn at least to like the man. He was the key that had unlocked for her the gates of influence; at this time, of course, it was perhaps the only key available to a woman, particularly an aristocrat, and for a woman of Daisy's flexible morality it was unthinkable that she would not seize it and try to use it.

In 1893 her father-in-law died and Daisy became Countess of Warwick. She entered into her – or, strictly, her husband's – inheritance with her usual energy and, indeed, extravagance. The simplicities of Warwick Castle were overtaken by a flood of *objets d'art*, by electric light, by flunkeys in smart uniforms. Easton Lodge was redecorated – and 3000 of its acres were auctioned off to help pay for the work. Two years later, Lord and Lady Warwick celebrated their new position in the world by holding a spectacular costume ball. Guests, summoned by white and gold invitation cards, were expected to appear dressed for the courts of eighteenth-century France; Daisy herself received them in the guise of Marie Antoinette. Four hundred guests danced minuettes and gavottes until at midnight trumpeters summoned them to a banquet at which a scurrying concourse of servants heaped *recherché* French dishes on the plates of diners seated at forty tables. A fortnight later some of the guests were still at the castle, enjoying the last fading echoes of this baronial celebration.

As Lady Warwick, Daisy still delighted in having attention paid her. She read with avidity the reports and accounts which newspapers and magazines hung like garlands about her activities. One such, however, struck through the haze of her self-admiration: 'Thousands of pounds spent on a few hours' silly masquerade; men and women strutting before each other's envious eyes, in mad rivalry of dissipation. . . . Other men and women and children the while huddling in their ragged hovels, their meagre shrunken flesh pierced by the winter's cruel sting; without food, without clothes, without fire. . . . Pitiful are the torments of the dying, but there is nothing more pitiful in all the world than the callousness that mocks and laughs at misery . . . upon my life, I pity the poor rich Countess of Warwick.' Nothing was more calculated to enrage her – partly, one suspects, because she herself had had just such thoughts as these. Most of her life she had mixed with politicians – as a child she had met Gladstone, Disraeli had nearly arranged that royal marriage, her husband had been a Member of Parliament, as had Lord Charles Beresford and many of the other young men she had entertained at Easton Lodge. Over the years she had developed the glimmerings of an understanding of just how appalling the condition of the poor of England was, and had even tried to do what she could to alleviate matters. In one of the rooms at Easton Lodge she had opened a needlework school for delicate or physically handicapped village girls and had aroused thereby a great deal of opposition – in town, when she displayed the work the girls had done, she was accused of having 'gone into trade', and in the country the squirarchy thought the girls were getting above themselves, as well as being drawn from that pool of impoverished labour from which they recruited their own servants.

In 1892 Daisy had first met W. T. Stead, a journalist and moral crusader who had become famous in 1885 by buying a thirteen-year-old virgin in order to attract attention to the trade in such girls for prostitution, which was one by-product of the disparity between the classes (the Establishment had responded in time-honoured fashion – they had not stopped the trade, but imprisoned him for dabbling in it). As editor of the *Pall Mall Gazette* and, later, the *Review of Reviews*, Stead had started one campaign after another, perhaps the first 'modern' journalist in Britain because the first properly to understand the potential power of the Press to sway opinion. The son of a Congregationalist minister, he was also a great rationaliser, able, for instance, to explain away Daisy's association with Edward by seeing it as the means by which the Prince would come by 'moral improvement'. She was to be 'the priest of the parish', he her 'parishioner'.

Once in contact with Stead, Daisy's own generous and by no means unintelligent awareness of the differences between her situation and that of most of her fellow-citizens became keener and more conscious. She had not, of course, altered her way of life; the centre of fashionable London provided a stage she would not give up lightly. Nor would she give up the Prince, and he had always been easily bored and thus needed elaborately arranged, expensive, although in essence quite simple, entertainments: riding, shooting, cards, plays and charades – and, of course, the nights rendered uneasy by the light step of heedless lovers making their way down creaking corridors to the bedroom doors of their current beloveds. None of this would appeal to Stead and as a result when he visited Easton Lodge he came alone, usually when no other guests were present. He was therefore one of the few who had seen the other face Daisy could present to the world, that of a woman concerned with social questions, possibly guilty about the wealth she had inherited, eager yet uncertain how to act upon these feelings. In 1894, as Countess of Warwick, Daisy stood for election as a Poor Law Guardian, one of the board which concerned itself with the administration of the local workhouse, and thus with the state of the local poor in general. She had never stood for election before – she was, after all, a lady born and bred – but in her addresses she had stressed not her aristocratic birthright to authority, but her woman's qualifications to deal with such subjects as nursing and child-care. She had been elected.

Now to be accused of indifference and unconcern, therefore, threw her into a fury she could remember thirty years later. Where had the piece appeared? In the *Clarion*, a Socialist periodical, perhaps the most widely read of all Labour publications. Without a word of warning or farewell to the guests who still remained, Daisy set out immediately for London; and at the end of Fleet Street and the top of an ancient flight of stairs she had the confrontation she had come for – with the *Clarion*'s editor, Robert Blatchford.

Blatchford was the archetypal self-made man of the epoch. Apprenticed to a brushmaker at fourteen, he ran away at twenty and walked from Yarmouth to London, to starve there until he enlisted in the Army. He came out a sergeant, and then by chance and luck and good, hard endeavour began to sell stories, found himself in journalism, became leader-writer on the Manchester *Sunday Chronicle*, where his Socialist convictions eventually cost him his job, founded the *Clarion* with a capital of £400 and established it with a circulation of around thirty or forty thousand. He sold a collection of his reprinted articles under the title of *Merrie England* and found himself author of the principal left-wing bestseller of the day, doubling his paper's circulation as a result. At this time, therefore, he was a man of some influence in Labour circles, although no platform speaker and not on good terms with the official leadership.

Daisy was probably the first aristocrat he had ever met, certainly the first furious Countess to invade his office. Diffident at first, he eventually began to harangue her, but did so with both conviction and style. Always one to take to masculine energy, she seems to have succumbed to the power of his beliefs and even to that of his arguments, dimly as she could perceive their economic logic. She wrote later, 'During the journey home I thought and thought about all I had been hearing and learning. I knew my outlook on life could never be the same as it had been before this incident.' It is difficult to be sure if she had really found her road to Damascus in Blatchford's dingy office – she was, after all, writing with the benefit of hindsight. Yet, even if it was to be ten years later, a Socialist she did become, and if she saw that the roots of this new certainty lay in that encounter with the working-class journalist, she is more likely to be right than anyone else. Blatchford, however, almost by definition an anti-patriot, would not have approved of the stand she took in her first political pronouncements. These were to record her approval of the Jameson raid, a cut-throat operation mounted by Cecil Rhodes with the implicit co-operation of the powerful Joseph Chamberlain at the Colonial Office in London, ostensibly to rescue the English-born settlers, the so-called *Uitlanders*, from political domination in the Boer republic of the Transvaal, in practice to extend Rhodes's sphere of influence – which he equated with the influence of Britain – over wider and wider areas of Southern Africa. During the three years of crisis which followed the failure of this adventure and culminated in Kruger's ultimatum to the British and the consequent Boer War, Daisy seems to have lost much of her jingoist fervour; when the war came, she accepted it as something which had simply to be borne and even supported as a loyal act, despite any personal misgivings one might have.

By then, however, she had continued on the path of practical help and education which she had started with her needlework project. She was a great believer in the value of education, particularly a practical and technological education, for the working classes; she thought this would help them directly to personal development and social achievement. At the edge of the Easton Lodge estate, therefore, she turned a small farm into a coeducational boarding school specialising in science and particularly agriculture. Bigods School was intended for children over twelve, paying a small fee each; although interesting as an experiment, it always met with a great deal of opposition, country people preferring children of that age to be out at work and the educational establishment being suspicious of the bias against the arts. However, with a practical example behind her of what might be done, she became a more and more powerful campaigner for working-class and particularly rural education.

In the meantime Daisy's position as Edward's unofficial consort had been modified. She remained very close to him, but they were no longer lovers, and she therefore decided to maintain her influence by developing as close a relationship with his wife Alexandra as she could. She wrote both to Edward and to the Princess and was doubtless delighted to discover with what warmth and magnanimity her overtures were received. Alexandra was, after all, a very forgiving woman, cut off from much normal contact with people by her deafness and probably rather cold sexually. Aware in her diffidence of these shortcomings rather than of her clear-cut, precisely defined beauty, she had always accepted Edward's widely known adventures with a loving humility – although at the time of the tensions over Lord Charles Beresford and Daisy's letter she had been irritated enough not to come home from a visit abroad, allowing Edward to explain as best he could her absence on his fiftieth birthday, finally returning only to nurse her son George through an attack of typhoid. Now, however, she sent Daisy what the latter described as 'a small crucifix wrapt in a piece of paper on which was written these words: "From one who has suffered much and forgives all".'

The change in Daisy's position was, however, soon common knowledge. Edward, not a man to be without an ancillary 'wife' – lovers in his circle used to call their mistresses this, and often exchanged rings with them – had met the beautiful Mrs George

Keppel at Sandown races and seems immediately to have fallen in love with her. She remained his mistress throughout the whole of his reign, and was with him when he died in 1910, summoned to the death-bed by the magnanimous Alexandra. For the Palace this quiet and dutiful woman must have seemed a great comfort after the anxieties they had been put through by the widely publicised activities and opinions of the energetic Countess of Warwick. Daisy herself had formed a new liaison, this time with a man five years younger than herself, a captain in the Army named Joseph Frederick Laycock. Vital and powerfully built, Laycock was a man of some intelligence and ability (he ended his Army career as a Brigadier-General) and he seems to have approved of many of Daisy's schemes, certainly contributing generously to some of them. There is no question, however, that in this relationship it was he who held the whip-hand; for the first time, perhaps, Daisy found herself more loving than loved. Not that she did not still throw her tantrums and make her scenes – nothing could ever change her temperament – but in the end it was she who needed him rather than the other way about. Indeed it seems fair to say that Laycock was the one real love of her life, the only man for whom she had more than the casual desire she had felt for so many or the rather matter-of-fact affection she knew with her husband.

It is around this time, just before the turn of the century, that one can discern the beginnings of a real anxiety about the financial status of the Warwick household. She and Stead wanted to publicise a new cause they had taken up, that of a closer alliance with the United States. In this she was following the ideas of Cecil Rhodes, a man she still idolised, who had written in Stead's journal, 'You can't get over the fact that the two peoples are of the same race, and that the trite saying that "blood is thicker than water" is a true saying.' (Given the heterogeneous origins of the population of the United States, this opinion, still popular today, has always seemed to me stronger on wishful thinking than on logic.) Daisy much desired to propagate this cause, but her income now was only £6000 a year – an enormous drop from her original fortune if one remembers the slowly declining value of the pound itself. Somewhat sanguinely, she suggested to Stead, who wanted to found a paper devoted to these views, that he went to America 'to find a millionaire who simply wants a motive given him for spending his hoards'. This was perhaps typical of the view then prevalent, and one not entirely without foundation, that American millionaires could be separated from their dollars with ease, provided that they were given an opportunity of consorting with people, and particularly ladies, of title.

The Earl, too, attempted in varying ways to mend his family's fortunes, taking trips to different parts of the world, as the years went by, in the hope of acquiring some kind of lucrative concession. Few of these journeys were ever to show any profit, although they seem to have afforded his lordship, who remained a shooting and fishing man, a considerable degree of pleasure. In 1899, however, he made his first real attempt at setting his finances on a business footing, turning his still enormous holdings in land into a limited company called Warwick Estates, an example which several other members of his class subsequently followed, despite the unpleasant tang of 'trade' that must have hung over such an operation. Pragmatism, allied with the frequent good fortune of owning coal or building land, has been the saving of a large proportion of Britain's aristocracy.

Notwithstanding her financial problems, however, Daisy continued with her educational schemes – as she did, of course, with her extravagant entertaining. Towards the end of 1898 the Lady Warwick Hostel opened in Reading. This was the first practical consequence of Daisy's projected agricultural scheme for women and was intended 'for the benefit of gentlewomen and the daughters of professional men'. For a fee of £50 a year young ladies were to be trained in horticulture and agricultural techniques and it was intended that each such hostel should be attached to an agricultural college. Despite the usual jeers and accusations of promiscuity – even the suffragettes were not yet, after all, in full cry – it soon became clear that these hostels fulfilled a need and later two more were opened. Five years and over 200 successfully trained students later, the Reading hostel was moved to Studley Castle in Warwickshire, there to attempt to establish itself as a full agricultural college.

By the turn of the century, too, Daisy had moved closer to an openly socialist position. Certainly trades unionists were frequent visitors at Warwick Castle and in both speech and writings she warmly supported their efforts – although she still tended to do this in an unconsciously condescending way, never conceding very much of her *grande dame* status. That, however, was now to be threatened from another quarter.

By attempting to win Alexandra's friendship, Daisy had hoped to remain in close contact with Edward and thus near the centre of affairs. She had always, one suspects, thought of herself as one who might manipulate kings, statesmen and their decisions, a power, naturally for the good, which was to be indirect but effective. Her relations with Edward remained good – indeed, he remained friendly to her until his death. But in 1901 Victoria died and he became the King at last. His advisers now exercised a much more rigorous guardianship over his associations, and it was inevitable that the remaining ties between Daisy and the King must be broken. Not only were her love affairs common knowledge and her extravagances a rich source of material for the gossip columns, but her opinions were beginning to outrage more and more members of her own class. Indeed, anything might have been forgiven her but her social conscience. Lord Esher, a senior civil servant who always exercised more power than was at first apparent because of his close friendship with Edward, came to see her. As she put it herself, 'He told me, with charming courtesy and frankness, that he thought it would be as well for all concerned if my close association with great affairs were to cease ...', sentiments echoed, one does not know with what secret satisfaction, in a letter which Queen Alexandra herself sent to Daisy at more or less the same time. There was no way round these powerful prohibitions; her days of power at court were over.

It is clear that Daisy Warwick did not turn to socialism out of pique at her own fading beauty and the loss of her influence with Edward, although this has been suggested. On the other hand, her separation from the highest levels of the hierarchy to which she belonged may well have helped to direct her towards the more and more powerful alternative of working-class radicalism. As always it was, however, in the area of education that she mounted most of her attacks; the educational system had to be overhauled, because, as she wrote, 'men will not always rest content in the positions in which they were born'. Scholarships brought an illusory equality: 'What about the child who must be a wage-earner out of school hours?' she asked.

Daisy worked hard for her women's agricultural scheme, trying to supplement by public subscription the money she herself was spending on it. In this she was always less successful than she must have hoped – the people who benefited rarely had money, the people who had money rarely understood or liked what she was up to. She tried to get public support, too, for Bigods School, particularly from local government, but again received very little. By dint of very hard work, by spending time with the constant stream of influential visitors, by writing, speaking and appealing, she did however manage to put both Bigods and the Reading hostel on a more solid footing. In the lull that ensued, she began to write a history of Warwick Castle, closely helped by Harvey Bloom, a clergyman of Bohemian appearance, great intellectual and physical vitality, but somewhat secular appetites. In 1902, despite a great deal of opposition from people who thought its objectives dubious and its methods vulgar, she supported the Salvation Army by employing some of those they were helping in a project to revitalise the Easton Lodge gardens. After this, she appeared on platforms for the Army, as she did for unions, to propagate her ideas on education and for various left-wing causes. Now over forty, the pressure of this work and the strains of keeping some kind of control over her financial situation were proving almost too much; the disaster which now overturned her emotional life brought her to the brink of breakdown.

In the spring of 1902 she discovered that Laycock, her 'Joe', was being cited as co-respondent in a divorce suit which the Marquis of Downshire was bringing against his wife. They had, he alleged, met on the hunting field and the situation had developed from there. Laycock offered no defence; Daisy, who understood these things, at first accepted with some sympathy Laycock's situation, a sympathy which did not survive the news that he was to marry the ex-Marchioness and which descended into fury and despair once Lady Downshire had irrevocably become Mrs Laycock. Distressed and ill, she left for Italy, where – and it says much for her stamina – she used the enforced holiday which followed to finish her *Warwick Castle and its Earls*.

Early in 1904 Marjorie, Daisy's daughter, got married, a ceremony made slightly bizarre by the bride's mother being seven months pregnant. When, in March, a new daughter was born, she was christened Mercy – it was apparently with the exclamation 'Oh, mercy!' that Daisy had received the news of her pregnancy. This domestic chore over, however, the revived Countess returned to the field of politics. In August of that year the International Congress of Socialists met in Amsterdam and Daisy decided to attend. Almost a quarter of the delegates there were British, but the one she wanted to meet was Hyndman, leader of the Social Democratic Federation, himself rich, with an aristocratic background and Cambridge-educated. 'Lady Warwick, apart from her natural advantages, was extremely well-dressed, looked full of animation and vigour, and appeared as if she had not a care in the world,' Hyndman remembered her at their first meeting. He and his wife took her back to their hotel with them, and there, rather as Blatchford had done a few years earlier, Hyndman harangued her at great length about his beliefs and convictions. One may well guess that one of her great attractions to men of distinction must have been this capacity to listen while they expounded their fondest theories, and not only listen but take them in. In any case, as he said later, 'she had manifestly studied Socialism before, and her criticisms, questions and objections were those of a capable mind'.

The effect of this meeting, and the excitements of the Congress itself, proved enough to sway Daisy's last formal hesitancy. In November 1904 she joined the Social Democratic Federation. Apart from the abolition of the monarchy – she could hardly be expected to take such a stand on what was almost a personal matter – she had now accepted a programme of an almost revolutionary nature and allied herself to one of the most radical of all the various Socialist groups. She travelled up and down the country, speaking at meetings of all sorts, perhaps not aware of the misgivings and mistrust she often aroused, or of the fact that many who crowded into the halls where she spoke did so as if to a freak show: during the Edwardian decade a Socialist aristocrat was a curiosity not to be missed. Her husband seems to have been as equable about her new, avowed politics as he had always been about her lovers and her extravagance; her older children, on the other hand, show signs of having been extremely embarrassed by what must have seemed mere publicity-seeking antics. In those days, after all, Socialism even of the mildest sort was equated with violence and barbarism, with barricades and bloody revolution, by almost the entire class to which Daisy herself belonged.

By 1907 twenty-five years of heavy spending were more than beginning to catch up with the Warwicks. Not only did a creditor (Sir John Willoughby, for long a close friend of Daisy's) seize much property at Easton Lodge, but Bigods School, Daisy's first and in many ways most exciting educational experiment, had to close for want of funds. The Board of Education, although in principle in favour of the school, was forced to end its support because of the narrowness of the curriculum, and local government was not slow to follow suit. Thus Dunmow lost its only secondary school, a school which, according to the Board itself, offered 'a type of education afforded by no other school in this part of the country'.

In 1909 Daisy suffered another financial reverse. She had been trying to raise funds for a left-wing periodical to be entitled *The Outspoken Review*, and had fallen eagerly and rather gullibly into a trap set by a swift-moving financier of dubious background named Hooley, a close associate of the ubiquitous Horatio Bottomley. She signed bills of exchange, in effect Hooley's debts to others, in exchange for shares to that amount in one of his companies. Since he had for some years been in and out of the law courts, it tells us something of Daisy Warwick's approach to the whole question of money and may go some way towards explaining how the fortune of her youth had come to slip so spectacularly away. The shares naturally proved worthless and Hooley's debts were added to her own. Not only that, but in the actions which followed her name was linked with his, something which did her little good when in 1911 he was sent to prison for a year. Her socialism, however, continued to absorb her. Rather paradoxically she used one of her aristocratic privileges, the right to install clergymen of her choice in livings on the Warwick estates, to settle there vicars of a markedly left-wing turn of mind – to the consternation of the parishioners, who several times threw the first of them into a convenient horse-pond. More substantially, she used her friendship with H. G. Wells, who had rented Little Easton rectory, to involve him as one of the editors of a miscellany of essays on socialist subjects, *Socialism and the Great State*, a book which had a surprising impact and was translated into several languages.

In 1912, still worried by the need to make money, Daisy embarked on what must have seemed to her a somewhat desperate venture: a lecture tour of the United States. She sailed in some state on the liner *Mauretania*, and arrived in New York in March, to be met by the usual wild pack of reporters which await any European celebrity. The first question, setting the tone for most of the rest, was 'Are you an anarchist?' From then on reporters seem hardly to have left her a moment's peace; audiences, on the other hand, were less responsive and, as her curiosity value declined, so did the numbers of those prepared to listen to her rather gossipy little talks about high life in England. Long before the tour was officially over, she was on her way back, hiding her humiliation in a smoke-screen of conflicting stories about why she had left America so abruptly.

From now on her manoeuvres to gain money became increasingly complicated and even sordid. There are sales of land, of property, of pictures. There are sums held back, objects of value which disappear, court actions, injunctions. The Official Receiver appeared in July 1913 and reported that some of the most valuable items at Easton Lodge had gone unaccountably missing; the sheriff of Essex arrived on the same errand in the same month. More

lawsuits were pending. Daisy, desperate, turned to writing films –
she turned out a drama entitled *The Great Pearl Affair* – and to
journalism – she became editor of the woman's page of the *Daily
Sketch*. But by June 1914 she was some £90,000 in debt, all the
Warwick and the Maynard estates were heavily mortgaged, most
of her valuables were sold or impounded and – unkindest cut of all
– Warwick Castle had been let to an American. Only a desperate
remedy could save such a desperate situation. Possibly the final
spur was the refusal of shops in Warwick to serve her, but more
plausibly it was the insistence of the Tory MP, Arthur du Cros,
that she pay the annual interest on the £16,000 he had lent her two
years earlier. Certainly he became one of her two principal contacts
in the game she started to play early in 1914 – a game that might
have been entitled 'Blackmail the Palace'. She got in touch with
Frank Harris, a journalist of dubious reputation, whose biographies
of various of his friends, Bernard Shaw and Oscar Wilde notably
among them, had shown his skill in doctoring the truth, and whose
autobiography, *My Life and Loves*, detailing his adventures in high
society, the Wild West and with women, was to become one of the
notorious books of the century. Having established her partnership
with him, she sent for Du Cros.

When the financier, a millionaire who had benefited from his
early awareness of the importance of the pneumatic tyre, came to
see Daisy, she told him her troubles were over, for she had found a
way to become solvent again: she would sell her memoirs for
£100,000. When Du Cros suggested she was being a little optimistic, she played her trump card: she had letters from Edward,
loving letters, indiscreet letters, letters which babbled not only
about his daily life, but about the people he had met and what he
thought of them – people like Tsar Nicholas of Russia, for example,
or the Kaiser. She knew very well what the worth of these letters
was, she said – and now she played what she must have hoped
would be another winning card – because Frank Harris had told
her. The combination of the letters with a man of Frank Harris's
reputation made a mixture explosive enough, she must have felt, to
send a loyal Tory like Du Cros scurrying with warnings to the
highest places.

She was not wrong. Du Cros had soon been to see Lord Albe-
marle, George V's ADC and, incidentally, George Keppel's
brother; from him he was passed on to Lord Stamfordham, once
Queen Victoria's private secretary, and to Charles Russell, the
King's solicitor. It was Russell, in a lawyerly way, who hinted that

Du Cros ought perhaps to find out what Daisy really wanted – and what Daisy really wanted, it turned out, was £85,000. She could, however, make no arrangements without Frank Harris's approval and Harris was in Paris and unlikely to return, since he had fled a step or so ahead of the bailiffs. Thus it was at the Ritz Hotel in Paris that, on 14 July, of all days, Du Cros faced Harris and the by now perhaps complacent Countess. Harris immediately poured contempt on Daisy's asking-price – with the offers he was receiving from America, he said, nothing less than £125,000 made any sense. Du Cros, perhaps commendably, negotiated the figure down to an even hundred thousand.

By coincidence he found himself travelling back across the Channel on the same ferry as Daisy herself. They took the opportunity to talk; Daisy outlined for him the full extent of her debts – and then suggested that he might take them over and, as a businessman, reduce them; the letters, she hinted, would then be handed back to the Palace. The alternative was publication; so sure of herself was she, in fact, that she scribbled out then and there an ultimatum to the Establishment. But the Establishment is not where it is for nothing – it was on the move itself. (Elsewhere, so were armies: Europe was less than three weeks from the war which would carve its history in two.) Back in London, Daisy now took on another businessman as her direct agent: a man named Bruce Logan. Through him she began to put heavier pressure on the Palace. Logan had a friend, Charles Hatry, another financier to end his career in jail, and it was in his safe that Edward's letters were now kept. It must have disturbed both men somewhat to find they were being followed wherever they went; Daisy, however, pressed resolutely forward. On the day Austria presented its ultimatum to Serbia, Daisy let Du Cros know that she had received the first instalment of the money now due to her from America. Whether this was true or not is unknown; what is certain is that, before the end of the month, the Palace had struck its decisive blow. A Judge in Chambers (thus avoiding the mess of an open court) granted an interlocutory injunction to prevent her publishing the papers (George V's name nowhere appearing, nor the nature of the 'documents'). No one knows the arguments presented, nor is any trace of the action to be found in the Public Records Office.

Daisy threatened to tell at least how she had been gagged, but a year later a final injunction was granted by Mr Justice Low; he ordered that 'all further proceedings in this Action be stayed until further Order and ... that the documents contained in a sealed envelope deposited in Court . . . be handed to Sir Henry Paget Cook the . . . Defendant's Solicitor forthwith to be destroyed by him.' So Daisy had come to the end of her association with Edward, this last sordid unwinding of the story ending in defeat, his letters to her lost. There is no question that she had attempted blackmail; but then, in the Marlborough House set, perhaps that was not as rare as we would like to believe. One remembers the Beresford affair, for example. And Daisy herself always justified her action by pointing to her relationship with Edward as the root cause of her financial troubles. Certainly a Royal visit has always been expensive, and Edward's were more expensive than most – he brought several of his friends close to bankruptcy. But Daisy must have known that her constant entertainments on the one hand and her philanthropy on the other had contributed more to her present condition than any expense the Prince of Wales had caused her.

Not that she was finished, by any means. Du Cros, who seems to have been curiously good-hearted considering how he had been used by both sides – he had hoped for a knighthood – waived his right to interest on his loan to Daisy, agreed not to ask for the principal back during her lifetime, and took over nearly £50,000 of her debts (there is a suggestion that she made him uneasy because of things she knew about him and hinted she might tell; it is hard otherwise to explain his unexpected generosity). After the war she sold off much of what remained of her estates, receiving nearly a quarter of a million for them – gratifying, but not by then enough to bring her into solvency.

She developed her love of animals, until the 800 acres of Easton Lodge became a sort of zoo, and certainly a sanctuary. She herself was surrounded by pets both conventional and bizarre, and while retaining the air of the great lady nevertheless persisted with vigour in pursuing her Socialist principles. She had, for example, moved a long way from the jingoism which had aroused her admiration of the Jameson Raid; during the war, she had taken a stance very close to pacifism, her most bellicose pronouncements being those made in support of the Russian Revolution.

In 1923 she split her family (and, indeed, sections of Labour opinion) by standing as the Labour Party's candidate in a by-election for the Warwick and Leamington constituency. Her opponent was Anthony Eden (now Lord Avon), her son's brother-in-law. In a largely rural area her only hope might have been to modify her opinions. On the contrary, she gave public support to Communism, said if she had been a man she would probably have refused to fight and – perhaps worst of all – declared herself opposed to hunting. Eden, with his handsome face, his Military Cross, his new wife and, above all, his totally conventional opinions, was an opponent impossible to beat. Her only hope lay in the agricultural vote, but that was heavily eroded by the Liberal, a man named Nicholls who had once been a labourer on the land himself. Thus the result was inevitable – Eden first, Nicholls respectably second, Lady Warwick, ten thousand votes adrift, nowhere.

In the late twenties Daisy tried to give Easton Lodge to the Labour Movement for use as a college, but despite a great deal of early interest eventually fell foul of the puritanism and class-pride of the movement. The principal of Ruskin College, the successful working-class college at Oxford which was to be incorporated in the proposed new Easton Lodge, said, 'The furnishings and decorations are lavish and ornate and do not lend themselves to the simplicity which is desirable for a Socialist institution' – the very tone of the Levellers and the haters of pleasure and colour who spent so much of the seventeenth century whitewashing the walls and smashing the stained-glass windows of the churches of England. For Daisy this attitude must have been a devastating shock; she had stepped away from her own class and taken up and worked for ideas far removed from those to which her childhood had conditioned her. She was often foolhardy, sometimes unscrupulous, on occasions autocratic, but she had made a long journey in the forty-odd years since Lord Rosslyn had brought flowers from the South of France for her eighteenth birthday, and perhaps she deserved better treatment than she got at the hands of all these self-righteous working men and bigoted intellectuals.

She did not waver in her beliefs, however, uncertainly based though they sometimes were. But she withdrew more and more from active work, and became, indeed, something of an eccentric, with her animals and her family treasures about her. She lived into her seventies, her death forcing her son desperately to try and turn back a trainload of Highland cattle she had just ordered for her park. She had led a complex, paradoxical and often self-indulgent life. She had evolved her own standpoint and stubbornly defended it. She had been forced by circumstances into many dubious manoeuvres, despite her forty years or more as a public figure. It is as young that one remembers her, slender, fair-haired, vivacious, her blue eyes snapping, waiting for the soft footfall in the corridor – Laycock, Beresford, Lonsdale – who would be a Prime Minister, Haig – who would be a Field Marshal, Edward – who would be a King.